TRACKING THE SPIRIT OF YELLOWSTONE

Recollections of Thirty-One Years as a Seasonal Ranger

Elk Along Firehole River During Winter

TRACKING THE SPIRIT OF YELLOWSTONE

Recollections of Thirty-One Years as a Seasonal Ranger

By

Orville E. Bach, Jr.

Illustrations by Margaret C. Bach

Blue Willow Press

Library of Congress Control Number: 2005925671

ISBN: 978-0-9767473-0-7

Published by
Blue Willow Press
197 Lamplight Lane
Bozeman, MT 59718

Printed in the United States of America by
Morris Publishing
3212 East Highway 30
Kearney, NE 68847

To

Ernestine Parker

TABLE OF CONTENTS

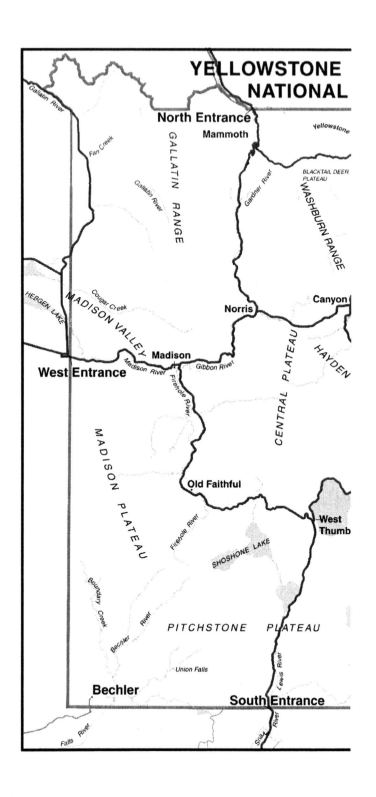

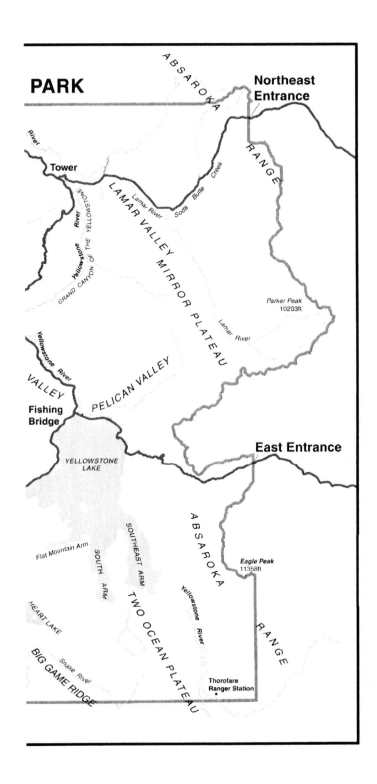

PARK

ABSAROKA

Northeast Entrance

RANGE

River

Tower

Yellowstone River

GRAND CANYON OF THE YELLOWSTONE

LAMAR VALLEY

Lamar River

Soda Butte Creek

MIRROR PLATEAU

Parker Peak
10203ft

Lamar River

Yellowstone River

VALLEY

PELICAN VALLEY

Fishing Bridge

East Entrance

YELLOWSTONE LAKE

Flat Mountain Arm

SOUTH ARM

SOUTHEAST ARM

ABSAROKA

Eagle Peak
11358ft

Yellowstone River

TWO OCEAN PLATEAU

RANGE

HEART LAKE

Heart Lake

BIG GAME RIDGE

Snake River

Thorofare
Ranger Station

Preface

The stories and commentaries in this book derive from over three decades of working in and exploring the Yellowstone country. On many occasions when I have shared stories to visitors of my adventures and misadventures in Yellowstone, as well as discussing issues and challenges facing our park, I have been told, "you should write a book!" So, I did. Obviously, these stories represent my personal views, and do not necessarily represent the official opinion of the National Park Service.

May the stories of my *adventures* serve to increase your appreciation and awareness of what a wild and magical place Yellowstone is. I trust that the stories of my *misadventures*, will serve to prevent you from making the same or similar mistakes I have made while trekking the park's backcountry. And of utmost importance, may these stories reinforce your conviction to protect and preserve the Greater Yellowstone Ecosystem for our children and grandchildren!

Kindred Spirits and Acknowledgements

In over thirty-five years of exploring Yellowstone's vast backcountry, I have held on to an old, tattered topographic map. Each time I take a trip, I mark my route in red on that map and place a small x where I camped. According to my count, I have had the good fortune of spending around 400 nights out in the Yellowstone wilderness. Rarely have I been alone on these trips. I have been blessed with the company of some wonderful people on my explorations of Yellowstone. The stories that follow will contain references to these fine companions.

Teddy Roosevelt once made the statement that you really don't get to know someone well until you spend some time around a campfire with him or her. I couldn't agree more. Allow me to introduce the folks with whom I have enjoyed many evenings around a campfire in Yellowstone:

Margaret, my wife—Margaret loves the natural world. As an artist, she has an amazing talent for capturing its beauty in watercolors. We discovered the West together, and she has accompanied me on many trips into Yellowstone's backcountry. She has also put up with a lot of inconvenience over the past thirty-five years. Moving back and forth from Tennessee to Yellowstone is not a simple thing to do.

Caroline and Alison, my daughters—Both of these girls inherited their parents' love of the wild outdoors. They spent every summer of their lives up through age seventeen in Yellowstone, except for two in Great Smoky Mountains National Park.

Jim Lenertz—Jim worked or volunteered in Yellowstone from 1967 through 2003. Medical problems prevented him from returning in 2004, but hopefully he will be back soon. In 1987, at the age of 47, Jim suffered a stroke that curtailed, but did not eliminate his wilderness adventures. He is the epitome of a great outdoorsman and has taught me most of my backcountry skills. He is a trusted partner when paddling a canoe.

John and Deb Dirksen—Just when I thought I was pretty good with my backcountry skills, I met John and Deb in 1989. They have taught me so much, especially how to slow down, make the backcountry more comfortable, and truly enjoy and appreciate it. Most of my great Yellowstone trips since 1989 have been with this couple. They probably know more about Yellowstone's backcountry than anyone. John figures he has spent nine years of his life in the backcountry, and most of that has been in Yellowstone.

Al Duff—I met Al when we were officers in the Air Force stationed at Malmstrom AFB in Great Falls, Montana. Al and I have spent considerable time together in Yellowstone's backcountry. Al is a strong, quiet, confident, extremely intelligent man. One simply cannot ask for a better companion than Al on a backcountry trip.

Tom Gerrity—I met Tom when I was stationed at Malmstrom AFB in Great Falls. Tom is a sensitive man with a great sense of humor. Spending time with Tom in the backcountry is sheer pleasure.

Sam Holbrook—Sam is the senior seasonal interpretive ranger in Yellowstone. The 2004 season marked his 38th summer in the park. He served as my mentor when I first arrived at Old Faithful in 1976. Sam is the epitome of a Yellowstone interpretive ranger. In recent years we have enjoyed some great backcountry trips with John and Deb.

Hank Barnett—Hank is truly a kindred spirit from our home state of Tennessee. I've never known another CPA with his backcountry skills. In fact, he may be the only CPA to serve as an NPS law enforcement ranger in three different national parks. Whether it's accounting, law enforcement ranger duties or hiking the high country, Hank exemplifies giving it his best.

Rick Hutchinson—Rick was my good friend in Yellowstone from my early days of NPS employment. He died much too young. Rick was truly an extraordinary person, and was outstanding in his position as Park Geologist. I have devoted a chapter to my special memories of him in the park.

Rod Busby—Rod was my first hiking buddy and companion in Yellowstone. We were two greenhorns learning how to travel the backcountry together. He totally shared my love for Yellowstone. Rod now works as an economist for the U.S. Forest Service in Louisiana, but still visits Yellowstone

Brian Severin—Brian and I were crewed together in the Strategic Air Command at Malmstrom AFB. Brian was a key member of my eighteen-day Yellowstone ski trip. I never met a stronger man in the backcountry. I have lost track of Brian. I last heard that when he retired from the USAF, he turned to ranching somewhere along the wild Missouri River in Montana.

Rick McIntyre—Rick is the most passionate wildlife advocate I have ever known. Knowing him during the wolf reintroduction in Yellowstone was truly a blessing.

I am grateful to all of these fine companions who were part of my Yellowstone stories. I am deeply indebted to my mother, Margaret K. Bach, for her wonderful wisdom and inspiration. She and my Dad, Orville Bach, Sr., instilled within me a deep love and appreciation for the natural world. I would also like to acknowledge all of the Yellowstone employees I have worked with over the years, including those with the National Park Service, Yellowstone Association and the park concessions. Tami Blackford was kind enough to customize the map that we included in the book. Thanks to Amy Ross and Dianna Pearson for their expertise in the design and layout of Margaret's line art. Hank Barnett contributed his technical skills in solving several formatting problems.

The following people read over the manuscript and offered helpful comments: Margaret Bach, Al Duff, Dick Gordon, Bill Lewis, Jo Ann Kell and Nelson Ross. I am in debt to the following folks who pored over the manuscript in detail, and contributed many valuable suggestions: Steve Hixson, Jim Lenertz, Gary McKenna, Kathy Russell, and Mike Yochim. John and Deb Dirksen helped me sort out the details from our many excursions into the backcountry. Even with all of this wonderful assistance, I take full responsibility for any errors.

Margaret's aunt, Ernestine Parker, offered continual encouragement for the writing of this book. It is therefore my pleasure to dedicate this book to her.

Introduction—The Spirit of Yellowstone

It is early morning in mid-June, and I am on Geyser Prediction duty in the Upper Geyser Basin. I have 2 ½ hours to study and observe the major geysers and post the day's first predictions. Standing near Daisy Geyser, over a mile from Old Faithful, I cannot see another soul. The air is still and cool, and the smell of new grass from the meadows mixes with a tinge of sulphur from the springs and geysers that surround me. Night has finally given way to the new dawn, but the transition was slow.

The only sounds to be heard are the gurgles of boiling springs and hisses of steam vents. I am looking at an ethereal world. The grasses are covered with a frosty dew. A hundred columns of steam are slowly drifting vertical. Steam is also rising from the many runoff channels and the Firehole River itself.

Suddenly the spell is broken. The sun begins to ease above the Central Plateau, spilling its first rays into the basin and eerily backlighting the steamy setting. The soft, low angle rays of light produce a much more vibrant green in the meadows. The waters of the Firehole River glimmer in the new light. The basin begins to awaken. A chorus of coyote howls erupts to the south from the vicinity of Black Sand Basin.

When I turn my head in that direction, I marvel at the huge snow drifts still remaining atop the Madison Plateau. Another howl pierces the solitude behind me. The coyote walks from the forest out into the meadow west of Daisy Geyser, raises its head and again answers the call.

Bison and elk are grazing in the meadow below. Above me, a honking formation of Canada geese flies over the basin. This enchanting scene is bombarding my senses. Such is the "spirit" of Yellowstone. It has to do with one's personal experiences, emotions and interrelationships with incredible natural phenomena in a magical place. A geyser basin early in the morning is just one piece of the fabric of Yellowstone's amazing diversity. Its canyons, waterfalls, big lakes, rugged peaks, populations of big animals and petrified forests—all situated on a high, wild, rolling volcanic plateau, provide a feast for the human spirit.

There is something utterly exhilarating about strolling through the Upper Geyser Basin at dawn, hiking along the edge of the Grand Canyon of the Yellowstone, sharing the trails with the grizzly bear, observing large populations of wildlife in a wild, natural setting and climbing to a mountain summit where the views contain nothing but wild country as far as the eye can see.

I have always closely identified myself with John Denver's great song, *Rocky Mountain High* where Denver describes the young man who was "born in the summer of his 27th year coming home to a place he had never been before." For me it was my 22nd year. The year was 1968.

I first came to Yellowstone with my wife Margaret to work for the Yellowstone Park Company at Canyon Village. My sister, Alice, had worked at Canyon during the summer of 1959—the summer of the big earthquake—and had compiled an impressive scrapbook. Her scrapbook pulled me in the direction of western adventure. So from Alabama, Margaret and I journeyed to a land that has been called "A World Apart" for good reason.

Approximately three million people a year visit Yellowstone National Park. To most, the visit provides a wonderful vacation experience from which to move on to other prime vacation spots. But to some a visit to Yellowstone becomes a life-changing event. It might be the geysers, or the abundance of wildlife, the waterfalls, the canyons, the mountains, or simply the wilderness quality of the place, that truly captures their soul.

I never dreamed that first summer would eventually become the first of over thirty spent working in Yellowstone, mostly as an interpretive park ranger for the National Park Service. In this capacity I have been blessed with many memorable experiences, consisting of both adventures and misadventures. I have learned some valuable lessons and insights from exploring the park's vast backcountry, for Yellowstone is a great teacher. It demands that you pay attention.

Three decades in the park have also provided me with a baseline for examining the health and integrity of the park and ecosystem regarding serious resource issues and park management. The following chapters represent some of my more memorable experiences combined with a smattering of philosophical offerings.

Part I

Adventures by Land

Union Falls

"Discovery" of a Waterfall

Yellowstone has long been famous for its many waterfalls. Given the many steep-edged, volcanic plateaus and abundant surface water, there are dozens of large waterfalls scattered about the park's road system and many more in the backcountry. The most famous is the magnificent 308-foot Lower Falls of the Yellowstone River at Canyon. I had developed a penchant for waterfalls during my second season working with the Yellowstone Park Company at Canyon Village. Margaret and I and several of our friends were attempting to visit all of the park's named falls depicted on official U.S. Geological Survey topographic maps.

Most of the park's waterfalls are located in the southwest corner of Yellowstone known as the Bechler area, named for Gustavus R. Bechler, the chief topographer of the 1872 Hayden Survey. This region of Yellowstone had become our favorite area in which to hike, and we found ourselves returning to it week after week, despite the long driving time from Canyon.

The Bechler country is so different from the rest of Yellowstone. As a native southerner, I naturally have a fondness for lush vegetation. Most of Yellowstone consists of a typical western environment with somewhat sparse vegetation, but the Bechler country is the exception. While many areas of the park may only receive five to twenty inches of annual precipitation, the Bechler region may receive forty to sixty inches.

Winter storms sweep in from the southwest, and heavy snows accumulate high up on the huge lava flow known as the Pitchstone Plateau, which then acts as a giant sponge throughout the summer months with water seeping and flowing out all over the place; hence the incredible abundance and variety of plants. With so much water flowing over the Pitchstone Plateau, this country is a waterfalls enthusiast's paradise! The area is also called the Cascade Corner for good reason.

On July 4, 1969, my friend and co-worker Rod Busby and I set out on a mission. Rod was my first hiking buddy and companion in Yellowstone. We were two greenhorns learning how to travel the backcountry together. Over the past two summers, we had visited all of Bechler's named waterfalls except one tucked away off the beaten path all by itself—Union Falls. We could not find much information on this waterfall. We were unable to locate any photos of the falls, and we could not find anyone who had ever been there. Ranger Tom Griffith at Canyon had not seen Union Falls, but told us that it was considered to be one of the park's "major" falls. "How high is Union Falls?" we asked. "Don't know," Ranger Griffith replied. "Why don't you take along some rope and measure it for us?"

The first decision Rod and I had to make consisted of which trail to take to Union Falls. According to maps, there appeared to be two primary choices: a twelve-mile hike in from the Bechler Ranger Station/ Cave Falls trailheads or an eight-mile hike in from Grassy Lake, situated along the very primitive forty-mile long Reclamation Road that skirts the park's southern boundary. We opted for the former because of the easier drive, more level terrain and more diverse scenery.

The fact that Union Falls was located off the beaten path and was situated so deeply in the backcountry only added to its mystique. Most of the other big waterfalls in the Bechler region were much more accessible to the hiker. Ouzel Falls, Iris Falls and Colonnade Falls were all located right along the very beautiful and popular Bechler River Trail, and Dunanda Falls was a fairly easy side trip from this trail. But Union Falls was the pariah. Rod and I were very anxious to see it once and for all.

Rod and I started from Cave Falls, which is one of the most unique waterfalls in the park. Cave Falls is very wide and contains a cave adjacent to it. It is possible to actually walk back into the cave and view the Falls River plunging over the brink from there. Just upstream from Cave Falls is the confluence of the Falls and Bechler Rivers.

The forest here is quite lush along the river with an abundance of shrubs and bushes. The trail follows the old Marysville Road, which the Mormons built in the 1880s from Marysville, Idaho, to Jackson Hole, Wyoming. The wagon tracks may still be visible in places though trees have grown up between the tracks.

The first of July is typically very early to visit the Bechler country. The snow up on top of the Pitchstone Plateau is still melting, resulting in a tremendous volume of water flowing off the Cascade Corner into the Bechler lowlands. The good news is that the many waterfalls in the Bechler region are truly stunning at this time of year with the streams' volume at a peak. The bad news includes standing water in the trails in places, many mosquitoes, and some very difficult stream fords.

Many hikers wait until mid-August or later to take advantage of the dry trails and absence of bugs, which is fine. But they are really missing the show when it comes to waterfalls. The delightful scenery along the way featured several moose sightings and lovely stands of aspen.

Since Rod and I had never seen a photo of Union Falls, we did not know what to expect. I will never forget hearing the initial roar from the trail. It was so loud that we assumed the falls must be right around the next bend in the trail. But as we continued to walk, the roar just continued to become louder until it was almost deafening. I glanced down into the little valley below us and took note of Mountain Ash Creek. It appeared relatively small and so tame. "How could this little stream possibly produce such a thunderous roar?" I asked Rod. It was becoming obvious to me that this waterfall would not come into view until the last possible moment. Many falls become visible from a fairly good distance away, but not this one.

As Rod rounded a bend in the trail ahead of me I heard him exclaim, "My God!" Suddenly we were staring at basically a cliff of whitewater. We had apparently caught Mountain Ash Creek at its peak flow in a heavy snowmelt year, and it appeared to be *flooding* over its precipice! We were mesmerized by the sight and sound of this stupendous falls, and we spent several hours exploring it. We now understood the name "Union" as we took note of the two forks that united at its brink. Before actually seeing it, I had guessed that perhaps the falls were named after some Union soldier.

We took photos from the overlook and then hiked down to the foot of the falls. We eventually hiked around and up to the brink and lowered the rope that Ranger Griffith had suggested we bring in an attempt to obtain a rough measurement of its height. We had brought along 150 feet of rope and it did not come close to reaching the bottom. We, therefore, estimated that the height of the falls was 250 feet, which is the figure that most publications use today, though I have read some that estimate 260 feet.

We hiked out the same trail that we had come in on and completed the trip without seeing another soul. I suspect that the early date had something to do with that, but it only added to our wilderness adventure. The Bechler country was not the easiest place to drive in and out of. We had driven down from West Yellowstone to Ashton, Idaho, and on into Cave Falls. We decided to go back on the Reclamation Road. Today, this road is usually referred to as the Ashton-Flagg or Grassy Lake Road.

As we neared Grassy Lake, we noticed a young man hitchhiking. Knowing that this road receives very little traffic, especially during the middle of the week, we stopped to pick him up. When we told him about our great hike to Union Falls, he pointed out that he had also been to the falls before and agreed that it was one of the best in the park.

But then he asked us if we had seen the other splendid falls in the area. We did not know what he was talking about. There were no other waterfalls shown on topo maps anywhere near Union Falls. The fellow told us that this "unknown" falls did not appear on any topo maps and that there was no trail to it, but he enthusiastically added that it was truly outstanding. "It's got to be 100 feet high and 100 feet wide!" he exclaimed. "It has only been recently discovered and only a handful of people have ever seen it," he added.

Rod and I pulled out our topo map, and the fellow pointed out a tributary that flowed into Mountain Ash Creek. "Just follow this tributary for about one mile and you'll come right to it," he said with a big grin. We knew exactly where the confluence of the tributary was. I had stopped to fish there because there was such a nice hole where the two streams joined. When we arrived at Flagg Ranch, the young fellow thanked us for the ride and departed. I will always regret that I did not get his name or quiz him on how *he* had come to know about this mysterious waterfall.

Rod and I had been attempting to visit and photograph every named waterfall in the park, but now we had the report of a large falls about which no one knew; neither was it shown on a topo map. Was this fellow pulling our leg? He had certainly *seemed* sincere. "How could a falls that big not even be on the map?" Rod asked. "I mean, I can accept that there might be an unnamed falls back there, but there isn't even a slash shown on the detailed fifteen minute USGS topo map," he added. Nevertheless, Rod and I were now hooked. We *had* to come back on our next day off and try to find this mysterious secret waterfall!

All during the next week of work, Rod and I could hardly wait for our next day off to arrive. When it finally did, we decided to drive down to Grassy Lake and hike in over Heartbreak Ridge to save a few miles. Of course, they don't call it "Heartbreak" Ridge for nothing, as there is a 700-foot difference in elevation from the top of the ridge to Mountain Ash Creek. Once we came to the tributary, we began to follow it, and at first the going was not too bad; in fact, we were able to follow an animal trail for about half a mile.

But, then, we entered a very boggy, swampy area where the going was horrendous. Not only that, but the vegetation became tangled and the terrain quite rugged. We were sinking in the bog and had to climb uphill away from the stream. Trouble is, away from the stream, we promptly ran into a dense forest replete with blow down. There just was no easy way to bushwhack through this mess!

Several times upon reaching fairly decent cascades and falls along the stream, we almost turned around. But we pushed on because the fellow had seemed so enthusiastic and sure of himself in describing the size of this waterfall. On the other hand, his estimate that it was only one mile up the tributary was obviously incorrect!

Finally, after 2 ½ hours of tough going, we were amply rewarded. First we heard the loud roar, and then the full breadth of the falls came into view as we rounded a bend in the stream. This young fellow had not exaggerated. For the second consecutive week, Rod and I had experienced the exhilaration of viewing a magnificent waterfall deep in the wilderness of Yellowstone at full volume! This waterfall was indeed 100 feet wide, though we estimated it to be closer to 80 feet high instead of 100 feet. Others have since estimated the falls to be 60 feet tall and 150 feet wide. Suffice it to say, this falls deserved to be ranked as one of Yellowstone's major waterfalls.

Rod and I had endured great difficulty in bushwhacking to this off-trail waterfall. In the process, we experienced a feeling of mystique and discovery that must have accompanied early Yellowstone explorers such as Colter, Bridger, Cook, Folsom, Peterson, and W.C. Gregg, who actually did explore and name some of the falls in the Bechler region in the early 1920s.

In subsequent years as other off-trail hikers found this waterfall, it became rather interesting to hear and read of just who the actual "discoverer" of these falls was. One guidebook writer, who suggested the excellent name of "Morning Falls," (the falls catches the early morning rays of the sun), claimed that *he* was the "discoverer" in 1977, despite the fact that Rod and I had visited it in 1969. Of course, Rod and I knew that *we* weren't the first to see this falls either. I recall Mary Meagher, Yellowstone's long-time bison researcher, once scolding me for my suggesting that Rod and I were among the first to ever see this waterfall in 1969.

She reminded me that park rangers, Army scouts and explorers had been venturing across Yellowstone's wilderness since the late 1800s, and while it is wonderful to *imagine* that we were among the first people there, it is altogether something different to claim to be the first. Yellowstone Park Historian Lee Whittlesey made this same excellent point in a book he co-authored, *Yellowstone Waterfalls and Their Discovery* when he wrote, "…it is more likely that Morning Falls has been known far longer than any historical record will ever show." Well, as I was to find in the summer of 2001, little did Mary and Lee know just how true their statements turned out to be!

While making a multi-day hike across the Pitchstone Plateau with ranger Sam Holbrook, and long-time Yellowstone backcountry explorers John and Deb Dirksen, we discovered irrefutable evidence that this splendid waterfall had indeed been known for well over 100 years. The four of us were hiking along an animal trail atop a ridge just upstream from Morning Falls when Deb discovered a large and very old blaze mark in a sizeable tree. The tree had long been dead; in fact, the top half of the tree was missing—probably due to a lightening strike.

It was obvious that the blaze had been made while the tree was living because the bark had grown over a good portion of the blaze before the tree died. We estimated that the blaze must have been made well over 100 years ago. Who could have made this blaze sometime around the turn of the century in this location so far removed from any trail? The Army established an outpost in Bechler in the late 1800's, but they would have had their hands full with duties far from *this* spot. Was it some Army scout out exploring on his off-duty days? An early unknown explorer? A poacher working far from established trails? And why did this person blaze a tree on this particular ridge? Obviously, we'll probably never know the answers to these questions. But this only adds to the mystique surrounding the "discovery" of this waterfall.

Island of Discovery

Deep in the wilderness at the southern tip of the South Arm of Yellowstone Lake is tiny Peale Island, named for Dr. A.C. Peale, a renowned mineralogist and member of the 1871 Hayden survey. As an avid paddler, I have enjoyed many canoe trips on Yellowstone Lake and have often wished that there were more islands scattered around the lake—for safety's sake as well as for camping possibilities. But, alas, such is not the case. There are only five named islands on the lake, and two, Molly and Carrington, are but piles of rocks.

Peale Island is a special place, and I have canoed there several times. The views of the Absaroka Mountains from its shores are spectacular, and the marshy meadows at the mouth of Grouse Creek are teeming with waterfowl. My first experience at Peale Island was to become my most memorable as more was "discovered" than just an island.

It was early September of 1969, and Margaret and I had just completed our second season working for the Yellowstone Park Company at Canyon. In those days, summer concession employees received only one day off each week, which made extensive excursions into the backcountry quite difficult.

Canyon Ranger Tom Griffith had instilled within me a great desire to visit the far reaches of Yellowstone Lake with his exquisite descriptions of the region. So Rod Busby and I arranged our employment termination dates in early September so we could have time for a four-day trip before we all had to return to our college fall terms. Our plans were to make a loop hike, starting from the South Entrance road and traveling past Heart Lake to the south tip of Yellowstone Lake, then over the Continental Divide to Fox Creek and out along the Snake River and South Boundary trails. We would have to cover seventy miles in four days.

We packed along a small inflatable raft because we wanted to explore the waters of Heart and Yellowstone Lakes and also try some fishing. At Heart Lake patrol cabin, we met a park service fire technician who issued us a fire permit, which in those days allowed flexibility in choosing a campsite. Once we arrived at the southern tip of the South Arm of Yellowstone Lake late in the afternoon of our second day, we began setting up camp. Suddenly we heard a high-pitched, blood-curdling growl—almost a scream, emanating from the forest behind us.

To this day I have no idea what animal made that sound, but it literally sent a chill up our spines. Was it a mountain lion? Rod and I walked over to the lake shore to see if we could spot any sign of animal activity, and to our dismay we found a fresh set of grizzly tracks near where we had planned to camp. While we certainly did not think the scream came from a bear, the combination of hearing that sound along with seeing fresh grizzly tracks unnerved us.

It was at this point that we gazed out across the waters of the South Arm and saw a densely forested island not that far from where we were standing. From our map we realized that we were looking at Peale Island, a mere dot on the lake. With our inflatable raft though, it seemed to represent a safe refuge. We decided to take the short paddle out to the island. Maybe it was a false sense of security, but we just didn't think that grizzlies, cougars or anything else would want to swim out to join us.

Our visit to this "island of discovery" did indeed produce several mysteries. The first mystery occurred when we struggled through the dense forest on the island trying to find an open space to pitch our tent. We suddenly came upon the last thing we ever expected to find twenty miles into the wilderness: a nice house complete with brick chimney! Yellowstone has many backcountry log patrol cabins, but this "cabin" was rather upscale. Apparently, having access to the lake allowed a few more modern materials to be used during its construction. In later years I found out that in addition to backcountry patrols, this cabin is used for various administrative uses, which might even include visits by distinguished visitors.

Our second mystery involved more sounds of the wilderness to which Rod and I had simply not been exposed before—the shrill, musical rattle of sandhill cranes and the raucous bugling of bull elk. There is always a first time, and this was our first time ever to hear sandhills and bugling bull elk in Yellowstone. However, it was our next mystery that perhaps would be the most compelling.

As we stood on the shore of Peale Island that evening to enjoy the alpenglow on the Absarokas, we noticed a very strange sight directly ahead of us. There was no visible beach across the way on the south tip of Yellowstone Lake. The lake's waters extended well into the dense forest surrounding the lake. This made absolutely no sense. Such a sight may not be unusual during the peak snow runoff in early summer when the lake is full to the brim, but this was September when the level of Yellowstone Lake is low. Extensive portions of the shoreline should have been visible. Adding to the mystery was the fact that the trees were still green. How could coniferous trees survive with their trunks being submerged in water?

We scratched our heads at this strange sight, but just dismissed it as another one of Yellowstone's mysteries. If only Rod and I had pursued this mysterious sight, we might have accelerated the discovery of a major phenomenon in Yellowstone.

About the same time that we were exploring Yellowstone in 1969, Bob Christianson of the U.S. Geological Survey had been given a daunting assignment: find the "Yellowstone volcanoes." Although scientists had long known that the geological origin of Yellowstone featured significant volcanic activity, no actual volcanoes had been found. Of course, Christianson was looking for something along the lines of a Mt. St. Helens or Mount Mazuma, now filled with Crater Lake. No such craters could be found.

Then Christianson had a stroke of luck. A friend from NASA called to ask Christianson if he would like to see some photos taken from outer space of the Yellowstone region. When Christianson viewed the photos, he could not believe his eyes. There was the volcanic crater for which he had been looking, but it was of massive size—measuring thirty by forty miles! No wonder he couldn't find it searching from the ground! Now that this huge Yellowstone volcanic caldera had been identified, the next question to be answered had to do with whether this enormous volcano was active or extinct.

In the summer of 1973, four years after Rod and I had gazed out at that strange mystery, someone else was on Peale Island scratching his head. It was Dr. Bob Smith, Geologist with the University of Utah. However, Bob had a theory to explain the mystery. He wondered if the huge Yellowstone volcanic caldera was still active, and the magma underneath was bulging up causing Yellowstone Lake to tilt. This would explain the water running into the forest on the southern end.

To test his theory, he decided to check elevations around the huge caldera to see if there had been any changes since they were last checked fifty years earlier. It came as no surprise to Bob to find that there had been some dramatic changes in elevation, especially near LeHardy Rapids of the Yellowstone River about six miles north of Fishing Bridge. Here the ground had actually lifted almost three feet since last checked in 1923, tilting the lake to the south, flooding the trees we had seen. In recent years, the earth's crust here has risen, dropped, and is now slowly bulging up again. Thus, much of Yellowstone Lake is actually in the middle of a living, breathing super volcano!

The next morning, Rod and I paddled our small raft off of our little island of discovery to the tip of the South Arm and continued our backpack trip up Passage Creek and over the Continental Divide. Old Ranger Griffith's descriptions of this region had been right on the mark. The trees were big, and the country was wild and spectacular. Standing on the divide at an elevation of over 9200 feet, we stopped to survey our surroundings. In the distance to the north, we could see the arms of Yellowstone Lake and the silhouette of Mount Washburn forty-five miles away. To the east rose the impressive slopes of the Two Ocean Plateau.

We realized that we were now over twenty-five miles from the nearest road. The only human being we had seen during the entire trip was the fire technician at Heart Lake patrol cabin. In this, only my second season in Yellowstone, I was totally in awe of the sheer size of this wilderness. I felt a sense of joy and freedom that I had never felt before in my twenty-three years of life.

Up until this trip my outings had consisted of only a single night spent in the backcountry, but this journey was different. It was an emotional time for me. The combination of being this deep in the wilderness and hearing its sounds, observing its sights and catching wild cutthroat trout had a profound effect on me. Visually, I could not get the sight of the distant peaks bathed in alpenglow out of my mind. The bugling of bull elk and calls of the sandhill crane were likewise embedded in my memory. Up until this trip, I had received some wonderful glimpses of Yellowstone's wilderness. However, now I felt as though I was discovering its very spirit, and it was very moving.

Rod and I had a strong interest in visiting all of the park's named waterfalls, and we were nearing the most remote one of all, Plateau Falls, situated on Plateau Creek near Mariposa Lake. We had to hike over a mile off-trail to reach it and arrived barely before dark. Compared to the named falls in the Bechler region, Plateau Falls was a disappointment, but it completed our goal of having visited every named falls on the USGS Yellowstone topo map.

By the time we reached Fox Creek, it was dark. Our last day we had planned to follow the Snake River all the way out to the road at the South Entrance. We had floated the Snake River through the Tetons earlier in the summer, and I was looking forward to hiking along it for this distance. The next morning we awoke to a temperature of twenty-two degrees and we had to build a fire to warm up.

We had expected to see the mighty Snake River in view, but it was nowhere to be seen. Rod looked around the area. "I don't get it," he said. "According to the map the Snake River ought to be right here in our camp, but all that's here is this little stream we hopped over when we came in last night." Then we looked at each other and laughed. We realized that this little stream in front of us *was* the Snake! It suddenly dawned on us that we were not that far from its headwaters, plus it was fall and streams were running low.

Our investigation of Plateau Falls had caused us to get behind our original schedule, and now we faced a thirty-mile hike out on our last day. Margaret was expecting me back at Canyon Village that evening, and we had to leave the park the next morning. Our forced march along the Snake River began. We found it fascinating to watch the Snake continue to grow in size and volume with every tributary that flowed into it. When we finally reached the confluence of the Heart River, the Snake began to take on the appearance of the large river we had expected.

We reached Snake River Hot Springs just as dark was settling into the forest. It was an eerie sight. The thermal basin was enshrouded in fog caused by the steam from the springs and the cold night air. A herd of elk was grazing in the basin, and a big bull was rounding up his harem.

Unfortunately, there was no moon, and we still had six miles to hike in the dark.

Walking down a pitch dark trail through the forest in grizzly country is just asking for trouble, so Rod and I talked and sang nonstop. We would take turns singing college fight songs or anything else just to make noise. Finally around 11:00 p.m., we reached the shore of the Snake River across from the road at the South Entrance. There would be no stepping over it here! We pulled out our little two-man raft, pumped it up once more and paddled across the river.

Since our car was parked fifteen miles up the road at the Heart Lake trailhead, we had hoped to hitch a ride. But trying to hitch a ride after Labor Day weekend at midnight is a losing proposition. Once we realized there was simply no traffic coming north from the Tetons, we decided to walk over to the ranger's residence at the South Entrance Ranger Station.

We knocked on the door, and a ranger finally came to greet us. Rod and I told him of our plight, and he asked us to repeat from where we had hiked on this day. "Fox Creek," Rod said.

"And you followed the Snake River all the way to here?" asked the ranger. "Yes sir," we said.

"That's damn near thirty miles!" he exclaimed. I'm sorry that I did not get this ranger's name because he was most gracious in meeting the needs of two tired backcountry travelers. He drove us to the trailhead, and Rod and I finally arrived at Canyon around 2:00 a.m. Our longest Yellowstone adventure had come to an end. It was truly an adventure of discovery for both of us. I have been back to Peale Island on numerous occasions, but by canoe, not backpack and raft! Up until a few years ago, there was a designated backcountry campsite on the island, but it was closed in order to reduce impact and allow the vegetation to recover along the delicate bay on the south end.

Since Peale Island is the only real island in Yellowstone Lake's three wilderness arms (the Molly Islands in the Southeast Arm are but scraps of gravel and rocks and are off-limits to protect waterfowl), it made for a popular campsite for wilderness paddlers. It was on this island that I truly began to discover the spirit of the Yellowstone wilderness as well as mysterious clues that eventually led to the discovery of Yellowstone's super volcano.

Granite Park and an
Indian Summer Snow in Yellowstone

After two wonderful summers working in Yellowstone in 1968 and 1969, Margaret and I faced a dilemma in 1970. I was due to graduate in December, enter the U.S. Air Force, and spend the month of June in basic camp at Charleston AFB, South Carolina. This did not leave us the necessary three months available to again work in Yellowstone. During the late winter of 1970, I was looking through a National Geographic guide to U.S. national parks, and happened across a photo of a rustic chalet called Granite Park, situated in a magnificent setting in the backcountry of Glacier National Park. Since it was located high in the mountains, the snow prevented the chalet from opening until July, which matched our available season perfectly.

According to the article, the chalet was managed by Ross and Kay Luding of West Glacier, Montana. I decided to write Mr. Luding a letter informing him that Margaret and I would like to work there. I really did not even expect a response, since I assumed that local folks were hired to work there. However, I was rather shocked to receive a letter from Mr. Luding two weeks later that read, "It just so happens that we need a married couple to manage Granite Park this summer. Can your wife cook?"

I excitedly showed the letter to Margaret. It appeared that we might yet be able to spend most of a third consecutive summer in the Northern Rockies! I quickly replied to Mr. Luding, telling him that we had been married for a couple of years, and as far as I was concerned, Margaret was an excellent cook. Within a few weeks Ross Luding sent us a letter of congratulations—the jobs were ours!

Margaret would be a cook, and I would be the "Man About the Place," which basically consisted of keeping the chalet's water pump working, hauling firewood and propane tanks and, in general, helping to supervise the daily operations. We would each receive $500.00 plus all our meals, for the two months' work. That might not sound like much, but in today's dollars it would be $2500. We were going to live on a mountain in the backcountry of Montana for two months. There would be no rent or living expenses, so we knew at the end of the summer we would have $1000.00 to deposit in our savings account.

A few weeks after we accepted the job offers, we received some disturbing news that I was afraid would wreck our summer plans. First, my summer camp dates were postponed to a later date, such that I could not get to Glacier until July 15. Second, Ross expected us at the chalet by June 20,

A Summer at Granite Park Chalet

since so much work had to be performed to get things ready for opening day on July 1. I wrote Ross with the bad news and expected the worst, but he replied that he had a handyman he would use in my absence as long as Margaret could still arrive on time.

Margaret and I decided the opportunity to spend a season at Granite Park was worth the travel inconvenience. Margaret flew out to Great Falls, Montana from Montgomery, Alabama, and then took a bus to West Glacier. I would drive our trusty 1964 Chevy II out as soon as my basic camp was completed, and expected to arrive July 15. Margaret, wearing a sharp, yellow, double-knit suit, arrived at the tiny bus stop in West Glacier. She was not dressed like someone about to spend a summer working as a cook in a high country chalet.

Ross Luding, a huge statuesque man, greeted her at the bus stop. A few pleasantries were exchanged before Margaret asked, "Has the other cook arrived?" Margaret and I had assumed all along that she would be assisting a primary cook or chef at the chalet. "Honey, you are *the* cook," Ross replied. "Oh my," Margaret moaned, "I didn't even bring a cookbook." "That's okay," Ross assured her, "My wife Kay will help with that." Kay was the cook at the park's other backcountry cabin, known as Sperry Chalet.

Since Margaret was the first employee to arrive, she was escorted up to a large old log building in the woods called Belton Chalet, and was shown to her room for the night. The place almost appeared haunted. There were large packrats running around in the attic all night, but Margaret was too tired to worry, and slept right through it. After she helped clean at Belton Chalet for another day, the rest of the crew arrived, and it was time to head up on the mountain. Ross, Kay, and the crew headed for the horse corral at Packers Roost. There, a wrangler had a pack train of supplies ready and horses for each of the eight crew members, plus Ross and Kay.

As the group headed up the seven-mile long trail, Margaret became somewhat alarmed by the fact that there were some steep drop-offs along the way, and so much of the trail was still covered in snow. About two miles out from Granite Park, Kay's horse slipped in the snow, and both went down. Kay, a spry sixty-nine-year-old lady, got up cursing and said, "I never did like horses. I'll just walk the rest of the way!"

Upon arriving it was obvious to all that there was much work to be completed during the next week before the chalet could open for customers. For one thing, snow was piled up to the second balcony, and shovels had to be used to dig through to get the doors open. Kay stayed for a couple of days and showed Margaret the meal plan. Dinners would consist of roast beef one night, ham the next, and turkey the next. These three menu items would rotate for the entire summer. Breakfast was the same every day— pancakes, ham, bacon, eggs, toast, coffee, and hot chocolate. Soon, Margaret added grits—a southern delicacy, to the breakfast menu. Trail lunches would consist of sandwiches primarily made from the food left over from the previous night's dinner.

A baker by the name of Annie would bake eight loaves of bread and several different kinds of pies each day, and would also prepare specialty a la carte items, such as tuna and egg salad sandwiches. When the chalet was full, about forty people were served with these meals. On most occasions, Margaret only had to cook one turkey with dressing, but on very busy nights, she would have to cook two.

Propane tanks (hauled in by mule) provided fuel for the kitchen's stoves and refrigerator. There was a small, gas-heated water heater for one shower, but this had to be rationed. With eight people it was not possible for each person to shower each night. Showers were rotated just like the ham, roast beef and turkey. Every three days you would get ham, and every three days you could take a shower! The really tough job was getting the sheets washed for forty customers per night. There was an old wringer washing machine but no dryer. The sheets would have to be hung out on clothes lines. Of course, during rainy weather the sheets just had to last a few extra days without washing.

Once each week the pack train from Packers Roost would arrive with fresh supplies, propane tanks and mail. Margaret had to get up at 5:30 a.m. each day, and did not retire until it finally got dark after 10:00 p.m. Each night at 9:00 p.m. the crew served the guests coffee and hot chocolate. If the weather was nice, guests would take their drinks outside to soak in the gorgeous views. If, on the other hand, the weather was cold and inclement, folks would gather around the wood stove. Occasionally, our crew would sing songs and perform humorous skits for the guests. Our favorite skit consisted of twisting two of the girls' arms and legs into one character we called "Freddy Friddle."

Despite her busy schedule, Margaret was able to keep a steady supply of letters coming to me at Charleston, South Carolina, where I was melting in the heat and humidity. Her descriptions of Granite Park depicted a magical, almost heavenly place. In fact, the primary view right out from the chalet was of "Heavens Peak." As soon as my basic training ended, I drove across the country as quickly as I possibly could. I made it from Charleston to West Glacier in three days.

When I arrived fairly late in the afternoon, Ross' son, Lanny, showed me where to store my car, and then took me inside to where the two-way radio was located. All transmissions to the chalet could be heard by everyone in the dining room. It just so happened that dinner was being served when Lanny got on the radio and transmitted, "We have one more late guest coming up." One of the girls at the chalet answered, "We're sorry, we are full for the night. We have no more room." Lanny replied, "This guest says he will sleep with the cook!" Margaret said the entire dining room erupted as she turned a deep shade of red.

Lanny then drove me up to the Alder trailhead. "This is the steepest trail up, but it is also the shortest," Lanny told me. He knew I was anxious to get up the mountain and see Margaret. I had four miles and over 1000 feet of elevation to gain, but I was in the best shape of my life. I had been running a fast two miles each morning for the past thirty days. I hit the trail practically running, but in a few minutes fell flat on my face heaving for air.

I suddenly realized that my training had all taken place at sea level, and I was now trying to run up a mountain at an elevation of 7000 feet. My body would need time to acclimate, so I slowed down. The trail switched back and forth straight up the side of the mountain, until it joined with the Garden Wall trail, a level trail from Logan Pass, but one which opens later in the summer due to lingering snow drifts. Once on the Garden Wall I could see the tiny chalet in the distance. The setting was everything Margaret had described in her letters. The chalet sat on a knob with incredible views in every direction.

Across the broad McDonald Creek valley to the west was situated the majestic, appropriately named, Heavens Peak. To the south were the hanging gardens and the Garden Wall. To the east was Swiftcurrent Peak and to the north were the rugged peaks of north Glacier. It was this view that Margaret had told me she enjoyed out her kitchen window, where she spent most of her time each day. As I hiked along the Garden Wall trail, little did I know that Margaret and the girls were sitting up on the roof with binoculars watching my every step.

Once I arrived, to my and Margaret's surprise, the crew performed a wedding ceremony for the two of us! The crew had actually made a wedding dress out of old, white sheets. Margaret had wondered why the crew occasionally asked for and took measurements of her frame. Most of the guests at the chalet that night actually assumed that the wedding ceremony was authentic, as they offered their congratulations!

The work at the chalet was grueling, and we had no days off. However, we could usually get in some short hikes during the afternoon. One day a visitor expressed dismay to me that we were working in a job that had no days off. "Well," I said, "you are off today and look where you decided to come for a visit. Just think, I am here at this heavenly place seven days a week!"

I found the history of the chalet as interesting as the surrounding mountains were beautiful. Although Glacier attained national park status in 1910, the Going-to-the-Sun Road was not completed until 1933. During the hiatus between those dates, much of the park's travel consisted of tourists on horseback, who stayed at camps and chalets spaced throughout the backcountry at one-day intervals. The small mountain structure was constructed of native stone in 1915, and became a popular stopover for guests on the famous sixty-five mile long North Circle trip.

During the 1920s this trip was one of the most spectacular and popular horseback vacation trips in the West. Granite Park is the only chalet that remains along that route, the others being razed after they were no longer in operation.

The china we used at the chalet was antique blue willow, having been originally stocked in 1915 by the Great Northern Railroad Company. On warm evenings, we served fruit drinks outside on the rock patio overlooking the valley. Margaret always cringed with worry that the beautiful pitcher might get broken or chipped. Thankfully, it never occurred on our watch.

During mornings and evenings we would often observe various species of wildlife from the chalet. With binoculars, we could spot mountain goats and grizzlies in the distance (walking around the grounds late in the evening was highly discouraged). Mule deer were common visitors to the chalet grounds, as they favored the vegetation. Our most frequent visitor was an animal that our crew became very attached to—a hoary marmot that we came to call "Johnny." The hoary marmot found in Glacier is a bit larger than the yellow-bellied marmot found in Yellowstone, but both are rather common around boulder fields in the Northern Rockies. Johnny actually learned to open the screen doors to the dining room, and would often join the guests for dinner on many evenings.

In addition to the magnificent scenery, wildlife, and fascinating guests, I enjoyed meeting the park rangers who stopped by Granite Park. One who stood out was backcountry ranger Eldon Bowman. Bowman always exuded an aura of regality as he rode in on horseback decked out, not in the green and gray uniform of the park service, but rather in leather buckskins. He had graying hair and looked like Jimmy Stewart's twin brother. I always felt that I was on the set of a western movie when Bowman was on the premises. He loved every minute of his patrols in the backcountry.

Then there was the young interpretive ranger, Joan Devereaux, who led hikes into Granite Park. Joan was staying overnight at the chalet on the terrible evening of August 13, 1967, when two nineteen year-old girls were tragically killed by grizzlies, one at Trout Lake and the other at the campsite below Granite Park. Even though that incident had occurred three years earlier, I quickly learned that she was reluctant to discuss details of that night.

Steve Frye occupied the fire lookout station atop Swiftcurrent Mountain, high above Granite Park. I enjoyed occasionally hiking up to visit Steve, and it was always good to see him down at the chalet. Steve eventually became the Old Faithful Subdistrict Ranger in Yellowstone before, in time, becoming Chief Ranger back in Glacier.

My favorite ranger was Bob Maury, because I had known him in Yellowstone during the summers of 1968 and 1969. Bob had just been transferred to Glacier, and it was always fun to chat about our Yellowstone backcountry adventures when he stopped in for a visit. Bob was particularly interested in our proper storage and disposal of garbage to prevent grizzlies from becoming habituated to human foods. Neglect in this area had perhaps contributed to the bear problems during the summer of 1967. The seven weeks spent at Granite Park were truly spectacular, and they quickly passed.

Our time spent there was a unique and wonderful experience, but by summer's end we longed for Yellowstone. Glacier is a spectacular, gorgeous, mountain paradise, but I guess it is Yellowstone's diversity that captures my soul. Our season ended on Labor Day, and Margaret and I hiked off the mountain. After seven weeks in the backcountry, I will never forget how strange automobile fumes smelled as I came out to the road.

Margaret and I had made plans to hook up with our friend and hiking companion, Rod Busby, for a late season trip before we all had to return to college. Rod had spent his summer working in the Grand Tetons. We agreed to meet at Jenny Lake Campground, and then head into the Bechler country for a four-day backpacking trip.

We should have known something was in the offing the first night at Jenny Lake, when high winds came up during the evening, and toppled lodgepole pines over like match sticks. Fortunately, we had camped in an open area, but the next morning we were shaken to see how many trees had come within only a few feet of tents in much of the campground.

September in the Bechler country is spectacular with the aspen trees turning yellow, and the huge meadows tinted a golden brown. The elk were bugling and the weather was picture perfect, as we camped along the Bechler River our first evening in. This was Indian summer at its finest. The following day we headed up the Bechler Canyon, and soon ran into a horse party. There were two men on horseback, with three additional pack horses. They appeared to have everything with them but the kitchen sink! We pulled off the trail to let the horse party pass, and one of the men stopped to give us some "good" news, "You folks will be glad to know that we left you a tarp and some eggs up at camp." I wanted to give the two men a lecture in backcountry etiquette, but thought the better of it.

Hiking across the Bechler Meadows, then turning up the Bechler Canyon rates at the top of my list for spectacular scenery. Near the mouth of the Bechler Canyon you can see the impressive 230 foot-high Ouzel Falls off in the distance, plunging over the plateau's edge. Once you enter the canyon itself, the trail follows the Bechler River, which merrily dances and cascades downstream.

After fording several streams thigh deep, we finally reached our camping destination at Three River Junction. Just as the horse party had promised, there was a big black plastic tarp left in camp. "They had five horses and could not pack it out," mused Rod. We sure didn't have room in our backpacks for it, so we hoped that the next horse party to come through would be more sensitive to no-trace camping and pack it out.

After enjoying viewing several of the major falls in the area, we returned back down the canyon to the Bechler Ford campsite for our last evening. Here the canyon opens up to meet the extensive meadows. We knew it was our last evening in the wilderness before returning to college, so we all soaked in this magical Indian summer day. The fishing was great in the river, and the low angle glow of the sun was lighting up the steep slopes of the Cascade Corner--the edge of the huge lava flow known as the Pitchstone Plateau. We spotted a huge bull moose with full rack, and the elk were bugling. The shrill, musical rattle of sandhill crane seemed to reverberate off the slopes. What more could anyone ask for? That evening, there was no moon and the stars were brilliant. We enjoyed sitting around our campfire, absorbing its warmth, as we shared more of our summer stories—ours from Glacier, and Rod's from the Tetons.

We had packed along an old Coleman canvas tent for the three of us. Rod was on one end, I was in the middle, and Margaret was next to me. Soon after we retired to the tent for the evening, the gorgeous, calm, weather conditions of Indian summer began to come to an end. The horrible winds from a few nights earlier at Jenny Lake Campground began to reoccur, but this time, the winds were twice as strong. Our designated campsite at Bechler Ford was in the middle of a mature lodgepole pine forest. As the night progressed the wind only got worse.

I've never heard an approaching tornado, but I had to wonder if it sounded something like the roar of these winds. Every few minutes we would hear another falling tree, known as "widowmakers," by those who spend a lot of time in the forest. When we had entered our tent, the night had been calm. Consequently, I was not even aware of the condition of the trees around our tent. As I became more experienced in the woods, I learned to survey the trees above me before pitching a tent. However, on this night, I'm not sure it would have mattered. The wind was howling so strongly that most of the trees going down were live trees, not dead ones.

Each time we heard the sound of another tree crashing to the forest floor, Margaret would tightly squeeze my arm in fear. As I lay in the tent, I considered our options. Should we try to move our tent? That would be tough considering the night was pitch black. We finally decided to say our prayers and get some sleep. Apparently our prayers were answered, because the winds seemed to gradually die down. However, for some reason the tent seemed to be closing in on us. At first I thought Rod and Margaret were just jamming into me, so I tried to push them away, but they complained that they had no room either. The next morning we discovered why. The winds had blown in a major snowstorm without our realizing it. As I emerged from the tent, I could see why we ran out of room during the night; there were seven inches of heavy snow weighing it down. We were lucky the tent had not collapsed!

Indian summer had given way to winter, at least for the time being. The golden meadows were now covered with snow. Heavy, gray clouds now draped over the edge of the plateau, replacing the brilliant deep blue skies from the day before. In its own different way, it was a beautiful scene. The weather had not dampened the enthusiasm of the sandhill cranes, judging from their incessant calls. Hot chocolate hit the spot on this frosty morning and soon, the three of us were trekking across the snow-laden Bechler Meadows on our way out of the backcountry for another summer.

The following summer, Margaret and I would find ourselves stationed at Malmstrom AFB, in Great Falls, Montana, from where we continued to explore the Yellowstone country in all seasons. I subsequently have spent hundreds of nights out in the Yellowstone wilderness, but I never experienced another wind-blown night quite like that night at Bechler Ford.

Twenty-five years after our magical summer spent at Granite Park, Margaret and I returned to the chalet with our daughters, Caroline and Alison, for a visit. At that time the chalet continued to operate with full meals prepared on the premises, just as Margaret had done. We found a logbook for former employees, and noted that all of our former friends and co-workers had made it back for a visit. We were the last ones to do so. As of this writing, Granite Park Chalet is still open for business, but, unfortunately, no longer provides the wonderful home-cooked meals like Margaret prepared.

Patrol Cabins and The Smooth One

In 1972, while I was in the Air Force stationed at Malmstrom Air Force Base in Great Falls, Montana, I was asked by the Sierra Club to write a trail guide for Yellowstone's backcountry. At the time there was a nice pamphlet available by Bill Chapman called "Yellowstone Backcountry," but there was no comprehensive guide to the park's over 1000 miles of trails. I had already covered quite a few of the trails during my summers working for the concession in the park, and now my unusual working schedule with the Air Force allowed me substantial time off for hiking. I would often work four straight twenty-four hour tours, and then have five days off. However, in order to have the sufficient time to schedule a backpack trip through Yellowstone's largest wilderness area, the Thorofare, it was necessary to take leave.

I needed at least a week to take the seventy-five mile-long trip I wanted, which was along the east shore of Yellowstone Lake all the way down to Thorofare Ranger Station, and then west along the South Boundary Trail, finally exiting at the South Entrance. My old hiking buddy, Rod Busby, arranged time off from graduate school at Washington State University to join me for the trip in mid-September. September has always been my favorite time of the season to hike in Yellowstone. All of the pesky insects are long gone. The streams are down and easier to ford (and to fish). The meadows are tinged a golden hue and the mountain peaks are often frosted white. Best of all the elk are in the rut and the incessant bugling by the bulls adds an exciting element to the wilderness experience.

However, there is one potential downside to hiking in September, and that is the weather. Long periods of cold, rainy, sleety weather can set in. Even snow can fall; not the nice, dry fluffy stuff that slides off of your parka in the winter, but rather the heavy, wet, sticky stuff. I'll be the first to admit that I'm a fair weather fan when it comes to wilderness camping. While I love a brief shower or even an extensive overnight thunderstorm when out in the backcountry, I just have a hard time enjoying myself during long periods of cold, rainy weather.

The day that we arrived at the west entrance to get our backcountry permit, we learned of the miserable weather forecast from Ranger Terry Danforth. When we told him of our plans to spend over a week in the backcountry, he said, "All you guys are going to be able to do is hole up somewhere in a tent and be miserable." That was bad enough to hear but to make matters worse he said it with a smile on his face. I explained to Ranger Danforth that normally I would just postpone our trip, but that I really had to take this hike for the field research for writing the trail guide, plus our schedules had to be arranged ahead of time so we were stuck with this week—bad weather or no.

I knew that Yellowstone maintained dozens of backcountry patrol cabins, and asked Mr. Danforth if he thought we could get permission to use some. He explained that with hunting season starting up in the surrounding national forests, rangers would most likely be scheduled to use them for poaching patrols. He did go on to say that it would not hurt to ask the District Ranger at Lake Ranger Station, though.

Rod and I secured our backcountry permit and headed for the Thorofare trailhead, located about ten miles east from the road junction at Fishing Bridge. On our drive over to Lake, the predicted miserable weather began to move in. Low clouds gathered overhead and a steady, cold rain began to fall. Rod and I decided to stop by Lake Ranger Station just for the heck of it, though we held out little hope that we would get permission to use the cabins. I walked into the historic log building and a ranger by the name of John Rapier came out to greet us. I told John of our plight—that I was in the Air Force and I had taken leave for a week to do some field research for a trail guide, and the weather forecast was grim. I asked him if there was anyway we might be able to use the cabins in the area.

I braced myself for the expected rejection, but John walked back into his office and returned with a key. "The first priority use of the cabins is to our backcountry rangers and trail crews, so if any of those folks show up you'll need to stay at your campsites," he said. "Just return the key after your trip." I shook Ranger Rapier's hand, thanked him, and walked out the front door of the station. "Rod," I said, "get in the car and let's head for the trailhead before anyone changes their mind!"

Frankly, in decent weather, the last thing I would want to do is use a NPS patrol cabin. I had stayed in one of Yellowstone's patrol cabins a few years earlier, when I had worked at Canyon for the Yellowstone Park Company. I had gotten to know Canyon Ranger Tom Griffith quite well. I was a greenhorn trying to get information about Yellowstone's vast backcountry, and Griffith had it. He had covered much of the park on horseback, including the Thorofare, and he had also participated in several lengthy winter ski patrols.

One day Griffith called me into his office and told me that he had received a report that the Mary Mountain patrol cabin had been broken into, and wanted to know if I would like to hike out, replace the lock, and stay for the night. Naturally, I jumped at the chance. The rustic old cabin, located next to Mary Lake, dated back many decades, and it was fascinating to read the cabin's official logbook, which detailed so many patrols in to the cabin.

Staying in a cabin is definitely a different experience from camping out. After all, I enjoyed sitting around the campfire, gazing up at the night sky, and easing into my tent in the evening. A cabin on the other hand, tends to provide a shield between a person and the wilderness. It's almost as though you "lock out" the wilderness. No, you don't have to worry about a bear or mountain lion walking over your tent, but hey, isn't that part of the wild experience in traversing the Yellowstone backcountry? Not to mention the significant chores involved in opening up and closing down the cabin.

Ranger Rapier had emphasized the importance of leaving the cabins in perfect condition, and had provided us with a checklist on how to properly secure the windows and shutters, lay fires in the woodstoves, hang the blankets and mattresses, sweep and mop the floors, bait and set the mousetraps, etc. The checklist that Rapier gave us was an old one, dating back to the 1940s. The substantial time it took to open up and then close down the cabins would take time away from being out on the trail. But, alas, the weather on this trip was most definitely *not* decent. In fact, it was absolutely horrendous!

The rain was falling heavily as we pulled on our ponchos and headed down the trail. In weather like this it is impossible to stay dry. After a couple of hours on the trail, our boots and legs were soaked, and the rest of our bodies soon became wet from condensation. Despite our discomforts the beauty of the wilderness was striking. I have often felt that some of the most gorgeous scenes in the backcountry occur during inclement weather. The misty clouds drift over the mountains and lakes and create an almost ethereal setting. The problem arises when it is time to make camp for the evening. By the time we reached Park Point patrol cabin at the eight-mile mark, we were absolutely soaked. The view of Yellowstone Lake from Park Point was stunning, but we were wet, cold, and physically, quite miserable. Even though we had planned to hike further down the trail, we knew this would be our last chance for a cabin on this day. The cabin was obviously empty so we decided to duck in and dry out.

After opening up the doors and shutters, we stoked up the wood stove and hung out all of our wet gear. On this rainy, dreary, day we would trade sitting around the campfire for sitting around the woodstove. Before leaving Fishing Bridge we had picked up some supplies, and without my knowledge, Rod had secretly purchased a half-pint of Calvert's sipping whiskey—"the smooth one"-- to enjoy in camp. After dinner while sitting around the stove still trying to dry out our gear, Rod surprised me by pulling out the flat bottle and offering me a cup. I recorded our day's observations in the cabin's official logbook, and pointed out that we concluded the evening around the woodstove with a sip of Calvert's--the "smooth one."

Each morning we would see a promising break in the skies, but by about 10:00 a.m., the rains would start up again, and continue throughout the day. By the time we reached the next cabin, we were in dire need of shelter for drying out our gear. After Park Point cabin (which unfortunately burned down several years ago and has not been rebuilt—some camper apparently was cooking on the porch and knocked the stove over), we stayed at Cabin Creek cabin, Thorofare Ranger Station and Fox Creek cabin. We had been fortunate that no rangers or trail crews needed them on the nights we were there. Each night we would take out the official cabin logbook, and record our day's observations. We always concluded our entry with the same comment, "Tonight we again enjoyed sitting around the woodstove and sipping Calvert's—the smooth one!" I also pointed out our deep appreciation to the rangers for allowing us to use the cabins, and that I intended to leave a nice portion of our prized Calvert's—"the smooth one" behind at our last stay for their enjoyment.

Reading the logbooks each night was a delight. Something I found particularly fascinating were the accounts of rangers on lengthy winter ski patrols. The one name that came up more than any other was Ranger Jerry Mernin. It was obvious that Mernin loved Yellowstone's wild country in any season. Frankly, I was amazed at the stamina and strength displayed on the long winter trips. Mernin and his colleagues would often rise at 4:00 a.m. to begin their ski trip of ten or so miles to the next cabin. This was necessary because of winter's short days, and also to take advantage of the hard, crusty snow frozen during the evening. Once the day warmed up the snow would lose its "set," causing skis to sink deep into the snow. Little did I know that the knowledge I learned from reading those entries by Mernin and other backcountry rangers would prove to be very valuable when I ventured out on my own lengthy winter trip across Yellowstone a couple of years later.

One entry that Mernin made at the Thorofare cabin that caught my attention was the night that he had gone outside to the small stream to get some water, and brush his teeth before retiring for the evening. Apparently a grizzly bear had the same idea, because the two of them met nose-to-nose at the stream. Mernin's entry stated that he jumped up, yelled, and ran back toward the cabin. The bear also jumped up, let out a wail, and headed back into the brush! Mernin told me in a recent conversation that he and the grizzly "simply had a mutual disregard for each other!"

Sometimes several decades of entries can pass before the logbook is filled and taken to be stored in the park's archives, located in the new Heritage and Research Center near the park's north entrance. One of the more memorable entries was from the Fox Creek cabin. Entries in the logbook dated all the way back to the 1930s, and apparently at that time the cabin was used on a regular basis by a backcountry ranger stationed there. Each day the ranger would record long, glowing reports of his patrols during the day through some of the wildest country to be found anywhere in the West. One day though, the ranger's entry was extremely brief: "Today I received my orders of transfer to Carlsbad Caverns. Shit!"

Of course Rod and I had many wonderful observations to record in the logbooks as well. A highlight was our experience in attempting to cross Big Game Ridge along the South Boundary Trail. The trail climbs all the way up to an elevation of 9700 feet, and traverses open meadows much of the way. Rod and I had taken note in the Fox Creek patrol cabin logbook of several harrowing fall patrols by rangers who became lost in snowstorms. Ranger Craig Johnson had made one entry that stood out.

Ranger Johnson had been crossing Big Game Ridge on horseback when a fall snowstorm hit. Normally, when traveling above timberline in Yellowstone, you rely on the orange trail markers attached to old trees that are held up by rock piles. However, according to Johnson the snow had blown in quickly and horizontally, and had covered everything, including the trail markers, in several inches of white. He simply could not find the way. He and his horse had to spend several unplanned hours in the dark out on the ridge as a result.

Two years later I began working for the NPS and was driving through the Northeast Entrance Station with Margaret and my sister Alice. As I looked at the ranger inside the station I noticed the name badge: "Craig Johnson." It was my day off and I was in my civvies, and could not pass this opportunity up. "Say, Ranger Johnson, are you the one who got lost in the snow on Big Game Ridge a couple of years ago?" I asked. He looked at me with the most puzzled look on his face and answered, "Yes, but how did you know?" I just smiled and said, "Oh, it's a pretty famous story you know."

After reading the entries about rangers getting lost on Big Game Ridge, Rod and I were a bit concerned as we began the 1500-foot climb from Fox Creek. The last time Rod and I had visited Fox Creek, we had followed the Snake River trail, rather than hike over the ridge on the South Boundary trail. As we began our climb the miserable weather kicked in on cue by mid-morning. This time though, the rain began to change to snow, as we continued our climb. "This is great." I thought. "Now *we* are going to find out what Big Game Ridge looks like during a snowstorm." However, the snow did not blow in horizontally, so the trail markers did not become covered, and also the snow was not falling heavy enough to block our ability to find the next trail marker once we climbed above timberline. Nevertheless, it was very easy for us to see the potential for losing the trail during a storm above timberline if visibility was reduced.

Once on top of the ridge we were disappointed to find ourselves practically in the clouds with no views. We had hoped to enjoy wonderful vistas of this southern portion of Yellowstone from this vantage point. Then just as we were mired in a pity party, an amazing thing happened. An opening appeared in the thick clouds, the sun shone through, and a full rainbow over Big Game Ridge appeared. We ecstatically reached for our cameras and began snapping photos of this magnificent scene. Mount Hancock suddenly appeared to the north so close that it almost seemed that we could reach out and touch it. The views were short-lived, however. After about five minutes of thrilling views, the clouds descended back down upon us, and we returned to basically trying to just locate the next trail marker in the fog. This was not easy and we continued to be haunted by Craig Johnson's log entry.

Years later I would think back to this trip when long-time ranger Bob Jackson told a friend and me that he would continue serving as a backcountry ranger, "as long as I can find the next trail marker."

As we descended the west side of Big Game Ridge toward Harebell patrol cabin, the snow turned back to rain, and the miserable weather that had plagued us the entire trip continued. At least we had navigated over the ridge without losing the trail, but it had not been easy. We had not seen another human on the entire trip, but as we neared Harebell cabin, we came across a hunting party on horseback about fifty yards away. As we approached the cabin the group eyed us with suspicion, especially when I unlocked the cabin's door. They must have assumed we were government employees, but probably wondered where our horses were!

This group was close to the south boundary, but nevertheless, park regulations prohibit guns within the park. Sometimes, hunters have been known to wander across the boundary in pursuit of that trophy bull elk, thus the need for fall ranger patrols along the boundaries. The confused hunting party promptly departed the area.

Once again the cabin was a lifesaver. We used the warmth of the wood stove to again dry out all of our gear on this our final evening in the wilderness. We recorded our day's adventure up on top of Big Game Ridge in the Harebell cabin logbook. The conclusion to our entry was the same as it had been at the previous four cabins: "After another great evening sitting around the wood stove, we enjoyed a few sips of Calvert's—the smooth one!" We kept our word and placed the bottle of Calvert's with at least one-third of the contents remaining in the food cabinet.

Harebell cabin was our fifth consecutive cabin to stay in. We were amazed at our good luck in finding each cabin empty during our six-day trip. The weather, while being variable enough to provide many memorable visual experiences, had been consistently brutal. It would literally take all night for our gear—boots, socks, pants, sweaters, etc.—to dry out next to the wood stove. If not for the cabins, we would have had to make a forced march to exit the wilderness. While I still preferred to camp in a tent, I had truly gained an admiration for these patrol cabins during inclement weather. From the log entries it was also apparent how important it was to leave a cabin in perfect condition. It was imperative that a "one-match" fire be laid in the wood stove in case someone struggled to the cabin on his or her last legs.

Once I started working for the Park Service in 1974, I was afforded the opportunity to stay in many of the park's patrol cabins. As I read the old logbooks and discovered details about the exploits of backcountry rangers such as Jerry Mernin, Dale Nuss, Bob Jackson, Ted Scott, Bob Maury, Tom Griffith, Pete Thompson, and others, I developed a true appreciation for these men. I could not help but wonder if Yellowstone's rangers in the future would be as tough as these men regarding their abilities to traverse the park's wilderness during all seasons, including the middle of winter.

During the early 1990s, Leslie Quinn, Director of Interpretive Services for the concession in the park (now Xanterra) and a longtime Yellowstone friend, stopped by to ask me if I had read *Guardians of Yellowstone* by Chief Ranger Dan Sholly. "No," I replied. "Well, you ought to, there are a couple of pages pertaining to you." When I asked Les what it was about he just grinned and told me to read it myself. I had met Chief Ranger Sholly on a few occasions, but could not imagine that he would have anything on me to write two pages about! When I read the pages Les was referring to, I almost fell out of my chair laughing. It had been almost twenty years since I had taken that trip through Thorofare, staying in the cabins during the dreadful weather. Yet it was only now that I learned "the rest of the story" regarding the bottle of Calvert's—the smooth one. The following is an excerpt from Sholly's book that detailed a trip he took into the Thorofare with Resource Management Specialist Stu Coleman, to meet backcountry rangers Jerry Mernin, Bob Jackson, and Andy Mitchell:

> After supper Jerry told of a time many years ago when he had been on a boundary ride to stock the patrol cabins with winter rations. ... Jerry had to push himself hard but had finally reached the Park Point patrol cabin on the east side of Yellowstone Lake as night was falling. Tired and wet, he settled down in the cabin and read through the logbook. One entry that piqued his interest was by a couple of hikers who had reached the cabin a few days before in a storm. Their day had been especially difficult, and they had written their thanks to the rangers of Yellowstone for letting them use the cabin. They had ended their report: "Really enjoyed a body-warming sip of 'Calvert the smooth one,'" and signed it "Orville E. Bach, Jr./1ˢᵗ Lt. U.S.A.F." Jerry remembered having given permission to a Mr. Bach to use the cabin. The young man had said he was doing some research for a trail book. Jerry traveled further south into the wilderness to the Cabin Creek patrol cabin. The weather had worsened considerably, and he barely made it to shelter before dark. As before, he wound down before going to bed by reading the cabin's logbook. To his surprise there was another of Lieutenant Bach's entries ending again, "And before we turned in we really enjoyed a few sips of 'Calvert the smooth one.'" And so the saga continued the next two days: terrible storms, struggling to get to a patrol cabin by sunset, finding lengthy entries by Lieutenant Bach in the log books—each ending "Really enjoyed a sip of 'Calvert the smooth one.' I plan to leave some for the rangers, for their hospitality, at the last cabin I stay in." Until at last, Mernin found himself thinking of that bottle of Calvert's whiskey constantly as his horse plodded across the Two Ocean Plateau.

He bounded into the Harebell cabin to see if Lieutenant Bach and his bottle of Calvert had been there. Sure enough, there was the entry. And—hurray!—the dear, kind fellow had written that he'd left the remainder of his whiskey in that cabin's food pantry. Mernin flung open the pantry door and—there it was! He grabbed the half-pint flat bottle and held it up to the light. His heart dropped to his socks; there wasn't so much as a drop in it. If he could have, he would have strangled Lieutenant Bach right then and there. But, as it turned out, the log entry made clear that Lieutenant Bach had been true to his word. For the final sentences in the book belonged not to Lieutenant Bach but to a young ranger Mernin had working under him. That ranger, it turned out, had ridden through the area only a day before Mernin and had just beat him to the whiskey bottle. "Sat around the stove as the wind howled outside, but found tremendous pleasure in sipping 'Calvert the smooth one,'" he had written with undisguised pleasure. Mernin closed the book and tried to sleep. But on that night sleep hadn't come as easily as usual.

After I stopped laughing, I walked over to the Hamilton's general store and purchased a small bottle of Calvert's, and mailed it to Mr. Mernin at Lake Ranger Station with a note: Dear Jerry: Here's your smooth one—twenty years late!

The NPS no longer allows the public to use patrol cabins; however, there are dozens of Forest Service patrol cabins within the Greater Yellowstone Ecosystem that are no longer officially in use, that the public can rent out. For information, check at any U.S. Forest Service Ranger Station.

Backpacking the High Country

Mystery at Parker Peak

I have always been intrigued by the stories of strange and mysterious noises occurring over Yellowstone Lake. These stories date back many decades. According to the 1966 Haynes Guide, "Strange overhead noises at Yellowstone Lake have been reported many times from the earliest days of exploration to the present. This strange noise...is not like the sound of a distant flight of birds nor any shore noise, but is weird and startling." Although I have spent many days and evenings paddling on Yellowstone Lake, I have never experienced this mysterious sound, reported to begin with a low roar, then rise in pitch, and then fade out.

The closest I have come to encountering a mystery on Yellowstone Lake occurred near Breeze Point. Jim Lenertz and I had just rounded the point on our way in to Grant. It was about sunset and the lake's waters were a paddler's dream--as calm and placid as a sheet of glass. There were no other boats anywhere in sight on West Thumb, but suddenly we saw a single wave about a foot high coming directly at us. It was the only wave on the entire lake, and it was hundreds of yards in length.

We just assumed that there must have been some kind of slight tremor to cause the solo wave, though I have a hard time understanding how only *one* wave would have been created, rather than several more. However, while I have never encountered weird noises on Yellowstone Lake, I certainly did once come across very strange and mysterious noises near Parker Peak.

Al Duff and I were on a lengthy September backpacking trip in 1976 along the eastern boundary of the park high in the Absaroka Range. Al and I had paired up several times for long September excursions into the backcountry. Our trip began at The Thunderer trailhead and took us up to Canoe Lake, Bootjack Gap, Parker Peak, down to Cold Creek, past Frost Lake, and eventually out at Pahaska Tepee near the East Entrance. We had set up our tents at a backcountry campsite near Parker Peak, and had just completed eating dinner. There were still a couple of hours of daylight left, so we decided to climb up to the summit of Parker Peak, and enjoy the views on this beautiful, clear fall day.

Once we reached the summit, the rich, low angle light was starting to bathe the mountains in a golden glow. We had a 360-degree view of the surrounding terrain. We could clearly see our campsite in the distance. Most of the terrain below us consisted of open high mountain meadows with only small islands of trees. Of particular interest was a herd of about thirty elk grazing in the meadow directly below us.

We had taken our field binoculars with us and were enjoying watching the elk when suddenly, without warning, there came a very loud, metallic, *clanging* sound that seemed to be coming from below us in the vicinity of our campsite. The noisy *clang, clang, clang* continued for about fifteen seconds! Al and I briefly looked at each other with puzzled expressions on our faces.

The view below us was completely open as far as the eye could see. We were in the middle of a very wild area. There was no one else around. My first thought was that a bear was ransacking our camp, but I glassed the area closely, and everything was peacefully intact. Of course, we only had a few aluminum pots, and this noise sounded more like someone ringing a school or dinner bell. I also wondered if there was a horse party in the area, and perhaps a pack mule had bolted away. Again, no sign of any such activity below us was apparent. Then it struck me. This loud, clanging sound had made quite an impression on Al and me, but the entire herd of elk below was completely oblivious to the noise. Not a single animal raised its head to acknowledge the sound or look around.

Al and I hiked back down to our campsite and searched around for any evidence that anything had passed through camp. Nothing out of the ordinary could be found. Now if I had been out by myself, I guess I would have just dismissed the sound as maybe something that I had somehow imagined. But since Al was there with me and we both heard the same, inexplicable sound, the experience had to go down as a genuine Yellowstone backcountry mystery.

I have told this story many times to others, and no one has ever offered up a good solution to the mystery. Several folks have told me that we were just hearing bull elk fighting each other, but that could not have produced the noise we heard. First, elk antlers clashing would produce a "clacking" not "clanging" noise, and second, the only elk in the area were directly below us and as mentioned they were calmly feeding all during the time this loud noise was heard. So there you have it—an unexplained mystery. Maybe one of these days I will hear the oft-reported mysterious noises over Yellowstone Lake, but until I do, my mystery sound location is near the summit of Parker Peak.

The Thunderstorm

During the summer months the Yellowstone plateau is home to some of the most violent mountain thunderstorms in the West. An August day can start out refreshingly clear and cool in the morning, but by mid-afternoon the day can degrade into a hair-raising, ear-splitting, electrical storm, complete with a couple of inches of hailstones. For this reason, it is imperative that hikers, backpackers, climbers, and paddlers always keep an eye on the clouds, and be prepared for sudden changes in the weather.

Hank Barnett and I were once only a half-mile from the summit of Yellowstone's highest mountain, Eagle Peak at 11,358 feet, but a dangerous storm sent us scurrying back down the mountain for cover. Just as golfers know to get off of a golf course during an electrical storm, so should paddlers get off lakes, climbers get off peaks, and hikers avoid high points and single trees.

The most dramatic thunderstorm I ever observed in Yellowstone was made even more spectacular by the unique mountain setting that it occurred in. Jim Lenertz and I were on a backpacking trip northwest of Mount Chittenden in 1978. We had hiked over Avalanche Peak to join the trail between Crow Creek Pass and Jones Pass, and had planned to camp at a small lake along the mountain crest that forms the boundary between Yellowstone and Shoshone National Forest.

The summer had been unusually dry, and consequently, there were no snowbanks remaining along the ridge this late in August. However, according to our topo map, the lake, which was situated around 9000 feet, was a permanent body of water. But, when we rounded the bend on the ridge where the lake was supposed to be, all we saw below was a brown depression in the forest. The lake was completely dried up!

We were low on water so obviously it was time to go to "plan B." We had about two hours of daylight remaining, so we opted to drop down off the ridge into what appeared to be a small meadow surrounded by mountains. We were betting that the meadow would have some springs originating in it, but first we had to descend about 1000 feet to find it. We reached the meadow barely before dark, and found just what we were looking for.

As we had hoped, there were some springs flowing, so we knew we had water for the night. However, the terrain was not exactly level to accommodate a tent, but we had to make do. After pitching our tent we boiled some water for our freeze-dried dinners, and then retired for the evening. Our day had been a long one with many more ups and downs than expected. The evening was relatively warm and our tent had a full view out the front door.

As we settled in for the night we began to notice some bright flashes of light above the surrounding peaks followed by distant rumbles of thunder. It was at this point I realized the unique setting we were located in. We were basically in the bottom of a natural horseshoe-shaped amphitheater. For this reason we were hearing some incredible reverberations from the thunder, as the sound bounced back and forth across the mountain walls.

The thunderstorm built up more strength, as it rolled up on top of the mountain. I had been caught in many thunderstorms over the years while hiking and camping in the Yellowstone backcountry. However, this thunderstorm was different from all the others. Typically, a mountain storm violently rolls up and over you and only lasts a few minutes. But not this one.

Once the full fury of the storm was above the mountain amphitheater, it remained there for what must have been two hours. There was no way we could have slept had we even tried. But there was no way we would have missed this brilliant show. Jim and I gathered at the front door of the tent on our hands and knees, and took in nature's performance. There were sheets of rain coming down, but we could clearly see the bolts of lightning bouncing off the mountain's amphitheater walls—right where we had been hiking during the late afternoon.

The resounding claps of thunder were deafening. Each lightning strike was immediately followed by rolling claps of thunder that would bounce back and forth and back across the horseshoe. Fortunately for us, the lightning strikes remained up on top of the mountain, and did not appear to represent a threat to our safety down in the meadow along the forest's edge.

Jim and I became almost giddy as the storm refused to budge. I thought about the stories I had read about John Muir climbing high up in a tree in Yosemite Valley to fully experience a storm. This storm was a total play on our senses. Our eyes were wide open, as each lightning strike would brightly light up the entire mountain above us. The sound of thunder was almost constant, given the echo effect. The rumbles of thunder literally vibrated through our bodies. Even the pungent smell of the forest was intense from the sheets of rain flowing down. With our adrenalin flowing, Jim and I actually cheered on the more intense strikes above us on the mountain.

We could not help but laugh about the fact that we had actually attempted to camp up on top of the ridge at the small lake, and indeed, we would have had it not been dried up. If we had been camped up on that high ridge, our evening may not have been very enjoyable. "Thank goodness that lake was dry!" I yelled at Jim in between claps of thunder. In fact, I told Jim a little story about a backpack trip Rod Busby and I took in 1971 in northern Glacier National Park. We had camped at Janet Lake and were ridiculed by some other backpackers for not accompanying them on the climb up to Hole in the Wall for the night.

That evening there was a heck of a storm—not as lengthy as this one mind you--but still, very impressive. Rod and I looked up where the bolts of lightning were hitting, and it was right where our hearty friends had headed to camp! The next morning Rod and I were sitting around camp enjoying a late breakfast, and to our surprise, here came the group of four. "Say, how was Hole in the Wall last night?" Rod asked with a big grin on his face. The four hikers did not utter a word, but shook their heads as if to imply they had suffered through a tough night. They appeared rather haggard and pale. After I related the story to Jim, I told him that the little lake could have easily been *our* version of "Hole in the Wall," except much worse.

Eventually, the storm finally began to die down, and we drifted off to sleep. The next morning we found that the storm had produced a dense fog over the valley. As we climbed back up on the ridge, we soon emerged above what seemed like a dense cloud cover, to find sunshine and a bright blue sky. After climbing 1000 feet, we followed the ridge up to the summit of Mount Chittenden. Below us to the north Pelican Valley was completely enshrouded in fog.

The breathtakingly beautiful scene before us took on the appearance of flying above the clouds in an airplane. The vista simply reinforced the notion that each trip into Yellowstone's backcountry is rewarding in a different way. The combination of this intense storm with the unique mountain setting had produced an unforgettable experience.

The Doctor and the Hippies

In 1976 the Yellowstone interpretive program took a large and very creative step into uncharted territory. District Interpretive Ranger Dave Pugh wanted to provide visitors with more than just one-to three-hour hikes. For the first time ever, rangers would lead visitors on a two-day, twenty-mile, overnight, backpacking adventure. Ranger Jim Lenertz was given the responsibility for working out the field details. Dave asked me to transfer from Mammoth to Old Faithful to help lead the hikes. A third ranger with extensive backcountry experience, Jeff Later, was also asked to lead the trips.

Jim put together quite an adventure. The first day consisted of a ten-mile hike up and over the Continental Divide to Shoshone Geyser Basin, where the group would establish a no-impact camp for the night. The second day consisted of six miles of trail hiking, and another four miles of cross-country travel with the use of maps and compasses.

Even though our hikes were limited to only fifteen participants, some of the more experienced backcountry rangers were skeptical that we could pull this activity off without running into serious problems, such as injuries requiring a rescue party to transport visitors out of the wilderness. There were also concerns that we would lose a visitor during the four-mile cross-country, off-trail hike through dense spruce and fir forest. However, I am proud to say that in the several years we conducted this program, we never had a single serious problem with any of the participants.

Perhaps the most *memorable* trip I ever led though, involved a serious clash between cultures and values. During the mid-1970s, our nation was divided by those who supported the Vietnam War and those who opposed it. This was also a period of occasional severe gas shortages. There was kind of an anti-establishment feeling among many of the young people who would come to Yellowstone in their small energy efficient vehicles, who camped with small tents and backpacked the park's trails. They resented many of the wealthy "establishment" who came to Yellowstone in their gas-guzzling, thirty-foot trailers and motor homes. Some of these gas-guzzlers even had the audacity to sport bumper stickers that read, "Don't be Fuelish, Drive 55!" (Congress had enacted a national fifty-five mph speed limit on all highways, including the interstates, to conserve fuel).

I was able to observe this cultural clash up close on our last backpacking trip of the season in early September. Jim and Jeff had already left to go back to their winter jobs; my college was still on the quarter session, so I was able to stay on into mid-September. With Jim and Jeff gone, I decided to take an easy trip for the season finale.

Rather than the rugged twenty-mile roundtrip trip to Shoshone Lake, I opted for a trip about half that distance. I decided to take the group out to the Fountain Flats road, and hike into the headwaters of Sentinel Creek, where we would camp. From there we would head cross-country to the Twin Buttes, and pick up the trail to Imperial Geyser and Fairy Falls. We would exit the backcountry just south of Midway Geyser Basin. Our trip was already booked full when the day preceding the outing, a gentleman and his eleven year-old son approached me at the Old Faithful Visitor Center asking to be added to the trip.

We had always strictly adhered to the fifteen maximum limit, but this fellow absolutely *refused* to take no for an answer. The visitor described how he was a doctor from southern California, and he had dreamed of taking his son out into the wilderness of Yellowstone, but was very concerned about the risks of going out by themselves. The doctor came close to shedding tears, as he begged me to make an exception, and add two more for the trip.

The tough old mountain ranger, Jim Lenertz, would have never granted this man's request; for that matter, Jim would have led the group on his twenty-mile marathon hike for the last trip of the season. But Jim was back in Arizona, so I decided to do a good deed for this man and his son, and add them on to the trip. As soon as we had retrieved the necessary information to add the two to our list, the doctor began asking where he could purchase the necessary equipment for the hike. He had no sleeping bags, tent or backpacks. This fellow really *was* a novice! I directed him to the local concession store, which had some fine equipment, though at premium prices.

The first part of our hike was relatively easy. We had a versatile group, which was fairly normal, though it seemed that on this trip we had more young hikers than usual. Several of the young folks proudly pronounced themselves as "hippies," and advocated a simple life style with a strong land ethic. These young men and women, mostly in their early twenties, appeared to be enamored with the wild country they were walking through. We followed a trail over level terrain for about three miles, before traveling another mile cross-country to the headwaters of Sentinel Creek.

One of our main goals for the first evening was to demonstrate how to establish a no-impact camp. I showed the group that it was possible to build a small fire without leaving any evidence, by digging out a small depression in the soil, and using small sticks for fuel. This way the ashes could be easily covered over and concealed. I was beginning to notice that while the young folks hung on my every word around the campfire, the doctor was turning a deaf ear. Rather than listen to any of my instructive words, he seemed determined to set up his camp his own way. The doctor and young people had already clashed on several of their philosophical differences, but things soon began to deteriorate even further.

The doctor began to put on quite an entertaining show for all of us. Looking back on his behavior, I have to attribute it to his not being able to slow down, unwind, and tune in to the natural setting during our trip. He seemed to still be caught up in the fast-paced stress of the big city, and the pressures of his profession, which were certainly understandable.

I had just finished my little spiel about how to build the fire, when I heard a strange "kerchunk, kerchunk, kerchunk" sound coming from behind us. We turned to see what in the world the doctor was up to. The poor man had his pocketknife out and was hammering his can of pork and beans. "Hey man," said one of the hippies, "What are you doing? Why don't you use a can opener, man?" he asked. The doctor stubbornly ignored them, and eventually pried open his can of beans.

Several minutes later the hippies and I were enjoying sitting around our small evening fire trading observations about the great Yellowstone wilderness, when suddenly the doctor walked up to the fire and emptied several cans of leftover food along with some unburnable trash into the fire. I had just finished explaining to the group to not dump such trash in the fire all at once, lest we lose the opportunity to leave absolutely no trace of our fire.

"Hey man," what do you think you are doing?" asked the hippies incredulously. "Didn't you listen to a single word the ranger told us? You just totally trashed our nice campsite, man!" Normally, I would have said something about what the uncooperative visitor had just done, but I figured the young folks were doing a much better job.

Later in the evening most of our group had retired to their tents, except for the young self-proclaimed hippies and myself. We were enjoying the peace and solitude of the evening, and our small evening fire. Suddenly, a rather brisk wind began to blow through our camp. Again, we heard a strange sound off in the woods—in the vicinity of the doctor's tent. We walked over to see what was causing the noise, and we found the doctor was at it with his knife again, this time stabbing holes in his tent! As it turned out the doctor may have spent a substantial sum on his sleeping bags and backpacks, but his tent was a real cheapo—a simple plastic tube. The wind was causing the cheap plastic tent to flap, causing an incessant noise, so the doctor theorized that cutting holes all through the tent would somehow allow the wind to quietly blow through it! Of course, it made no difference. The tent flapped as loudly as ever.

The hippies really got on the poor doctor. "Hey man, what are you going to do now if it rains tonight? Is it quieter yet, man?" they asked with sharp ridicule in their voices. Sitting at the fire I just quietly chuckled to myself and wondered how someone who is smart enough to make it through medical school could continue to display such poor judgment in the outdoors. Fortunately for the doctor and his son, it did not rain during the evening.

The next day we traveled cross-country using our maps and compasses to the summit of the South Twin Butte. From the top we overlooked the face of the peak. I pointed out to the group our route of descent, which would take us along the ridge down to the saddle between the South and North Twin Buttes. As I was describing our route down, I looked over in disbelief as the doctor walked to the face of the cliff and tossed both of his backpacks off the top.

We watched the packs sail several hundred feet through the air, and then crash on the rocks below. As expected the hippies immediately registered their opinion. "Man, what in the world are you doing now? Are you crazy?" they asked. The doctor angrily retorted, "I don't see why my son and I should have to carry these heavy packs all the way down to the saddle when gravity can do the work for us!" I did not even bother to reply. "Does this poor man possess any common sense at all?" I pondered to myself.

Once we reached the bottom of the cliff we found to no one's surprise that the two expensive JanSport backpacks were severely damaged. The sharp rocks had ripped several holes in the cloth pack, while the aluminum frames were all bent out of shape. We helped bend them back enough so that they were at least usable for the last four miles of the hike.

We negotiated the final portion of the hike without further incident. The doctor and his son had completed the two-day trip, but I felt that they had never really experienced the Yellowstone wilderness. My interpretive skills had failed me on this trip. No matter what I tried to do I could not succeed in getting the doctor to slow down and take a closer look at the magnificent ecosystem that we were traveling through.

Our interpretive staff continued to offer overnight trips for several more years, until eventually budget constraints forced an end to them. I never had another trip where we had a participant like the doctor. I saw many a visitor become truly enthralled by the experience. A few years later in the 1990s, our full-day hikes were also terminated. The rationale given was that we needed to focus more on the quantity of visitors rather than having a ranger go out for several hours with a small group of people. Though the budget problem was very real, I always felt that the longer hikes really won the visitor over as a strong constituent of supporting the preserving of Yellowstone. However, there was at least one doctor from southern California that I was unable to reach.

Fortunately, in recent years, the National Park Service in Yellowstone has brought back longer hikes through the "Adventure Fee Hike" program. Though no longer free, the program allows rangers more time to introduce the visitor to the unique wilderness qualities of Yellowstone. The overnight trip has never returned, though many visitors have requested it. Nearly twenty years after the overnight hikes were discontinued, we continue to have former participants return with the hope of taking their sons and daughters on the trip that they fondly remember taking in Yellowstone. Given the realities of today's federal budget constraints, it may be a long time, if indeed ever, that the overnight interpretive trips return, thus remaining an interesting and missed part of Yellowstone's history.

Grizzly Bears

Are You a Stander or a Runner?

Hikers in Yellowstone tend to have a little extra spring in their step just knowing that they are sharing the trail and the backcountry with a powerful, imposing predator. In fact, some people refuse to hike and backpack in the park for this very reason.

My first summer in Yellowstone in 1968 followed one of the worst summers ever for grizzly-human encounters in the West. During the summer of 1967 in Glacier National Park, two female concession employees were killed by two different grizzlies in separate incidents on the same night. Jack Olson detailed the frightening and tragic details in his classic book, *The Night of the Grizzlies.*

Excerpts from the book first appeared in *Sports Illustrated*, and like most first-time concession employees in grizzly country, I read the details of that fateful night about three times. As a result, each time my friends and I hiked or camped that summer, we always had grizzlies on our minds. During those first couple of summers, I didn't even have a tent! We would just carry bedrolls and sleep out under the stars. When a shower came along we would just duck under the canopy of a dense stand of trees until the rain had ended.

On a dark night in the woods a tent at least seems to offer some measure of psychological comfort. However, when we would lay down under the stars, every little sound out in the woods would cause us to look up and ponder, "Is it a grizzly?" This reaction was only normal for anyone who had read Olson's terrifying account of the two grizzly killings in Glacier. Both attacks occurred at night while the victims were in camp in their sleeping bags.

I will never forget the moonless night in 1968 that Rod Busby and I were camped near Douglas Knob, while on a backpacking trip into Bechler. We had started at Old Faithful, and had reached our campsite well after sunset. We had been unable to locate our camp's water source in the dark, and both of us had retired into our bedrolls that evening with a powerful thirst. As usual, Rod nodded off to sleep ahead of me as evidenced by his snoring.

I kept hearing strange noises in the woods and each time I would lean up, look out into the pitch darkness and assert, "Rod, did you hear that?" It did no good. He was still snoring. The sounds continued to alarm me, but I finally must have nodded off.

At some time in the middle of the night I was rudely awakened by the sound of someone shouting. I leaned up, dazed, half-asleep, and saw Rod sitting up. The faint glow from the embers of our campfire illuminated his face. He appeared to have a wide-eyed, crazed expression. He pointed off into the pitch-black woods and shouted at the top of his lungs, "Look! Right over there!" "Oh my God!" I thought. "We're dead. Rod must see a grizzly coming at us!" I looked where he had pointed and saw nothing but darkness. "Where?" I shouted. "What do you see? "Where is it?" I was terrified but when I turned to look back at Rod, he had curled back up in his bedroll and had rolled over! I crawled over and shook him. "Rod, what is it? What did you see?" Rod groggily opened his eyes for a brief moment and muttered, "I must have had a dream. I thought I saw water gushing out of a spring." He then rolled back over and began snoring again. "Great," I thought. "Rod has a dream about finding some ice-cold water to quench his thirst and goes back to sleep." I was so wired there was no way I could go back to sleep. So I just lay there in my bedroll and listened to the sounds off in the dark forest. And imagined there was a grizzly behind every tree surrounding our camp!

I eventually overcame this extreme fear of camping in grizzly country. Sleeping inside a tent helped, but I also did quite a bit of reading on bears, and finally convinced myself that the odds of a wild bear coming into camp are pretty slim. It's kind of like folks who attend seminars to overcome the fear of flying. I found that most human-bear encounters involved bears that had become habituated to human food. Both of the bears involved in the terrible killings in Glacier in 1967 had been habituated bears. Of course, there are no guarantees in grizzly country. I still think about grizzlies when I retire for the evening out in the backcountry.

Recently while visiting the Moose Visitor Center in Grand Teton National Park, I walked over to a stuffed grizzly on exhibit. Standing only a foot away I just could not imagine the terror one would feel if attacked by such a large, impressive animal. The live weight of this bear was 600 pounds, according to the staff at the visitor center. Many hikers now carry canisters of bear pepper spray, which has been proven to be effective in warding off an attack of a grizzly, but clearly this would be a last resort option.

I once read Steve Herrero's excellent book, *Bear Attacks*, and promised myself that I would not read it again. It had about the same effect on me that Olson's *Night of the Grizzlies* had sixteen years earlier. Herrero's book details many gruesome bear attacks in North America. But he points out, "If grizzly bears readily attacked people then there would be far more injuries and I, for one, wouldn't care to try to coexist with them." I guess I am living proof of that statement. I have hiked all of the park's 1000 miles of trails, some many times over, and have spent over 400 nights out in Yellowstone's backcountry, but have had very few encounters with bears.

When you consider how many folks do hike and camp in the park each summer, it is rather comforting to know that the number of human-bear incidents is really quite small. So the odds are pretty good you won't have a serious encounter if you take the proper precautions. However, it is the grizzly's unpredictability and physical strength and power that send chills up the spine when you see a bear or its fresh sign in the backcountry. I should also point out that Herrero concludes in his book that "The challenge of continued coexistence...does require that we accept some small chance of injury, and even death." A couple of summers ago I was enjoying a presentation on the grizzlies of the Greater Yellowstone Ecosystem by Yellowstone Bear Biologist Kerry Gunther. Kerry has spent many years in the field observing grizzlies, and is an expert on the animal. When someone in the audience asked him what to do if you encounter a grizzly while hiking, Kerry had an interesting reply, "Well, first you have to find out if you are a stander or a runner!" I couldn't help but chuckle to myself thinking back on how I once reacted when I had my first serious bear encounter, and also the way my good friend and fellow interpretive ranger Sam Holbrook responded when he had a close call a few years ago.

Experts on bears recommend that you attempt to avoid an encounter by taking preventative measures, such as making sufficient noise along the trail, especially if the wind is in your face. Bears have a very keen sense of smell and will normally turn away from you if they detect your presence. I was once backpacking with John and Deb Dirksen near Beaverdam Creek south of the Southeast Arm of Yellowstone Lake, when we heard a loud crashing noise in the willow brush ahead of us. We had obviously spooked a large animal, which is fairly common when traveling the trails. The question was, was it a moose, elk, grizzly, or what?

The trail was muddy that day and as we rounded the next bend in the trail our question was answered. There in the mud were the large tracks of a bear traveling north on the Thorofare trail. The distance from the pad of the front paw to the claw imprints told us the tracks were those of a grizzly, and a big one at that. We were traveling south and were headed for a head-on collision if the bear had thankfully not detected our presence and veered off the trail. Since we were not making much noise and there was little if any wind, we assumed that the bear had picked up our scent with its keen nose.

A bear has relatively poor eyesight. Sometimes a bear will stand on its hind legs in an attempt to identify something in range of its nose. The hearing of a bear is thought to be roughly equivalent to the hearing of a human. So if you are hiking into the teeth of a stiff breeze, it is important to make some noise. This is especially true if you cannot see very far ahead. A trail that traverses rolling terrain or enters dense patches of timber does not allow for good views. Some hikers hang bells on their packs, but personally, I think this might be overkill. The constant clanging of bells is probably not what you prefer to listen to in the wilderness, plus, you will likely frighten off every other wild creature in the forest.

If there is not a wind in my face and the visibility ahead is good, I usually do not make much noise because I like to view wildlife, and I'm confident a bear would smell me coming (especially if I have been out on the trail for a few days!). On the other hand, if your visibility is limited, and you are hiking into the wind, then you are playing a bit of Russian roulette by not making some noise. Some experts recommend that you break small sticks or clap your hands. Or you can sing, recite poems, give speeches, or just pull that bell out of your pocket.

On one trip I had just run into a fresh, steaming pile of bear scat in a densely-vegetated area. I usually carry a small harmonica with me to play around the campfire. I decided to play some of my favorite songs while hiking through the dense undergrowth on that day!

If you are hiking with several friends or family you probably don't have a thing to worry about. Bear encounters with groups of four or more are very rare, probably because of the noise and smell that a group constantly emanates. If you have kids with you then you can probably relax, given their proclivity for chatter!

If you come across a grizzly at a distance, then you can probably enjoy the thrill of just observing the bear. Obviously, you want to make a wide detour or back away from the bear to prevent the bear from getting too close. But suppose that one day you do encounter a grizzly bear at a very close range. What then? This was the question Kerry Gunther was responding to. Experts recommend that you remain calm and not make any sudden movements that might provoke a charge.

If the bear does charge, then you are down to your last alternative: playing dead. By laying flat on your stomach, extending your legs and digging in to prevent the bear from rolling you over, you are protecting key parts of your body, and trying to convince the bear that you are not a threat to it. There have been numerous incidents where hikers survived a bear encounter by taking this action. If you have pepper spray then this might be the time to use it if the charge turns into an attack.

Pepper spray should only be used as a last resort incident. Some hikers seem to feel invincible once they strap on a canister. Such confidence is not justified when you consider unpredictable variables such as wind, distance between you and the bear, your marksmanship, and the quality of your canister. I recall my good friend Carl Sheehan, a long time artist-in-resident at the Old Faithful Lodge, once telling me the story about his experience in testing his own canister of bear spray. He took off the locking device and depressed the switch. He had expected to see a rapid spray of twenty feet. But instead the contents dribbled out of the can and fell on his foot. As Carl would later ruse, "If a grizzly had been after my big toe, then I would have nailed him!"

The best way to escape "pepper spray overconfidence" is to stroll into the Moose Visitor Center and walk up to that stuffed grizzly. Then try to convince yourself that some cayenne peppers will actually repel a grizzly of this size. Perhaps it will, but there are no guarantees. Clearly, we are talking about a last resort alternative. Hopefully, your preventative measures will avert a close encounter.

The reference to "stander or runner" typically refers to whether the hiker who has a close encounter with a bear thinks he can get to and up a tree in time. When I had my serious confrontation with a grizzly, I guess I found that at least on that occasion, I was a "runner" according to Gunther. Rod Busby and I were hiking across the Gallatins on a very windy day during September of 1972. Our trail traversed large open meadows and islands of dense forest.

With the wind in our faces in prime grizzly habitat we knew that we were hiking in a potentially dangerous situation, so we attempted to make noise by talking loudly to each other. Apparently, our voices were muffled by the groaning of the swaying, wind-blown trees, because as we rounded a sharp bend in the trail, there stood a grizzly cub. Obviously, in hindsight, we should have made more shrill noises by clapping, whistling, playing a harmonica, breaking sticks, or whatever. When we saw the cub we immediately knew that we were in serious trouble. Surprising a grizzly sow with her cubs is about the worst thing you can do to invite a bear encounter.

A grizzly can clip along at speeds equal to that of a horse for short distances, so it is impossible to outrun a bear. There is an old bear joke about how you don't really have to outrun a charging bear; all you really have to do is outrun your companion. This may be humorous but it is also true. I found out the hard way! The moment the grizzly cub saw us it let out a loud wail, and ran away from us back down the trail. It appeared to be as frightened of us as we were of it. We knew that Mama was going to be intervening rather quickly.

Rod immediately shed his pack and disappeared down the trail. I attempted to do the same by flinging off my backpack, and also turned to run down the trail in search of a tree to climb. However, I had made a serious mental mistake by forgetting to unfasten my waist belt. So, I had a forty-pound backpack flapping along my backside, as I tried to run. Rod later told me that when he looked back up the trail he thought I was performing one of those exquisite Russian dances, where you bend your knees and practically sit on the floor. I was only able to take a few steps before I fell to my knees to remove my waist belt, which by now had become tightly cinched.

As I was frantically attempting to unfasten my waist belt, I looked over my shoulder to see if the Mama was in sight yet, and my worst fears were confirmed. There about thirty yards away, I saw a sow grizzly running straight toward me. Her teeth were bared, she was growling, the hair on her neck was standing up, and she was bearing down on me. I will never forget her beady eyes, which were ringed by black circles of color against the blonde color of her head and face.

After I managed to get my backpack with waist strap off, I murmured, "Oh God" and began running toward a tree. In retrospect, I really had no chance to outrun this charging bear to a tree. At this point, I basically had two choices: play dead or run for a tree. My instincts took over. I'm sure that most experts would agree that I made the wrong decision. After all, even your Mom probably taught you not to run from a growling dog. It only releases the natural instinct of the animal to aggressively pursue its prey. As I began to run I could almost feel the vibrations of the big bear's growling in my upper body.

I was racing for a tree about ten yards off the trail. My eyes were focused on the limbs I was hoping to latch onto when suddenly, I tripped over a fallen log and fell flat on my stomach. During the split second that I was on the ground I will never forget the thought that raced through my mind: "Why isn't the bear on top of me?" Prior to tripping over the log every instinct in me had told me that the bear was right behind me. In another split second I was into the tree practically flying from limb to limb, nicking my arms and chest along the way.

Trees in Yellowstone are not designed for easy climbing. In fact, the omnipresent lodgepole pine has been compared to a telephone pole with a Christmas tree tied on the top. However, you would be surprised at how easy climbing a tree can be when you are highly motivated! Once I was about ten feet up the tree I looked below me expecting to see a bear inches away from my feet, but there was no bear in sight.

I could now barely hear over the rapid beating of my heart, and Rod's shouts, "Butch, are you okay? Butch, where are you?" Rod told me later that he had caught a glimpse of the bear chasing me, but lost sight from his viewpoint high in another tree. I quickly answered him to let him know I had managed to climb a tree. "Do you see the bear?" he asked. As I looked down to the forest floor below me, I could see no evidence of the sow or cub. I was literally shaking like a leaf and it took me several minutes to calm down and capture my wits. Rod and I stayed up in the trees for about fifteen minutes before we decided it was safe to climb back down.

We retrieved our backpacks and were relieved to see that the bears had not torn into them. Although we had discarded our packs out of necessity in climbing the trees, experts strongly recommend against throwing down a pack containing food during a bear encounter. This can condition a bear to aggressively attack hikers to obtain food. At this point Rod and I tentatively continued our hike. The trail was wet and to our dismay we could see that both the sow and cub were traveling the trail ahead of us.

Our senses were so alert we probably appeared to be wired. Every now and then a red squirrel, known as "boomers" for their ability to emit a loud chatter, would send us several inches into the air, as we reacted to the shrill sound. After about twenty minutes we were very relieved to see the bear tracks move up a hill away from our trail. Rod and I now had a very easy decision to make. We were about one mile from our designated backcountry campsite, and it was now about 4:00 p.m. We were also about seven miles from our exit trailhead. Given the close proximity of this disturbed grizzly sow, we decided to forego our last camp and simply hike out on that afternoon.

Looking back at the close encounter, I will never know at what point the grizzly sow abandoned her charge. Once I began running for the tree I never looked back. I do know that there is no way I outran the bear to the tree. I can only assume that the sow made a bluff charge, and had probably stopped just before I tripped over the log. I believe the fact that the cub turned and ran back in the direction of the sow, and did not run past me, placing me between the cub and sow, probably saved me from a physical attack.

I have described this incident many times in my interpretive programs in an attempt to emphasize the preventative measures necessary to avoid such an encounter. Clearly, we were not making enough noise on this day. Also, I learned to use a "quick release" method to connect my waist belt, so that I could quickly shed my pack if I ever again felt the need to climb a tree.

Of course, when I describe my inane attempts to run with a backpack flopping along my backside, and then tripping over the log, I have been the subject of some good-natured ribbing. "After watching you try to run with that pack and then tripping over the log, that old bear knew that you were no threat to its cub, and just left you alone," my friends would say. So I have had some good laughs around the campfire over this incident, but it was not funny at the time. It was a frightening experience that I would wish on no one.

However, I have seen bears on several occasions that were much more enjoyable. Typical is a June trip I took in 1971 across Hayden Valley with Margaret and Rod and Kathy Busby. Hayden Valley is prime grizzly habitat with great vistas. Spring was bursting upon the valley with lush green grasses and carpets of white and yellow flowers. The sky was a dark shade of blue, with white puffy cumulus clouds stacked on the horizon. To the north were the clear images of Observation Peak, Dunraven Peak and Mount Washburn.

We stopped for lunch in a small patch of trees near the gurgling flow of Alum Creek. All was right in our world. Suddenly, Margaret jumped up and exclaimed, "Here comes a bear!" My first reaction was to hope that she had spotted something else and mistaken it for a bear. That is not hard to do in Hayden Valley, given the bison, elk, coyotes, and hump-shaped boulders scattered about. However, when I saw Margaret start to climb a tree, I knew that she was not kidding. Sure enough, a medium-sized black bear was loping right at us. All four of us climbed up a tree. The bear ran right under us and just continued its trot on out into the valley. It seemed to be oblivious to our presence, and appeared to be enjoying an afternoon jog.

Later that afternoon we saw two grizzlies the way all hikers and backpackers relish--off in the distance, digging next to a snow bank. We were on the edge of the forest and the bears were about 150 yards away out in the open valley. The two bears were unaware of our presence. We pulled out our binoculars and enjoyed observing them for about half an hour.

Finally, the wind must have shifted, because both bears lifted their noses to the air, stood up, and apparently picked up our scent before running off.

After we watched the bears disappear over a distant ridge, we walked out to see what the bears were digging, and found little spring beauties just coming into bloom where the snow had receded. The little white flowers have a bulbous root that is a rich and tasty source of nutrients for bears in the spring of the year.

On another occasion I was watching a grizzly during early June in Lamar Valley. Grizzlies like to hunt for elk calves during this time of year. The bears have a couple of weeks when they can run down the calves, but after that the elk calves become difficult to catch. I noticed this grizzly following its nose through the sagebrush. It was totally relying on its olfactory senses to find food. As it got closer to the scent, the bear seemed to become very aggressive moving through the sage.

Suddenly, an elk calf that had been attempting to hide out in the sage jumped up to run off. It never had a chance. The mother elk ran over to the bear but realized there was nothing she could do and just left. This observation convinced me just how powerful a bear's nose really is, and it also proved that the old tale that newborn elk calves have no scent is simply a myth. Of course, these kinds of bear "encounters" aren't the ones that get the attention, but fortunately, these are the typical sightings that backpackers and hikers make.

Ranger Les Inafuka spent over twenty years in Yellowstone, much of it on backcountry patrols. One particular patrol that runs the risk of encountering bears is the annual poacher patrol during the fall. There are always a few hunters who seem to conveniently get "lost" along the park boundary, as they pursue trophy elk during the elk hunting seasons in the surrounding national forests. When on poacher patrol the ranger cannot make noise while traveling in order to protect his or her location from any unscrupulous hunters.

Fall is also the time of year when the grizzly enters "hyperphagia," a period where the bear is gorging itself in preparation for hibernation. During such patrols, not only in Yellowstone, but in Alaska as well, Les had his share of bear encounters. Les had success in being a "stander." He did not run, climb trees, or play dead. Once, while stationed in Alaska, Les was out for an afternoon jog along a dirt road, which ran parallel to an alder-lined stream. Suddenly, Les heard something behind him running through the alder brush.

He turned around just in time to see a large grizzly emerge from the alder, jump the stream, climb up on the road and begin a full charge directly at him. There were no trees in sight and Les knew that he could not outrun this grizzly. But rather than play dead, Les stood his ground. The bear continued its charge, but at the last possible second, it swerved off to the side, barely grazing Les' shoulder. Such incidents probably help explain Les' graying hair.

Fellow Yellowstone Ranger Sam Holbrook did not have a bear encounter until after over thirty seasons of work in the park. Sam was investigating some thermal features in a remote area about one mile from the road when the encounter took place. He said that he was leaning over to closely examine the colorful bacteria thriving in a runoff channel when, suddenly, he was overcome with the strange sensation that someone or "some thing" was behind him watching.

There was a sloping hill directly behind him so Sam turned around to take a look. There to his shock about twenty-five yards away was a grizzly bear sitting on his haunches watching Sam's every move. Sam admits that he probably should have carefully backed away from the apparently complacent bear, but his "runner" instinct took over, much as mine did in the Gallatins. He said that he turned, jumped over a small creek, and ran a full mile back to the road before he even looked back. The visual thought of that old bear just sitting there watching Sam sprint off has caused more than one of his colleagues to break out in a loud chuckle.

I think that part of the reason why Sam and I found ourselves as "runners" during bear encounters had more to do with our lack of mental preparation. I doubt seriously that either one of us would run off again under similar circumstances. Hikers and backpackers should carefully read the excellent handouts on hiking and camping in bear country that the NPS provides. By following all precautions, staying alert, and being mentally prepared, hopefully you will make the correct decision if you encounter a bear in the backcountry. Making noise and hiking with other people are your best insurance against being put to the stander or runner test.

The opportunity to share a wild area with the majestic grizzly bear is not only a thrilling experience, but it is also a rare one. The grizzly requires a very large and wild area in order to live, reproduce, and perpetuate the species. Yellowstone National Park measures roughly seventy by fifty miles, but the grizzly's range extends well beyond the park boundary. When Lewis and Clark headed west in 1804, the grizzly ranged all across the North American plains and mountains. However, as our civilization advanced westward, one state after another began to list the grizzly as extinct.

States such as Colorado, New Mexico, Arizona, South Dakota and Utah are examples of areas that used to support thriving grizzly populations that are now barren. California used to have the biggest population of grizzlies of any state in the nation—hence the nickname "the golden bear" state. The last grizzly in the golden bear state was killed in 1922. The grizzly bear population is extremely difficult to count, but there are probably only around 1000 grizzlies left in the contiguous forty-eight states.

Its last stand is basically the Greater Yellowstone Ecosystem and the northern Montana wilderness found in Glacier National Park and the Bob Marshall, Scapegoat and Great Bear Wilderness Areas. The estimated population of grizzlies in the Greater Yellowstone area ranges from about 400 to 700 bears.

Hopefully, our children and grandchildren who may return to Yellowstone fifty years from now, will still find the grizzly reigning as the true king of the wilderness. In order for that to happen most biologists who specialize in bears agree that three things must occur: First, the bears' habitat must be preserved and protected. That will involve critical decisions regarding real estate development, road-building, logging, mining, and drilling for oil and gas outside the boundaries of Yellowstone National Park, but within the ecosystem. The grizzly typically loses out when any of these activities occurs within its habitat.

Second, humans must learn how to coexist with bears. That includes following all precautions while hiking and camping in bear country, and taking extra care to not allow bears to obtain human foods (a fed bear is a dead bear).

And third, eventually the Yellowstone grizzly population will need some bears from elsewhere to breed in the population to provide the genetic diversity needed for long-term survival. The Greater Yellowstone Ecosystem is basically an island population. At present there is no link or corridor to another population. This was about to be corrected with the reintroduction of grizzlies into Idaho wilderness areas. The U.S. Fish and Wildlife Service had an approved plan with the support and cooperation of surrounding states and federal agencies, but Secretary of Interior Gale Norton canceled the plan during the summer of 2002.

For the time being the grizzly is thriving. Many bear experts appear to be optimistic about the next decade or two, but pessimistic after that. While it is true that the grizzly has all of the equipment necessary to make you think about whether you would "stand" or "run"—400 to 600 pounds of massive muscle, bone-crushing jaws, sharp three-inch claws and amazing speed, the fact is, there is nothing more endearing than the sight of a grizzly sow leading her cubs across a meadow in search of roots and berries. May this regal animal roam Yellowstone for many decades to come.

There's a Bison at my Window!

Until my two daughters reached college age I was able to proudly proclaim that they had spent every summer of their lives in a national park. Many years ago Margaret brought home a book from the library titled *Bears in my Kitchen*. As I recall it was written by the wife of a ranger and detailed their unusual family experiences working and living in national parks. The Bachs never had bears in our kitchen, but we *have* had some unusual experiences, including bears on our porch, bears at our bedroom window, moose at our front door, and bison about everywhere but inside our quarters!

At least once each summer I will wake up just after dawn to hear a munching sound accompanied with low grunts. I'll sit up, push back the window curtain, and there two feet away, is a baseball-sized eyeball of a bison staring back at me! There is something unnerving about gawking at a 2000-pound animal only a few feet away with nothing more than a small glass windowpane separating beast from human! For some reason there are always a few bison that like to wander around the housing area munching on tufts of grass amidst the obsidian gravel. Obsidian is a type of volcanic glass common in many areas of the Yellowstone plateau, including the concentrated assortment of trailers and apartments, which serve as housing for employees at Old Faithful. The employee softball field at Old Faithful consists of obsidian gravel, and each summer a game is delayed when a bison decides to stand on second base. If I were a bison, I would be out in the gorgeous meadows along the Firehole River. Go figure.

Obsidian gravel does not exactly fit the mold of the ideal moose habitat of marshy willows. Nevertheless, one day I came home for lunch to find a young bull moose blocking the entrance to the front door of our quarters.

I guess the biggest excitement we ever had with a bison occurred with our youngest daughter Alison. Alison had been "dog-sitting" a beautiful young Malamute for an employee one day. Alison had taken the dog out for a walk, and then brought it back and tied its leash to a tree at the corner of our cabin. We were sitting at the kitchen table having lunch when we heard something bumping against the back of the cabin.

Alison went to the door and let out a scream. A big bull bison had the dog cornered at the back of our cabin. The poor dog was paralyzed with fear. It was not moving or making a sound. The bison, however, was enraged. It appeared ready to gore the dog into the ground. Alison was screaming, "get away, get away," but to no avail. Margaret grabbed a mop and ran to the back bedroom and began banging the mop on the inside wall

Alison Examining a Bison Skull in Hayden Valley

opposite where the bison was standing. Luckily, this startled the huge animal, and it abruptly departed the area. I feel certain if Margaret had not quickly acted, the bison would have killed the Malamute.

Visitors mistakenly believe that the most dangerous animal in Yellowstone is the bear. More injuries occur from bison. You simply have to allow these wild 2000-pound animals plenty of space. Park regulations require that a minimum distance of twenty-five yards be maintained between humans and all large animals, except for bears, where the required minimum distance is 100 yards. This sounds simple, but at Old Faithful you have to constantly be on the lookout for these few strange bison that enjoy hanging out in the developed area. For example, a few years ago a bison was walking down a row of trailers in the Old Faithful government housing area. My friend, Bronco Grigg, who works for NPS Maintenance, usually lives in one of these homes on our street.

As mentioned previously, seeing bison wandering through the housing area is not unusual; however, on this day the bison walked over to Bronco's Nissan Stanza parked in front of his home, and gored the front door on the passenger side of the vehicle! The bison just lowered his head, slammed his horn into the car, impaling the door, and then lifted the entire front end of the car off the pavement. The bison then dropped the car and proceeded to casually continue his stroll down the street.

I have told this story to many visitors in an attempt to describe the damage that a bison can do to a human. Bronco still has his car and no, he never did repair the tennis ball-sized hole in his door. I don't blame him. Besides, if Bronco had filed a claim, I doubt that his insurance company would have believed his story!

Twice we had visits from bears. When I was working at Mammoth in 1975, we lived in a trailer in the upper housing area. One evening we heard a knocking sound out on the front porch. I assumed that someone had come by for a visit, so I opened the door. There standing in front of me was a blond-colored black bear. Before I could even make a sound or shut the door, I heard someone shout, "Get outta here!" and the bear jumped off of my porch. Close behind the bear was Ranger Don Frazier with a broom. Apparently this bear had received some human food, and Don was attempting to run the bear out of the area.

We never had a grizzly at the front door, but one evening at Old Faithful we heard something outside the bedroom window, followed by a slight movement in the middle of the night. At the time we were living in a trailer, and it was not uncommon to feel the flimsy structure shake from a tremor. There are over 2000 tremors recorded on seismographs in the Yellowstone area each year.

However, the next morning as I was leaving for work, I noticed that the movement had not been caused by an earthquake. I saw grizzly tracks in the mud leading up to our window, where for some reason the bear had reached up and placed its paw.

Not all of our family adventures with wildlife involved large animals. Once, when our daughters Caroline and Alison were very young, they were out riding their bikes one morning, and came across two baby squirrels that had apparently fallen out of their nest. The little squirrels appeared to be close to death, so the girls brought them home, fed them milk, and tried to nurse them to health. The squirrels made good progress and eventually they recovered and became quite active.

The girls named the two squirrels "Squeaky" and "Peanut Butter," because one made a squeaking sound, and the other had an affinity for peanut butter. The girls built a small pen outside and placed the little squirrels in it. But the next morning Caroline and Alison were horrified by what they found. The two little squirrels appeared to be frozen as stiff as boards. Their eyes were closed and their tongues were protruding from their mouths. Overnight, the temperature had dipped into the twenties, and even though the girls had prepared a nest for them, it appeared that the squirrels had succumbed to the cold. Alison and Caroline came in just bawling their eyes out.

However, it just so happened that Tom and Nora Gerrity of Great Falls, Montana were visiting with us at the time, and Nora is a pediatrician. She was not so quick to give up on the squirrels. She thought they simply had hypothermia, and told the girls to place the squirrels out in the sun. Sure enough, in a couple of hours "Squeaky" and "Peanut Butter" were scurrying around as good as new. The two little squirrels would stay around during the day, and would then go to their pen at night. They would jump on your shoulder and climb up on top of your head, and were great pets. However, a few weeks later the squirrels did not return to their pen at night. We just assumed that they had returned to the wild, though I suppose a predator such as a pine martin might have intervened! In retrospect, we should have taught the girls to not bother abandoned wildlife, since the mothers often return.

Living at Old Faithful does tend to deprive your family from some activities typically enjoyed in a town during the summer. For example, one summer when Caroline was seven years old, she wanted to see a parade on the Fourth of July. I had to work that day, so I explained to her that we would not be able to travel anywhere to see one. Caroline was always a determined little girl so this answer did not suffice. "Then I'll just have to make up a parade here," she said. Caroline proceeded to round up several other children and make plans for a parade.

The children prepared colorful signs, which were posted about a week ahead of time around the housing area to let residents know when and where the event would be held. When the big day arrived Margaret noticed that people were beginning to set up their folding chairs to enjoy the day's festivities, and asked Caroline if everything was all set. Caroline, having spent so much energy on making up the signs, had forgotten all about it! Somehow though, she rounded up the other children, obtained flags, wagons, and noisemakers, and pulled the parade off in front of a nice-sized crowd that was very appreciative. Even today, this tradition has continued. Each Fourth of July about 2:00 p.m., the children of the Old Faithful Housing Area present a parade. Although I can't be positive, I think it all started with Caroline.

Once each week I had the geyser prediction shift, which required that I get up early and head out into the Upper Geyser Basin to predict the major geysers. Most kids like to sleep in, but Caroline and Alison would frequently get up to join me on these special mornings. The geyser basin at first light is almost otherworldly; everything is enshrouded in fog and the bizarre, mineralized cones of Grotto, Giant and Castle are gushing forth columns of steam, which are backlit by the rising sun.

One of the prime benefits of being out in the basin early in the morning includes the opportunity to see an abundance and variety of wildlife, with bison, elk and coyotes being the most common. Living in Yellowstone was actually an education in ecology for my girls. They also developed a deep appreciation for wilderness and natural ecosystems. For this reason, they were usually eager to join me on lengthy backcountry trips.

Yellowstone is a very wild place and there are potential dangers. Margaret and I always taught the girls to respect the wild animals, and keep a safe distance. We urged them to respect the scalding water in the thermal basins, as well as the swift water in the streams.

Over the years I only recall three close calls with my family. The first occurred on the Snake River. The Snake River begins as a trickle coursing off the Absaroka Mountains in southeast Yellowstone, and flows some twenty miles before reaching the South Entrance. From here the Snake flows past one of the most spectacular mountain ranges in the world, the Grand Tetons. Friends John and Deb Dirksen had joined Margaret, Alison and me for the ten-mile float between Dead Man's Bar and Moose on that stretch of river in the Tetons. Even in late summer the Snake River flows at a very fast rate. For example, it only takes about two hours to float the ten miles. John and Deb were in one raft, and Margaret, Alison and I were in the other. Our trip had gone well and we had just taken our final break on an island, before concluding the trip at Moose. From the island we soaked in the views of the Grand Teton Range, which on this beautiful, clear day were stunning.

However, it was time to finish up the trip, because we had a big potluck to get to back at Old Faithful on that evening. As we neared Moose, the river split up into several channels. My experience reminded me to stay to the right in the largest channel. We rounded a bend in the channel, and immediately in front of us was a large cottonwood tree that had just fallen across the stream thanks to some work by beavers. The tree blocked most of the channel, but I thought I could maneuver our raft sharply to squeeze past the tree.

As I dug my wooden oars into the water one of them suddenly snapped! Now we were headed right for the middle of the big tree, and with only one oar, there was little I could do about it. I will never forget how calmly Margaret proclaimed, "We aren't going to make it are we?" At the last instant, Margaret pushed Alison all the way down to the floor of our four-man raft, and then she lowered herself down on top of her. That pretty much took up the bottom of the raft, so as we neared the tree I grabbed a limb and pulled myself up on top of the fallen tree. Margaret and Alison and the raft went under the tree and popped back up on the other side. As I looked downstream from my precarious perch on the tree, there were Margaret and Alison in the raft swiftly moving down the channel without any oars. I had heard the troubling statement about being "upstream without a paddle" many times, but now members of my family were living out that predicament!

John and Deb had seen the entire event from behind us so they continued past me to try to catch them. I had an approach to get off the tree, but I knew that Margaret and Alison could run into some serious trouble, such as floating into a logjam. In fact, Alison was screaming bloody murder. John quickly caught up with them though, and saved the day.

The second close call I had was in a backcountry thermal region north of Pelican Valley. Alison and I were on a trip across the Mirror Plateau with friends John, Deb, Hank Barnett, and Alan Martin, when we entered a thermal area along a stream. Just as we were preparing to ford across Broad Creek, John broke through the thin crust and suffered a bad burn to his leg. It would have been a critical injury if John had already removed his boots like the rest of us, and Alison and I were next in line! The details on this incident are included in the chapter titled "The Totem Forest."

The third incident involved a pot luck that was held at the Old Faithful Maintenance Shed during the late 1970s. Caroline was about six years old, and really enjoyed playing with little Kate, the daughter of Steve and Cyd Martin. Steve had just become the Old Faithful Subdistrict Ranger. It was a typical pot luck in that there were dozens of people scattered about grilling and conversing and the kids were all over the place playing. As darkness approached and it came time to sit down at the picnic tables outside to eat, Margaret and Cyd could not locate Caroline and Kate anywhere. We searched all around the shed. There was no trace of them.

"I guess we'd better get a search and rescue started," Steve mentioned to me. I could tell from his eyes that he was deeply worried, and given his law enforcement background, I knew that he had been through the grind many times regarding such incidents. The area was surrounded by woods, so we were gravely concerned that the girls had wandered off and gotten lost. However, just as we were about to start assigning grids to search the area, I heard someone exclaim, "Here they are!" Caroline and Kate had somehow propped open a door to a small paint storage area, and they were holed up in there playing games. I guess it was the parents who were "lost," but those two little girls sure put a fright into us!

Spending their first eighteen summers in a national park helped Caroline and Alison to develop not only a deep love for natural beauty, but also a healthy respect for its potential dangers.

As of this writing both of my daughters live and work in Montana within the Greater Yellowstone Ecosystem. Something tells me that they will never stray too far away from this land of their youth.

Lost!

For over a decade, Jim Lenertz and I offered an interpretive program in the Old Faithful area that we called "Exploring Yellowstone by Map and Compass." The half-day program was limited to fifteen participants, and we did our best to instruct each person on the important skills of using a topographic map and a compass in the wilderness to avoid becoming lost. This program, along with our backpacking demonstration, was highly recommended for those visitors who had made reservations to go on our two day, twenty-mile, overnight backpacking trip. All three of these programs were very popular from the mid 1970s up until the mid 1980s, at which time the NPS discontinued them due to budget constraints and a change in management objectives, which preferred shorter programs that reached a greater number of visitors.

Each week that I offered the map and compass activity, I would take the group into a remote region near Nez Perce Creek, where we would learn how to set and follow a compass course to several small lakes in the area. The first thing I did was ask each participant to describe to the rest of the group his or her most harrowing experience of being lost.

Everyone has been lost at some time. Perhaps a wrong turn was taken in a big city. Or perhaps you became separated from your parents in a department store as a youngster. However, I was amazed at how many of the participants had suffered distressing experiences of being lost in the woods somewhere, and it was always fascinating to hear their personal stories. The one that was the most unforgettable involved an Air Force pilot who was shot down over North Vietnam, and had to survive for weeks in the jungle while surreptitiously traveling at night toward the south and eventual safety.

When it came my turn, I first told the group about the exploits of poor Truman Everts, who wandered lost through the Yellowstone wilderness for thirty-seven days in 1870, when he became separated from other members of the Washburn-Langford expedition, yet survived the ordeal. Everts lived to a ripe old age and fathered children late in life. In fact, during the mid-90s a fifty-six year-old lady from Louisville, Kentucky approached me after I had just completed giving my evening program at the Old Faithful Visitor Center. She said she had a journal she wanted to donate to the park that had been kept by her grandfather. "And, who was that?" I asked. "Truman Everts," she replied! This experience helped me appreciate just what a recent human history Yellowstone enjoys.

Of course, the map and compass participants wanted to know of my "harrowing" tales of being lost in Yellowstone. I really didn't have much to tell them. One can certainly get lost in Yellowstone. The park consists of 3472 square miles, and 98% of that acreage is wilderness. I have been turned around a few times but never anything serious. I wandered around for about an hour once with Rod and Kathy Busby near Three-River Junction in Bechler, until we finally found the trail.

My most embarrassing experience of becoming "lost" in Yellowstone actually involved an interpretive activity. During the 1980s our Chief of Interpretation was George Robinson. George was a stickler for demanding that our staff constantly try new, innovative programs and activities. Each member of the staff was required to have at least one new program each summer in our districts.

I had discovered a chain of old beaver ponds complete with the dams and a lodge near Nez Perce Creek. From the hundreds of cut trees, it was obvious that beaver had been in the area for many decades. Although beaver were still active in the main pond, the stream connecting the ponds had dried up many years ago. I felt the area provided a great interpretive story. I called my walk "Backcountry Beaver Bopping." Looking back, the program title seems rather silly, but George Robinson was big on creativity, games, and catchy titles.

Beaver ponds are a story of succession. Beaver dam up a stream in order to provide a home for themselves. On dry land a beaver is vulnerable to being preyed on by a predator. They are slow and awkward. I have always compared a beaver on land to a porcupine *without* the quills.

However, in water a beaver is a splendid swimmer, and is generally safe from predation. In the process of building a safe home for itself, the beaver actually creates a home for many other species such as fish, frogs, ducks, and especially moose. A beaver pond is often shallow and tends to fill in and become a bog or meadow within a few decades. At this point the meadow provides good habitat for elk and bison.

My plan was to lead our group along the faint streambed to the chain of ponds, and allow the participants to pick out clues as to what had happened there. On my very first program my supervisor, Joe Halladay, showed up to audit me. Joe is a kind man who has a deep appreciation for Yellowstone's resources. He served as the district supervisor for over twenty years in the park. But Joe was notorious for auditing members of his staff on their *first* programs.

I was confident in the quality of my walk, but you never know how things are going to work out until you actually give that first program. I headed up the faint streambed with my group, and things were going along fine, but then the group began to concentrate on the abundance of animal signs. We began to examine markings on trees, animal droppings, bones and hair on the forest floor. Elk and especially bison migrate through this area as they travel back and forth between the high meadows of Hayden Valley and the lower ones at Fountain Flats.

The group kept finding trees that were freshly girdled by bison horns and elk antlers. There were several youngsters on the walk who continually asked me questions about the wealth of animal sign in the forest. We were all enjoying ourselves, but suddenly I realized that the old streambed was no longer in sight. All I could see was a maze of lodgepole pine trees.

I began to move the group back toward where I thought the streambed was, but after walking for another ten minutes, it did not appear. At this point I stopped the group and asked them a simple question, "Folks, remember that old streambed we were following about twenty minutes ago? Well, we need to find it again because it will lead us to the beaver ponds. Please point in the direction of where you think it is." Fifteen hands went up, each pointing in a different direction!

At this point I decided to follow my own instincts. I had a map (useless in the forest maze), but no compass. Fortunately, my instincts were accurate and we relocated the old streambed, and then followed it up to the chain of beaver ponds. After examining the ponds, dams and old lodge, we looped back to our starting point. The visitors bade me farewell and expressed their thanks for taking them on a walk through such an interesting area.

After the group had departed Joe escorted me over to a log, sat down, and began discussing the strengths and weakness of this, my *first*, interpretive walk to the old beaver ponds. "Butch," Joe began, "let's begin with your strong points. I really liked the sense of adventure you provided the participants when you led them to believe you were lost in the forest!" "I'm glad you enjoyed that, Joe," I managed to say. "Yep, you really had them convinced that they were lost, and I especially enjoyed the way you had them point the way out!" Joe chuckled.

Now, if this had been my first season, and I was trying to win over my new supervisor's confidence, I might have had a tough decision to make. But I had known Joe for fifteen years, and he was not only my respected supervisor, but also my good friend. "Joe," I sheepishly began, "I'm afraid that was no act. I really *was* turned around out there for awhile!" At first I don't think he believed me, but when he saw me start to laugh at the ordeal I think I convinced him. "Joe, this is what you get for always showing up on the first program," I whined. Even so, Joe never did change his habit of auditing our first programs.

However, for my Map and Compass participants, I did have a harrowing story to tell my group about getting lost—it just so happens that it did not occur in Yellowstone. During the summer of 1988 I spent the summer season in the Great Smoky Mountains with my family working as an interpretive ranger. Our permanent home was in East Tennessee where I taught at Walters State Community College, also known as the Great Smoky Mountains Community College, only forty miles from the Smokies.

We wanted to experience the full season of the beautiful flowering plants there, plus I really wanted to learn more about the area where we spent the majority of the year. Ironically, 1988 was the only year between 1967 and the present that I did not spend at least part of the summer in Yellowstone, and it turned out to be some summer to miss, given the great fires that burned.

East Tennessee is home to some of the finest wilderness canoeing in the country, so most of my outings in the fall and spring consisted of canoe trips. I had taken a few small backpacking trips in the Smokies, but the vast majority of my backpacking experiences were limited to the northern Rockies in Wyoming and Montana. While I had taken many off-trail trips in Yellowstone, Glacier, Grand Teton, and the Bob Marshall and Scapegoat Wilderness Areas, I had never traveled off-trail in the Smokies.

By late August I was becoming somewhat depressed at the daily reports about the fires raging in Yellowstone. Oddly, what had begun as a fire season that the biologists in Yellowstone thought the park needed, had turned into something altogether different. I knew from my Yellowstone training sessions that park biologists had become very concerned over the loss of diversity in the park's aging forests, as well as the decrease in nutrient levels in Yellowstone Lake. Forest fires would help restore the forest diversity, and release nutrients into the lakes.

So when the fires started to burn, I would often digress from talking about the Smokies' natural history to Yellowstone's, given the national publicity the fires were generating. On one of my interpretive walks in the Smokies, we discussed how fire was essential for the health of the Table Mountain pine. It was on this walk that I would cheerfully comment on the "good news" that Yellowstone's forests were finally experiencing some needed burns. However, as the fire season turned into Yellowstone's biggest burn in 200 years, I quit talking about it on my walks in the Smokies.

This fire was not "behaving itself." Rather than burning acreage well away from established roads and trails, the fires were consuming old growth forests along popular trails, such as Fairy Falls, and were seriously threatening developed areas. The beloved Old Faithful Inn, built in 1903, was directly in the path of the North Fork Fire. The thought of losing this magnificent building, in addition to the loss of so much old growth forest at one time, truly saddened me. At that particular time, Margaret and my two daughters were away visiting family in Alabama. What better way to get my mind off of the fires in Yellowstone, than take a backpack trip deep into the Smokies' wilderness on my days off?

I planned a great two-day trip that would begin at the highest point in the Smokies--Clingman's Dome at 6700 feet--and end right at the small government cabin where we lived during that summer on Little River at Elkmont. My plan consisted of hiking west along the famed Appalachian Trail past Silers Bald (where I understood the views were fabulous) for eight miles to Buckeye Gap, and then descend off the AT, and travel cross country for about one mile to designated campsite #25 on Upper Little River.

Campsite #25 appeared to have everything I wanted: a rushing river, mountains rising all around, and seclusion, since it was at the end of the trail with no through traffic. I tried without success to get a hiking companion for the trip; however, this did not concern me much. I knew that park personnel strongly discouraged hikers from traveling cross-country in the Great Smoky Mountains. But I thought my trip was a safe one for five reasons: First, my topo map depicted an *old* trail from Buckeye Gap down to Little River. In the Smokies such unmaintained trails are referred to as "manways." Second, several park employees had told me, "I've heard that's a good trail." I was told to talk to Ranger Dwight McCarter, who had been down this manway many times, but when I tried to contact him, I found that he was away from the park…fighting fires in Yellowstone! Third, it was *only one mile* from Buckeye Gap to campsite #25. Fourth, I had a very detailed 7 ½ minute USGS topo map, and a good compass. Finally, considering the distances I had traveled cross-country with Jim Lenertz in Yellowstone, I laughed at the idea that I couldn't successfully negotiate one measly mile.

The weather forecast also seemed favorable. My trip would begin on Thursday morning and end Friday afternoon. Severe thunderstorms were in the offing, but were not supposed to arrive until early Saturday morning. I would be out and back at work by then. But as a precaution, I packed my gore-tex parka and a pop-up umbrella—handy in the Smokies, since the humidity tends to get you if the rain doesn't!

The hike from Clingman's Dome out to Siler's Bald was heavenly, with views in all directions. Huge, puffy white clouds drifted above the high grassy balds and rocky ridgetops, both of which permitted unlimited panoramic views. These views helped me appreciate the vast size of the seemingly endless wilderness that the western half of the park contains. From the high balds and ridges, the trail would descend gradually into the cool spruce-fir forest.

I stopped at Siler's Bald for lunch, and while taking in the spectacular views, congratulated myself for selecting this trip on my days off. The berry crop was outstanding, more than anything I had ever seen in Yellowstone. Blueberries and blackberries were practically everywhere, and provided a constant source of snack food. I had yet to see a bear but the trail was like a barnyard—full of droppings from bears gorging themselves on the abundant berry crop.

From Siler's Bald I had about three miles to travel along the AT before reaching Buckeye Gap. I had been making good time, but for some reason my progress slowed along these three miles. I began to think that perhaps I had walked through Buckeye Gap without realizing it. I had been told that there was an old sign at the gap, but maybe it had been removed. Finally, I reached a gap full of buckeye trees. Surely this was it but there was no sign. I decided to play it safe and continue along the AT to the Miry Ridge trail junction, which according to my map was located a short distance past Buckeye Gap. In the process, I reached the real Buckeye Gap, complete with an old weather-beaten sign, barely hanging by one bolt on an old post.

I was beginning to realize that reading a topo map of the Smokies was different from reading a topo map of terrain in the northern Rockies.

I took a break and enjoyed a snack while evaluating my situation. I could see no sign of a path or "manway" leaving the AT from Buckeye Gap, but on the other hand, the forest was fairly open. I could see no reason not to leave the trail and drop down from the gap. As a precaution, I took out my compass and set a course heading down into the drainage. From the gap I could easily see the valley below, but I knew that such views would quickly disappear once I began my descent.

The descent was *very* steep and reminded me of some of my trips in the Absaroka mountain range of Yellowstone. I quickly picked up a stream. I studied my trusty map, which depicted two streams flowing down from the gap, joining, and then flowing for about a mile to where the trail and campsite #25 should be located. Once I had located the stream, I put the compass in my jeans pocket (I would later regret that move).

I continued to drop steeply into the drainage. The vegetation became thicker and thicker. Looking back, it was almost like the devil was tempting me into hell. The friendly open forest at the gap had gradually changed into a dense jungle. Soon, the vegetation was so dense that I had to walk down the middle of the streambed, which was shallow, and at first, presented few obstacles. But as I continued, even the streambed became totally entangled in rhododendron. No wonder the mountain pioneers referred to these rhododendron thickets as "hells." I was sure as hell in one.

There was no sign of a trail or a campsite. I had been traveling for almost two hours. Was I on the right drainage? Of course I was. Afterall, my topo map showed only one stream. But all I could see was the incessant green of rhododendron leaves. By now, I was completely enshrouded in a tangle—an absolute jungle!

I was shocked at how it was becoming almost impossible to make any progress. Groping through this jungle with a small daypack would be hard enough, but having a full external backpack on made it almost impossible. The best analogy I can provide is to imagine jumping into a swimming pool filled with salt-water taffy. Or trying to move after ten people had lassoed you with ropes. At this point I began to feel scared. The very fact that I felt scared, scared me more.

Several factors contributed to this sudden feeling of fear. Perhaps I am a bit claustrophobic. I had never, ever, felt so closed-in and oppressed. I could not even see the sky above me for the dense vegetation! Second, my mind was racing back to the training sessions in May, where I had learned of hikers who had disappeared in the Smokies, and were never heard from or seen again. I thought back to the huge expanse of endless green I had looked down on from Siler's Bald. I was now engulfed by it! I began to think of my lack of experience in traveling cross-country in this type of terrain and vegetation. I was not in my familiar Yellowstone lodgepole, or even spruce-fir forest. I began to realize that it could take an entire day to travel just one mile in these conditions, and it was physically and mentally exhausting! Finally, I'm certain that being alone in this predicament affected me. I had taken many arduous trips in Yellowstone over the years, but almost always with at least one companion.

At this point I decided to turn back, retrace my route, and climb back up to the AT on top of the ridge. I knew this would be an ordeal to climb over 1200 feet back up the drainage, but I was concerned that I might *never* find the trail continuing down the stream. Besides, it had become almost impossible to move in this jungle of rhododendron bushes, which are really tangled trees reaching a height of thirty feet.

By now it was 5:00 p.m. Sunset was about 8:00 p.m. Of course, in this jungle it gets dark about an hour before sunset. As I struggled back up the steep drainage, I could not believe how physically exhausted I was feeling. I was soaked from perspiration. It wasn't really that warm, but the late August day was quite humid. My profuse sweating caused me to become extremely thirsty. I had already depleted my two twenty-ounce water bottles, which I had filled from a spring. I hesitated to drink water from this particular stream, since I had observed evidence of wild hog activity nearby, but I had no choice.

As I continued my climb I began to feel more exhausted. I could only remember feeling this lethargic on a backcountry trip one other time when Rick Hutchinson and I had hiked in eighteen miles, and were attempting to find a flat spot for our tent near the top of the Absarokas overlooking the Southeast Arm of Yellowstone Lake. On that trip I became nauseated and had to sack out. I certainly did not want to repeat that!

I was now at a point where I would climb for six steps, and then have to stop and rest. I simply could not believe how far down I had come. Maybe I had gone *past* the trail and campsite, but being encased in the jungle could not see it. I had no way of knowing.

I decided to take off my pack, eat a snack, and just lie back and rest awhile. This helped tremendously. I began to try to put things into perspective. "I'm not going to die out here—at least not tonight," I thought to myself. If need be, I would bivouac down here for the night. The food and rest really helped. My energy level came back up a few notches. I slowly resumed my climb out of this hell. The vegetation was becoming *slightly* less dense, as I continued to struggle up the drainage. Then, for some reason, I decided to take out my compass and check my direction. My desired route should have been opposite from the compass bearing I had set up at Buckeye Gap.

What I saw on the compass dial shocked me. It showed that I was heading in a direction 120 degrees off course to the east! "This cannot be!" I thought to myself. "I am following the drainage back up to Buckeye Gap." I recalled what my frequent Yellowstone hiking companion, Jim Lenertz, had always preached to me: "One day you will look at your compass and not believe it. But you had better trust the compass over your own sense of direction!"

I dismissed Jim's sermon for the time being. I was so certain that my route was correct and the compass was wrong, that I rationalized that the dial had been turned while it was in my jeans pocket during all my struggling through the jungle. Besides, I was following the drainage. I *had* to be right. Of course, Jim had also preached to always write down your compass bearing, and then tie the compass on a string and hang it around your neck so as not to twist the dial. But once I had found the drainage I supposedly had it made as it would lead me directly to my destination. Not so!

I continued to follow the drainage and finally began to see some light toward the top of the ridge through the dense trees. "Thank the Lord," I thought. "At least I am finally getting close to the gap." Just seeing some light through the forest canopy lifted my spirits, though I *was* somewhat concerned that I had not recognized anything on the way back up. "Seems like I would've at least seen a footprint somewhere in the streambed," I thought. But then the place *was* a jungle—severely limiting visibility to only what you could see directly in front of your face.

Finally, finally, I reached the top of the ridge. There was no trail; just more jungle. This was not Buckeye Gap. It was not even the main ridge, which the AT followed. "Where in the world could I be?" I pondered. For the first time in a long, long time, I felt a wave of utter fear and panic beginning to sweep over me. I was lost. I reflected on the dozens of ridges to the north and the ocean of wild jungle of forest wilderness I had observed to the north while hiking atop the AT. Now I wondered if I had been swallowed up by it.

My pulse quickened and my rate of breathing increased. "My God," I thought. "I feel like I'm going into shock. Are you going to let your mind defeat your body?" I took off my pack, got out another candy bar, and stretched out. My mind drifted to a passage that I had written in my hiking guidebook to Yellowstone, "If you get to a point where you find yourself saying to yourself, 'I am lost, hopelessly lost,' the first thing to do is nothing. Sit down. Reconnoiter. Reconstruct your previous movements on the topo map and find your general location. The solution to your problem will probably become obvious. In any case, don't rush around frantically—you will get more lost, if that's possible. Plan first, then act."

I knew that this was not Yellowstone but I also knew that I needed to follow my own advice and calm down and think this situation through. The feeling of panic was incredible. I wanted to throw down my backpack and run off blindly in any direction ranting and raving. I began to get control of myself. "Okay," I thought. "If I don't find my way back to the AT I will bivouac here tonight, and tomorrow if I have to, I will start a fire. I had a stove full of fuel and plenty of matches (little did I know that before the next morning, over *four inches* of rain would fall).

I began to try to figure out what could have gone wrong. My best judgment, now that I had calmed down and knocked back most of the fear (and this was critical), was that I had followed another drainage up than the one I had descended. Perhaps there were other drainages *not shown* on my 7-½ minute quadrangle map. Then I remembered my compass! Maybe that darn thing *had* been correct! I decided to slowly traverse the ridge, heading west—the direction my compass had wanted me to go some time ago.

I hoped this ridge would join the main ridge that the AT and Buckeye Gap were located on. By now it was 6:30 p.m. I was doing some tall praying that the next ridge I came to would be the main ridge with the AT on top of it. I didn't even want to entertain how I would feel or what I would do if it were not. Finally, I reached the top of the ridge and there was the trail. I have experienced great feelings of relief before when finding a trail or landmark after wandering off-trail for many hours. However, it is impossible to describe the euphoria and ecstasy I felt when I realized that I had located the AT again.

I assumed that I had come out well west of Buckeye Gap, since I had angled sharply to the west traversing the ridge. I began hiking along the trail looking for the junction with the Miry Ridge Trail, which was now going to be my route to follow down to Elkmont. After forty minutes of fast walking I reached *Buckeye Gap!* I could not believe I had been that far off—to the *east!*

I suppose the rest of my trip would be considered an "adventure" to some, but to me it was a piece of cake once I had a trail to walk on, and was out of the grips of the hell-like jungle. My mental and physical states were soaring. I could not believe the energy I now felt. This experience helped me appreciate the power the mind has over our bodies. I decided now to camp at site #26, about three miles down this trail.

About two miles down the trail I jumped a bear. In the next three miles I would encounter four more! Talk about bear country! If this had been Yellowstone with its big grizzlies, I would have been shaken. But these black bears, while potentially dangerous, are mere pups compared to Yellowstone's big bears. Seeing so many bears did not faze me. I was still energized from finding my way back out of the jungle.

While on the Miry Ridge trail the skies began to darken, and the loud cracks and rumbles of thunder reverberated through the mountains. "Hmm," I thought. "Guess the severe thunderstorms have arrived about twenty-four hours early." I knew that this was par for the course for the weather forecasting business in East Tennessee. Suddenly, a direct lightning strike hit right over my head. "Here I am on an exposed ridge in a severe electrical storm," I mused to myself. But at least I knew where the heck I was!

I began to recall the park's backcountry description of campsite #26: "Special hazard during storms due to lightning." When I reached #26 it was almost dark except for the illumination from the constant lightning strikes. Amazingly, no rain was falling yet. I could find no source of water nearby in the dark. By now I had walked fifteen miles, but I decided to push on for campsite #27 on Jakes Creek. At a lower elevation, surely it would have a good water source, plus, I would not be common fodder for a lightning strike.

About fifteen minutes past campsite #26 all hell broke loose. I was afraid that a tornado had hit. A deluge of rain commenced. The lightning displays were so intense that I could easily see down the trail in what should have been a very dark forest. I put on my raincoat and pulled out my umbrella, but to no avail. This was truly a flood! Soon, the trail became a roaring stream itself. As I neared campsite #27, I began to realize that there was *no way* I could hope to get my tent up in this downpour. Then it hit me—why not just walk all the way out to my cabin at Elkmont? The idea of making it to my cabin, finding refuge from this deluge, and having a cold beer while I watched the raging storm from *inside* thrilled me.

I was now soaked from the sideways rain, but I surged on with renewed vigor and enthusiasm. The storm was now at full bore. The night would have been pitch black by now except for the incredible lightning display, which was the most outstanding I had seen since camped with Jim Lenertz in the cirque high above Pelican Valley in Yellowstone. Although it did not seem possible, the rain began to fall at an even heavier rate, which now began to concern me since I had two fords of Jakes Creek yet to make.

I passed campsite #27 and slogged on to the ford. The first was not too bad, but the second one appeared daunting. The normally clear creek was turbid and rising by the second. I was now soaked to the bone so I just charged into the stream, and managed to maneuver safely across the waist-high waters. If I had indeed camped out for the night, I would never have been able to make it across this stream the next day.

By 10:00 p.m. I was at the trailhead. The storm had not abated in the least. I had walked twenty-one miles and still had almost two more to walk down a road. As I slogged on down the road through the rain, my left heel was really beginning to bother me. I suddenly realized that I had needlessly carried my full backpack for twenty-three miles! "Dang," I thought. "I haven't pulled a stunt like this since Rod Busby and I hauled a two-man rubber raft thirty miles from Fox Creek to the South Entrance in Yellowstone!"

Upon reaching my quarters, I headed straight for the fridge, pulled out a cold beer, turned out all of the lights, curled up on the couch, and watched in awe the raging squall. I felt exhausted and ecstatic at the same time. After a couple of hours of being mesmerized by the continuing storm, and being ever so thankful that I was *inside*, I retired for the evening. I don't think I hardly moved until I awoke the next morning.

It was *still* pouring! The Little River was now lapping at the back door of my cabin. I walked up the Little River Road and could not recognize what I saw. The river was well out of its banks. Rangers were in the process of evacuating Elkmont Campground in those sites along the river. A total of four inches of rain had fallen since the previous evening according to the rain gauge at Elkmont. The rain total was surely much higher up on top of the mountains where I had been. Backpackers were stranded in several sections of the park's backcountry due to impassable stream fords.

Many "what ifs" began to go through my mind. What if I had been stubborn and not turned back in the jungle? What if I had stayed out and bivouacked for the night? Most frighteningly, what if I had not found my way back to the AT? What had started out as a simple overnight backpacking trip, turned into quite an adventure. And it could have easily turned out much worse.

In recent years I have had the good fortune of being able to again teach a full one-day map and compass course for the Yellowstone Institute. The Institute now offers courses similar to the long interpretive programs that the National Park Service used to offer. I have enjoyed telling the visitors of my most harrowing misadventure of "being lost" in the wilderness.

I have shared with visitors the two main lessons I learned from my experience. One, I vowed to never venture off-trail in extremely heavy vegetated areas like the Smokies again. I have friends who successfully negotiate the Smokies' wilderness off-trail, but for me I will let them have it. If I go off-trail it will be in the West. Second, I vowed to never go off-trail by myself again. Too many things can go wrong out in the wilderness, and being alone exposes you to the severest of consequences.

One Evening at
Turret Mountain Meadow

For several years I had encouraged my friend and teaching colleague, Hank Barnett, to join me on an extensive backpacking trip into Yellowstone's Thorofare Region. In 1987 Hank (who went on to become a seasonal ranger himself at Crater Lake, Great Smoky Mountains and eventually Yellowstone) and I finally arranged the time in early September, when the Yellowstone wilderness is special and the elk are bugling. I had just finished working my first season in Great Smoky Mountains National Park, and our college was about to switch from a quarter calendar to one using semesters. We knew this would be our last chance for a long time to take a lengthy fall trip, so we arranged for a ten-day trip into the Thorofare.

I have always considered the Thorofare to be the wildest roadless area in Yellowstone, because of its sheer size as well as rugged beauty. In fact, a few years ago, the Thorofare received the notoriety of being designated as the most remote area in the contiguous forty-eight states based on distance to the nearest road. I did not relish this special area receiving so much national attention, plus I was shocked to learn that the most remote area left in the country was *only twenty miles* to the nearest road! That fact alone should illustrate to any reasonable person just what has happened to wild country in our nation, and why we need to preserve what few wilderness areas we have remaining.

Hank and I decided to call our trip the "Eagle Peak Expedition," for we hoped to scale Yellowstone's highest peak at an elevation of 11,358 feet. We paddled our canoe eighteen miles down the Southeast Arm of Yellowstone Lake. The conditions were ideal for paddling. The weather was rather warm and winds were calm. There were some fires burning in the park causing the skies to appear rather hazy. "This almost reminds me of the Great Smokies," Hank commented.

We paddled our canoe to the Trail Creek outlet, and hid it in the nearby woods. Considering the fact that we were hiking in September, the ford across the Yellowstone River was surprisingly deep. All my trips into the Thorofare have been in September. I could not imagine attempting this ford in mid-summer, when the snow melt was still in progress. We had brought along some old tennis shoes to use for the ford, and once safely across, we hid them under a large log.

Our campsite for this evening would be near Trappers Creek in the Yellowstone River delta area, where the river flows into the Southeast Arm of Yellowstone Lake. After we set up our tents and hung our food, we decided to walk down the creek to its outlet, where it flows into the Yellowstone River. I thought I would enjoy some catch and release fishing for cutthroat trout. As we walked through the willow brush we came across several shed moose antlers. This area is fabulous moose habitat given the abundance of willow. When we reached the river I pulled out my fishing pole, but found that I had forgotten to pack any lures! That took care of my fishing plans.

On our next day we had planned to simply follow Trappers Creek up to the boundary line with Shoshone National Forest, and camp above timberline. From there we hoped to hike to the summit of Eagle Peak. We broke camp and hiked along the trail until it crossed Trappers Creek. We glanced to the east at our upcoming task of hiking off-trail. Just as we were about to leave the trail behind and disappear into the forest along Trappers Creek, a ranger on horseback emerged from the woods heading down the Thorofare Trail.

His wool ranger flat hat was stained and no longer quite flat, as it had obviously been in use for a long time. I had only seen one other hat like this one, and that belonged to Don Yestness, the long-time backcountry ranger at Shoshone Lake. I used to run into Don often during the late 1970s, when we were leading our two-day overnight interpretive backpack trips to Shoshone Geyser Basin.

As it turned out, the ranger was Bob Jackson. I had heard and read about ranger Jackson for many years. I had read his logbook comments in numerous backcountry patrol cabins as well, but this was my first time to meet him in person. Jackson was somewhat of a legend in Yellowstone ranger lore. He was particularly adept at catching poachers in the act. In fact, his normal tour of duty was mid-summer through late fall, to include the hunting season in the national forests around Yellowstone's remote southeast corner.

Bob politely introduced himself, and then inquired as to where we were heading. We told him of our plans. "Well, if you accept my advice, you will not go that way," he said. "Upper Trappers Creek is grizzly city, and they don't like to be disturbed this time of year. You fellows think it over and do what you think is best, but my advice is to stick to the trail and go up Howell Creek." At this point Bob and I traded comments on working in Yellowstone—me in the front country at Old Faithful, the busiest place in the park, and Bob in the most remote place in the park. Obviously, Bob thought he had the better work location. "I figure I'll keep coming to this job as long as I can see the next trail marker," Bob said with a chuckle.

With that, Bob disappeared down the trail as quickly as he had mysteriously appeared. Hank and I decided to sit down and discuss our options. While I don't always look for signs of divine intervention, the circumstances here were rather unusual. First, what were the odds that Ranger Bob Jackson would happen by on his thirty-two-mile ride into Thorofare Ranger Station at the precise moment that Hank and I were crossing the trail to head up Trappers Creek? Second, we could not dismiss Jackson's warning about grizzlies. I knew that most human-bear encounters occurred off-trail, and involved one or two hikers. Bear encounters with parties of four or more almost never happen. I also knew that grizzlies enter a period of hyperphagia during the fall, when they tend to be more aggressive as they are attempting to lay on the layers of fat in preparation for winter's hibernation.

Hank and I finally decided that perhaps the good Lord was trying to send us a message, so we opted to hike around via the trail up Howell Creek, and attempt the climb up Eagle Peak from that side. We camped at site 6-D-7, a beautiful spot in a meadow right on a tributary to Howell Creek. In fact, it was this tributary that we would follow in our attempt to climb Eagle Peak. However, the site did not contain a bear pole, and we had a terrible time finding a tree to use as one.

The next morning we were rather lackadaisical about getting up, since we had the entire day to hike the three miles up to the summit of Eagle Peak. Then the problem with hanging our food resurfaced. It took us almost a full hour to find a decent tree, and properly get our food and backpacks pulled up and stored. The late start would prove to be our downfall.

The climb up the tributary to the shoulder of Eagle Peak was really easier than I had expected. As we reached an elevation of 10,720 feet, we saw bighorn sheep grazing in the alpine meadows, and the summit was clearly visible and in reach. But we also saw something else that cast a pall over our climb. Huge, dark thunderclouds had quickly built up, and lightning strikes were beginning to appear all around the summit of Eagle Peak.

Normally these kinds of thunderstorms roll in later in the afternoon. But on this day, at around 2:00 p.m., they were already in full force. It was almost as if the spirit of Eagle Peak was speaking down to us, "You will not climb me on this day!" Indeed, given the severity of the storms that had materialized, it would have been extremely foolish to continue up on top of the exposed ridge. We had ascended over 2300 feet from our camp, and only had about 580 feet of elevation left when the storms hit. So we began our descent back down to Howell Creek, griping the whole way about how we had allowed ourselves to get off to such a late start on this day.

Given our time schedule we knew that we would not have the opportunity to climb Eagle Peak the next morning. We had to hike over ten miles back to our campsite at Turret Mountain Meadow. Looking at the map though, it appeared that we might be able to hike up to the top of Table Mountain, which at an elevation of 11,063 feet ranks as one of Yellowstone's highest peaks.

The next morning from our camp at 8400 feet we climbed over 1000 feet up to a shoulder of Table Mountain at an elevation 9490 feet. However, once we topped this shoulder, we could view the imposing southeast wall of Table Mountain. While the peak appeared very interesting on our topo map, in reality we could not get to the top from this angle. So we spent about an hour on top of the impressive shoulder of the massive mountain, eating snacks and simply taking in the incredible views into some of the wildest country in the West.

The main goal of our ten-day trip was to enjoy this wild country, rather than bagging peaks. True, we were disappointed to get so close, but not make the summit of Yellowstone's highest peak. Perhaps it was poetic justice then, that our next evening spent out in the wilderness would turn out to be the best one of the trip, and indeed one of the most special evenings I have ever spent out in the Yellowstone wilderness.

On our way back to the Southeast Arm we camped for the evening in a large meadow, tinted a beautiful September gold, situated beneath Turret Mountain, so named for the lofty knob rising out of the mountain mass. Our campsite was located in a small island of trees out in the meadow. As we prepared our evening meal, a wilderness spectacle began to slowly unfold before our eyes. First, the low angle of the late evening sun cast the entire meadow and mountain above a rich, golden tint. Then, across the meadow a huge bull moose walked out of the forest, and began rubbing his massive antlers on a tree. Overhead, a great grey owl glided over the meadow in search of a rodent scurrying out in the open grass. Our visual senses were being bombarded, yet there was an eerie silence hanging over the meadow.

Suddenly, the stillness was broken by the sharp barks and howls of coyotes. Even though we could not see them, their haunting chorus reverberated across the meadow. I began to feel a complete sense of exhilaration, as if we were sitting in the front row of a grand performance, and the curtain had just risen. "What's next?" I silently mused. I didn't have to wait long.

Directly across the meadow from our campsite an enormous bull elk emerged from the thick lodgepole forest. Standing with great dignity the bull raised his head skyward, and emitted a high-pitched shrill bugle, followed by a baritone grunt. His great rack of antlers almost rested on his broad tan back, as he seemed to issue his challenge to all competitors. We could now make out a small herd of cows beginning to emerge from the forest into the meadow.

Then without warning, the bull's challenge was answered as another smaller bull emerged from the forest into the meadow and quickly announced his intentions with a thunderous bugle of his own. The harem of fifteen cows appeared nervous, as the two bulls closed on each other. These two majestic animals locked antlers just as the low angle of the sun's rays were reaching a peak, illuminating them in a rich, golden hue. The owl was still soaring and the coyotes were continuing their serenade. Hank and I could only stand awestruck as the spectacle continued to unfold.

I was prepared for a long, rugged battle between these two warriors, but the contest was short-lived. The smaller bull found that his time would have to wait, at least with this monarch's harem. I turned to Hank and asked, "What will be next in this meadow, a grizzly?" But the magical moment was concluded as quickly as it had begun. The moose moved off into large willow and out of sight. The elk disappeared back into the forest. The alpenglow was gone, the sun having set behind the Two Ocean Plateau. The owl was still circling the meadow, but its form melted into the darkening scene. The wildlife spectacle at Turret Mountain meadow had really lasted but for a few fleeting moments. However, like so many of Yellowstone's experiences, the memory was etched into my brain for a lifetime.

The next morning marked the end of the unusually warm weather, as a cold rain moved in. By the time we reached the ford at the Yellowstone River, the rain had turned to snow. We decided to have lunch under the protective boughs of a large spruce tree before easing into the ice-cold waters. I looked under the log to retrieve my old tennis shoes, but was surprised to find only one shoe. I guess I learned a lesson about trying to hide such items on the forest floor.

Hank made the ford and then managed to toss one of his shoes across the river for my use. The snow continued throughout most of the afternoon. The thermometer on my backpack read a cold thirty-five degrees. Once we reached camp the snow was continuing, so we pitched a small tarp to prepare dinner under. We had packed it along for just such a use. By early evening the snow ceased, and the clouds lifted, revealing the newly-frosted peaks of the Absaroka Range. From our campsite near Trail Creek, we viewed a full golden moon rising above the Absarokas, as we warmed ourselves around a cheerful campfire. "Hank," I said. "It just doesn't get any better than this!" He nodded in agreement.

The next morning broke foggy and cold, but canoeing conditions were ideal as we paddled back up the arm to our last campsite at Park Point. That evening as we sat around the campfire, we began to recall the best moments from our ten-day trip. Then we became somewhat paranoid as we realized that we had a plane to catch the next afternoon. "Butch, what would we do if a storm blows up in the middle of the night?" Hank asked with a worried expression on his face. "I guess we would try to stash the canoe back in the woods and hike the eight miles out," I replied.

The weather had entered a period of instability, and I worried about winds coming up before we could get out. My friend and District Interpretive Ranger, Joe Halladay, had graciously offered to pick us up at Sedge Bay at noon the next day. I slept in fits worrying about the weather for most of the night. Typically, early morning is the best time of day to paddle the lake, as the waters are calm. However, during the night I heard the wind beginning to blow and the sound of waves starting to crash on the lake's shore. I looked at my watch and it read 4:20 a.m. "Hank," I groggily managed, "the wind has already started to blow. Let's get out of here. We can eat breakfast once we reach Sedge Bay."

By 4:45 a.m. we had packed up our gear and were in the canoe paddling. It was still dark and this was definitely the coldest morning of our trip. The temperature was in the low twenties. As the sun came up out of the east the lighting was beautiful out on the lake, but the sun's rays were blocked by the mountains for quite some time. As we neared Sedge Bay the winds had died down, which removed the threat of not being able to make it out, but we were freezing! The idea of waiting in the icy shade on Sedge Bay was not too appealing. So we pulled into a small cove prior to reaching Sedge Bay. The cove contained a thermal area with several steam vents.

Hank and I got out of the canoe and crouched around the steam vents to absorb their warmth. "Hank, you sure can't do this in the Smoky Mountains," I joked as we enjoyed our own personal steam radiators. Once we had sufficiently warmed up, we paddled the remaining thirty minutes to Sedge Bay, reaching shore at 7:15 a.m. We had a long wait in store since we had asked Joe to meet us at noon. Soon the rays of the morning sun reached the shore of Sedge Bay, and we relaxed on shore, absorbing its wonderful warmth. The long wait for Joe really wasn't so bad, as we used the time to just soak in the beautiful scenery and reflect on our trip. Our ten days in the wilderness had provided some magnificent memories, but the most special of all was the evening at Turret Mountain Meadow.

Elk in Meadow at West Thumb

Moonbow Over Divide Lookout

There are three lookout towers that are staffed during the summer months in Yellowstone: Mount Washburn, Mount Sheridan, and Mount Holmes. From these three peaks trained fire lookouts can see most of the park's terrain, and report smokes that may be caused by lightning strikes. Decades earlier, other lookouts were utilized at such locations as Pelican Cone, Purple Mountain, Observation Peak, Divide Lookout, and several others. Today, airplanes play an important role in looking for fires when conditions warrant. As a result many of the rustic old fire lookout towers are going the way of the drive-in movie across the Rocky Mountain West.

Divide Lookout Tower was situated about seven miles southeast of Old Faithful atop the Continental Divide at an elevation of 8779 feet. The steel tower was built in 1957, and was accessible by a short trail near Craig Pass on the Old Faithful—West Thumb road. When I transferred to Old Faithful in 1976, Divide Lookout was not staffed, though it could be in the event of an emergency, such as extreme fire weather conditions. However, we did utilize it for interpretive programs.

Each week we led a twenty-mile, two-day overnight backpacking trip that began at the Lone Star Geyser trailhead, traveled to Shoshone Geyser Basin for the night, and then concluded the next day by hiking four miles cross-country to the lookout. The lookout would provide our group with two thrills. The first was just finding it. Since the lookout was situated on a flat knob in a dense forest, it did not come into view until you were within 100 yards.

Because we were hiking cross-country with no trail, we had to be very accurate with the use of our map and compass. The GPS was not available back then. I'm proud to say the three of us on the staff that led this trip, Jim Lenertz, Jeff Later, and myself, never missed it.

The second thrill was obtaining the view. We would take our fifteen participants up to the lookout for a great overview of the trip just completed, and then hike the remaining 1.7-mile trail out to the road. From the base of the lookout on the forest floor, there was absolutely no view. But by climbing the sixty-eight-foot tower, you were able to get above the forest canopy, and the view was utterly spectacular. Below and to the south was a wonderful bird's eye view of Shoshone Lake. Further south in the distance were the mighty Tetons. Over to the southeast you could see Mount Sheridan, and beyond that the impressive Absaroka Mountain Range. The Gallatins were easily visible to the northwest.

Of particular interest were the views of the numerous thermal basins.

Columns of steam from Shoshone Geyser Basin could be viewed six miles to the southwest, as well as massive clouds of steam rising from Black Sand Geyser Basin and the Upper Geyser Basin only seven miles away to the northwest.

We also used Divide Lookout for a forest fire ecology hike. The NPS had initiated its natural fire policy in 1972, and Divide Lookout was a great resource to show visitors the role that forest fires played in the ecosystem. The short hike up to the lookout coursed through an old lodgepole pine forest, and one that is rather distinctive, in that the forest contains numerous burled trees. A burl is an unusual knotty growth on a tree. Many of the trees used to build the majestic Old Faithful Inn were apparently taken not too far from this area. Why there are so many burled trees in this vicinity is a mystery. From the top of Divide Lookout visitors were able to look out over much of Yellowstone's vast forest, and could gain an appreciation for the role fire played in regenerating the forest and benefiting wildlife.

One of the most spectacular sights I ever had the privilege to behold in Yellowstone was to experience the rise of a full moon from Divide Lookout. To see the huge golden sphere rise up above the rugged peaks of the Absaroka Range to the east was simply breathtaking. In August of 1983 I decided to take my ten-year old daughter Caroline, and friend Terry Holcomb and his daughter Wendy, fifteen, and sons Jimmy, thirteen, and David, eight, up to the lookout for the night to experience the rise of the full moon. As it turned out we experienced much more than we bargained for!

Divide Lookout was constructed of angle-iron supports with sturdy wooden steps leading the way to the top of the structure. Anyone with a fear of heights would not want to look down while climbing up the steps, but once inside the cabin on top you felt at ease. The lookout cabin was fairly roomy, and contained ample sleeping space for several people.

Even though the lookout was no longer used by fire lookouts, the rather thick lookout manual was still on hand. Looking through the lengthy document increased my appreciation for the many complex duties that lookouts are responsible for. I had always assumed that a lookout simply recorded the fire weather, looked for smokes, and if they spotted one, marked it on a map, and called it in via park radio. However, the manual clearly revealed that there was much more to the job. Of particular interest to us was the chapter titled, "What to do in case of lightning strikes." We put the manual back in the cabinet drawer.

That evening the full moon rose on cue above the Absarokas, and we were not disappointed. At first the moon was huge with a gorgeous golden glow, but as it rose higher, its color brightened up the entire countryside. Down below you could see the glow of several campsites around the shores of Shoshone Lake, where paddlers and/or backpackers were enjoying their evening in the wilderness (unfortunately, today fires are no longer allowed at Shoshone Lake). We played cards by candlelight, as we continued to soak in the beauty of the moonlit evening.

All four kids were excitedly giggling and babbling over the experience, but soon they began to tap out, and all we could hear was a bit of whispering. Eventually, the whispering gave way to total silence, as the youngsters nodded off to sleep.

I used the top bunk and everyone else slept on the lower level near the floor. The top bunk was even with the windows, and on this evening the moon was so bright, it was almost like trying to sleep in a room with the overhead light left on. Nevertheless, I finally joined the rest of the group and dozed off to sleep.

About two hours later that evening something caused me to wake up. A bright light was shining directly in my eyes. I remember thinking that the full moon must be brighter than normal on this evening, when suddenly the silence was shattered by a deafening clap of thunder. The bright light in my eyes had not been the moon; rather, it had been a flash of lightning. I rose up in my bunk and looked to the southwest to the Pitchstone Plateau beyond Shoshone Lake. There, I saw an ominous sight. A huge, dark thunderstorm was rolling over the plateau, heading straight for us.

I looked over toward Terry and noticed that he had also been awakened, and was sitting up looking out at the storm. Bolts of lightning were relentlessly being hurled down from the mushroomed shaped cloud. The cloud was eerily lit up by the full moon overhead. Terry and I felt very nervous about being exposed above the trees during an electrical storm of this size, and decided to wake the kids.

My first thought was for our group to simply climb down the lookout and wait in the dense forest for the storm to pass, but some of the lightning bolts were now right around us. "Quick," Terry instructed, "get the fire lookout manual!" We pulled the manual out and turned to the chapter that covered lightning strikes. Terry shone his flashlight on the book while I read. "My gosh, there must be fifteen steps to take," I said with anguish. I was alarmed because the menacing cloud was rolling directly at us, and would be over us in a matter of minutes.

"This thing looks like an upside down battleship with all guns blazing," Terry told me under his breath so as not to frighten the kids. I read from the manual out loud: "What to do in the event of a lightning storm—Note: this lookout tower is grounded for protection against direct lightning strikes, but be sure to check and tighten the connecting bolts periodically to insure the grounding rods have not come loose." This statement certainly did not reassure us.

There was no telling how long it had been since anyone had checked those connections. "Step One: In the event of an impending lightning storm, *do not* go outside of the lookout, as this would be very dangerous." This statement confirmed that it was too late for us to climb down the lookout. "Step Two: Go to the center of the lookout and stand on a rubber mat." We quickly pulled down our ensolite sleeping pads, and spread them in the middle of the floor and crouched down on them.

There were actually several more steps listed on the page, but with time running out on us, I quickly skipped to the last one: "Now that you have taken all of these required steps you may now relax with the comforting knowledge that no fire lookout has ever been killed during a lightning storm, except for those where the grounding rods were not properly fastened." Well, this did not exactly comfort us!

I felt as though we were playing a game of Russian roulette for I had no idea what shape the grounding rods were in. The thunderhead was now directly over the west end of Shoshone Lake near Shoshone Geyser Basin, only six miles away from us. The relentless lightning strikes were absolutely glorious. Too bad we were unable to enjoy the spectacular show because the storm was racing right toward us.

Given the frequency of the sky-to-ground lightning strikes, I expected the worst. The thunderhead that Terry had described as a battleship was moving toward us with a life of its own. The noise from the constant thunder and large rain drops and perhaps hail stones pounding the metal roof of the lookout was deafening. There was absolutely no way we were going to avoid taking a direct hit. Terry told me later that he was thinking that if we got hit, it would be like standing inside a giant incandescent light bulb!

We all had our minds on that last step in the manual. We were praying that this lookout tower was properly grounded. As the big cloud closed on us, lightning strikes were coming down all around us. We all hugged each other tightly in the middle of the floor. I think I even closed my eyes in anticipation of a strike. A few moments later I looked up and to my shock the big cloud had rolled right over us, and we had not received a direct hit. I now looked to the east and watched the lightning strikes continuing to come out of the cloud, and was amazed that we were spared.

The next phenomenon that we viewed simply qualifies as one of those fabulous magical Yellowstone moments. Along with the lightning, the big thundercloud had also produced a considerable amount of rain. As the cloud rolled over us, the rain was continuing to come down in sheets lagging behind. The full moon emerged back into full view and lit up the trailing curtain of rain. The result was a full moonbow over the lookout. I had heard of moonbows, but had never actually seen one.

On several occasions Margaret and I have watched Castle Geyser erupt late in the evening under a full moon, but we never observed a moonbow. I have read about rare moonbows at Cumberland Falls in Kentucky. The moonbow over us was simply incredible. From our perch high in the lookout, it seemed that we were looking *down* on the moonbow.

Unlike the many colors of a rainbow, this moonbow was bright silver in color, but the colors were striated in various shades. Just like a rainbow, the moonbow did not last very long, and soon disappeared. As far as the eye could now see, the sky was clear.

After the storm it was difficult to go back to sleep. Our adrenalin was pumping, given the close call we had just had, but we were also wound up over the magnificent sight of the moonbow. The kids were delighted. For Terry's three kids, this was their first primal wilderness experience. The group of six continued to chat excitedly about the event for a half hour, before we finally went back to sleep.

The next morning on the way down, we naturally checked the base of the lookout to examine the grounding rods. All appeared to be in good shape and tightly secured. How I wished we had known this during the storm!

Sadly, budget cutbacks during the late 1980s eliminated most of the longer interpretive hikes that we offered out of Old Faithful, including the fire ecology hike and overnight backpacking trip, both of which utilized Divide Lookout. The lookout was rather hastily removed in the fall of 1991. One of the most splendid views in all of Yellowstone is now gone forever.

At the time the lookout was removed, it appeared to be in fairly good condition; however, the rationale for removing Divide Lookout was sound. It was no longer being used for official purposes, and it was considered a safety hazard. There existed a concern that a visitor would fall and be fatally or seriously injured, and sue the government for damages. Unfortunately, this type of tort claim has become rather common; some of the claims border on the ridiculous.

Not all rangers were in favor of removing Divide Lookout, and some spoke out against it. I will always feel that if we had still been leading interpretive hikes up to the lookout, we might have been able to save it, because I think a fence around the base of the lookout would have eliminated the safety concern. Also, Divide Lookout was unique in the park, in that it was not simply a cabin perched on top of a peak such as at Pelican Cone, Observation Peak, Snake River, and the three that are still staffed. Of course, the fact that it was unique made its loss more significant.

After the removal of Divide Lookout in 1991, I did not return to the site of the lookout until the summer of 2002. There was really no reason to go there unless you wanted to see some burled trees or climb over 700 feet to merely gain a limited glimpse of the north end of Shoshone Lake. When I reached the top of the forested knob, it was hard to believe that a lookout ever existed. Today's visitors probably wonder why a lookout tower was ever built on this spot in the middle of a dense, old lodgepole forest, for there are simply no views. They would never imagine that right here, prior to 1991, it was possible to obtain one of the best views of the Yellowstone country to be found in the park. Many visitors over the years experienced this view. Personally, Divide Lookout will always hold a special place in my heart, and needless to say, I will never forget the night of the moonbow.

Note: The U.S. Forest Service maintains some lookouts, which are no longer in official use, for rent to visitors in the Northern Rockies. For information, check at any Forest Service Ranger Station.

The Trip from Hell

Fortunately, most folks who hike and backpack in Yellowstone's backcountry stay on the trail. There are, after all, over 1000 miles of trails that traverse the park. However, there are a few hikers who occasionally venture off-trail with map, compass, and in recent years, a GPS (global positioning satellite) unit in hand. This isn't always a good idea for several reasons. For one thing, most serious human-bear encounters in Yellowstone occur off-trail. Grizzlies often seem to seek refuge from the developed trails.

Off-trail travel is also a great way to get lost. Yellowstone covers nearly 3500 square miles, and you can get in serious trouble if that GPS lets you down. This can happen. A hiker was traveling off-trail during February 2003 in Great Smoky Mountains National Park, following his GPS, when the unit died. He wandered around for four days before fortunately, the GPS revived, and he managed to find his way out--cold, hungry, dehydrated and sick from drinking directly from the streams. He was lucky the weather was mild.

It is also much easier to sustain an injury off-trail, since you must often hop over fallen logs and boulders. I recall a ranger in Grand Teton National Park once telling me a story about how he was on an off-trail hike in Waterfalls Canyon, when he suddenly slipped and fell. He managed to catch himself before reaching the ground, but he noticed something fuzzy directly in front of his right eye. His eyes attempted to focus on a broken limb one inch from his eye. The limb was as sharp and pointed as a dagger. If he had fallen forward only a few more inches, he would have suffered a grave injury while deep in the wilderness away from any established trails.

Obviously, it is very important to be able to use a map, compass and yes, even a GPS. For example, there are numerous trails in Yellowstone that cross large meadows. With so many animals in Yellowstone making their own trails, a hiker can easily confuse an animal trail with the official trail. In order to help hikers stay on officially designated trails, the NPS mounts tall wooden posts in the meadows with orange metal tags attached. The problem is, bison just love to rub their heads and shoulders on these posts, and they frequently get knocked down.

So let's suppose you are hiking the Mary Mountain trail across Hayden Valley and lose the trail—you had better have a map and compass on hand and know how to use them. Yes, the GPS is nice to have too, but remember it is a high tech instrument, and we all know that Murphy just loves technology. Despite all of the problems that can occur with off-trail travel, occasionally the temptation gets the best of you.

For years, each time I would drive the Canyon to Tower road over

Dunraven Pass, I would gaze over to the west at the handsome Washburn Range, and fantasize about making a cross-country hike along its backbone. In 1989, Sam Holbrook, Yellowstone's senior interpretive ranger, introduced me to John and Deb Dirksen. While I was still venturing out with my old hiking buddy Jim Lenertz on canoe trips, Sam knew that Jim was no longer able to take the extended trips, and thought that I might enjoy hiking with John and Deb.

I will always be grateful for that introduction because of the wonderful friendship my family and I have had with John and Deb, and how they enriched my enjoyment of the backcountry. They basically changed my whole routine. While I always enjoyed a campfire where allowed in the backcountry, I rarely ever cooked on the fire. John is the master of tending a campfire, and Deb must be the best backcountry cook on the planet.

One of the first trips I made with them was in Bechler with Margaret and my two daughters, Caroline and Alison. John asked the girls if they had ever eaten "biscuit on the log." We had no idea what John was talking about. Biscuit on a log? My girls were familiar with the usual fare that I served up—granola bars, m&ms, and freeze-dried chili mac. John found a small log and peeled off all of the bark. Deb had made up some biscuit dough, and John wrapped it in loops around the log. He then rolled the log back and forth across the campfire, until the dough had cooked up into a wonderful, golden brown. Deb spread butter and jam over the dough, and we all took turns eating that biscuit right off of the log.

That was just the first of many fantastic culinary experiences around the fire with these two masterful Yellowstone explorers. You won't find freeze-dried dinners around these two! Some of the more memorable feature entrees on our backcountry menu that Deb has served up from scratch have included quesadillas, Navajo tacos, minestrone, pizza, turkey and dressing, and pot roast. Standard fare for breakfast has included egg McMuffins, French toast with homemade syrup, and fried egg sandwiches. Desserts have included huckleberry cobbler, and for salads, Deb often picks leaves from such plants as glacier lilies, spring beauties, and fireweed, topping it off with her own trail-made dressing.

Since 1988, most of my major excursions into the backcountry have included John and Deb. John's entrepreneurial activities usually allow most of the summer for backcountry travel, and Deb tries to mesh her academic schedule to include as many summer trips as possible.

So it was my bright idea to suggest to John and Deb that we attempt to traverse the Washburn Range. We have taken some pretty tough trips over the years, but John and Deb frequently refer to this one as the "Trip from Hell." In order to travel cross-country, you normally have to obtain permission from the sub-district ranger in charge of that particular backcountry region. Many off-trail regions in Yellowstone are part of the park's bear management areas. These areas were set aside for the purpose of restricting human entry and disturbance in high-density grizzly bear habitat.

The Washburn Range has this designation. The area is closed August 1 through November 10. Prior to August 1, the area is open by special permit obtained from the Tower Ranger Station. The trick is timing the trip to have enough snow to provide a water source along the way, but not have too much to impede travel. We received a permit from Tower sub-district ranger, Colette Dagle-Berg, to take the trip.

Our trip, as planned, would take us first to Grebe Lake, and then up to the summit of Observation Peak. Normally we would have hiked in from Cascade Lake, but this trail was closed due to bear activity. Consequently, we had to ascend the steep south slopes of Observation Peak, gaining over 1300 feet in the process. Ranger John Lounsbury had asked us to be on the lookout for an old U.S. Army cabin located somewhere north of the lake, and up against the slopes of the peak. He had read accounts of the army using this cabin in the early 1900s; however, we saw no evidence of one. Furthermore, if such a cabin did exist in this location, it appeared to us that the fires of 1988 would have reduced it to ashes.

From the summit of Observation Peak, it was easy to visualize our route along the ridge of the Washburn range. The named peaks that we would hike over after Observation Peak at 9397 feet would include Cook Peak at 9742 feet, Folsom Peak at 9326 feet, and possibly Prospect Peak at 9525 feet (if we decided to exit at Roosevelt, rather than Blacktail Deer Creek).

The first big surprise we encountered once on top was the substantial accumulation of snow remaining. Here we were in late June, and yet there were still several feet of snow piled on top of the ridge as far as the eye could see. However, the snow was set up very well, and walking across the top of it was not a problem. We had planned to make the remaining fifteen-mile cross-country journey in one day, but we knew that we would have to get an early start the following morning to make it.

The next morning broke clear, but amazingly warm. Normally, daybreak at 9400 feet in Yellowstone in June is going to be bitter cold. The warmth signaled coming out day for mosquitoes as well. As we began hiking north along the ridge toward Cook Peak, we encountered our second big surprise. We had assumed that most of this hike would be either above timberline or at the very least, through sparse timber. Instead, we were having to dig our way through dense spruce and fir, constantly climbing over blowdown.

About two hours into the day, we emerged from the dense timber, allowing some nice views of the wilderness below us on both sides of the ridge. But the unusual warm weather had caused a dramatic change in the snow surface—we were starting to sink several inches with each step. We stopped to re-evaluate our trip, and the three of us really blew it big time. Our better judgment told us to turn around and head back to Observation Peak; but our wanderlust overruled that decision. Six miles to the north, we could see the spectacular apex of Cook Peak looming seemingly oh so close; also, the ridge that we were now traveling on was somewhat wind-blown, so for the first time, we were actually able to follow a snow-free route along the ridge in places.

We rationalized that most of the rest of the trip would feature such conditions. We were wrong. As we hiked along this section of the ridge, we were being lured slowly into an insidious trap. By late morning we had re-entered dense forest with deep snow, and now we were beginning to "post-hole," meaning we would take about six steps, and then suddenly sink to our crotches.

The conditions deteriorated further, until we were soon post-holing with almost every step. We kept hoping that around the next bend we would find another wind-blown, snow-free ridgetop, but this did not happen. Turning back now was no longer an option. We were just south of Cook Peak, so we figured that we had reached the point of no return. It was now shorter to head over Cook Peak to lower, snow-free elevations than it was to return to Observation Peak.

John Dirksen is one of the strongest and toughest backcountry travelers I have ever seen, but on this day, he was a defeated man. So were Deb and I. To make matters worse, John was letting out a terrible groan with almost every step. He would step out on the snow, which appeared capable of supporting his weight, but when he transferred his load to make another step, he would sink to his crotch, and let out a horrible moan. I was also struggling terribly, but hearing John's groans weakened my psyche. Feelings of despair and hopelessness began to sweep over me.

The conditions were now impossible to travel in. We were at a standstill. With each step we would sink to our crotches. I had once taken a trip through the Bob Marshall Wilderness in Montana during the month of May with Al Duff, but we had anticipated lots of snow, and had taken along a couple of pair of small snowshoes. They had come in handy. "If only we had those now," I thought to myself. The three of us stopped, climbed up on a tree log to eat a snack, and discussed our predicament.

Clearly, we had to get out of the snow. We knew that our only hope was to drop down off the ridge to lose elevation, but as we looked down below, the scene was anything but inviting. As far as the eye could see was the rugged drainage of Tower Creek flowing amidst horrendously dense timber. From our view, it appeared to be dreadful to travel through, but we had no choice. Continuing to post-hole north or south on the ridge was out of the question.

So we abandoned our ridge-running trip. The trip that had held such promise had become a nightmare. We descended from an elevation of 9200 feet down to about 8400 feet, and finally escaped the snow and despicable post-holing.

At first we were extremely encouraged. For one thing, we were now in some open country, and the views of the majestic peaks, now above us, were gorgeous. Springs were bubbling out of the meadow, so we had some great drinking water, and glacier lilies and spring beauties were blooming everywhere. We took another snack and rest break and were in good spirits, but that would not last. Our plan now was to follow along north of the Tower Creek drainage until we crossed Lost Creek, which flows off of Prospect Peak. Lost Creek would eventually lead us back to civilization at Roosevelt.

As soon as we left behind our lovely little mountain meadow, reality returned as we entered the rugged, dense woods. Forest fires had swept through this region in 1988, and had left behind a maze of blowdown. If you have ever played "pick-up-sticks" as a kid, just magnify the sticks into fallen trees, and you can imagine what we were having to deal with. Climbing over the trees was bad enough, but many of the trees were charred and covered with soot. Most of the terrain was terribly muddy.

After a while, I began to actually wonder, "which is worse, post-holing in the snow up there on the ridgetop, or climbing over blowdown down here in this muddy maze of drainages?" I'm afraid that I surmised that one poison was as bad as the other. The three of us became very quiet as we trudged forward. This was not just a physical battle. It was also a mental battle. We tried to maintain a strong attitude. We had no other choice. Our only pleasant or positive thoughts had to do with how much we were going to enjoy eating a quart of Wilcoxson vanilla ice cream at the Roosevelt store if we ever made it out!

Deb began to really struggle. Like John, she is one tough wilderness traveler. However, she does have one limitation to deal with. Her legs are short. On a trail she just keeps them moving, and can set a fast pace. But climbing up and over the blowdown was an arduous task for those short legs. Each few yards Deb would come to a horizontal log about waist high. She would place her hands on the charred log, grunt as she lifted one leg up and over, and groan as she pulled the other one over. She would then walk about five yards and have to repeat this maneuver—over and over and over again.

As sundown approached, it was obvious that we were not going to make it out on this day as planned. From our map, it appeared that we were directly south of Prospect Peak, in rugged country, leaving us with another five or six miles of bushwhacking to reach Roosevelt. We had intentionally packed very light for the trip; in fact, we did not even have a tent, but instead packed a lightweight nylon tarp. Just before dark, we found a flat spot to bivouac for the night. Near our camp we observed a large buffalo skull along with most of the rest of the skeleton, the bones having been scattered by predators. We managed to joke that we didn't want *our* bones to end up in this spot.

We spent a very restless night. The warm weather had really brought the mosquitoes out in force. Late June into early mid-July is mosquito season in Yellowstone. Normally, we would have a tent with mosquito netting, but we had not planned to have to camp out down in this forest. The previous night up on Observation Peak had been mostly mosquito-free, thanks to the snow and cool weather. The constant whine of mosquitoes in our ears was almost unbearable.

We managed to cover our heads with clothing as best we could, and catch winks of sleep, but we were all anxious to see the first rays of morning's light. To make matters even worse, I was due back at work at Old Faithful the next day at 3:00 p.m. Once daylight arrived, we gulped down some granola bars, loaded up our packs, and continued our forced march through the maze of fallen timber. We soon emerged from the 1988 burn zone, and this helped immensely, as we began to encounter less blowdown.

By mid-morning we broke out into open meadows. Not only that, but we were gradually walking downhill. Even though we were not yet out, we felt a deep sense of relief. Our perseverance had paid off, for we knew that the worst part of our journey was finally over. Soon, we were sitting on the porch of the Roosevelt Lodge gulping down that ice cream. I even managed to get back to work on time that afternoon.

The strange thing about taking a trip like this, is how soon your mind displaces the harsh memory of hardships encountered. A few years later John and I attempted to hike the Washburn Range again. On this trip the snow was not a problem, but the weather was. We hiked through pouring rain most of the day, except for a brilliant respite on the summit of Cook Peak. The view from this summit, of some of the wildest backcountry Yellowstone has to offer, restored our good spirits, as we descended down to the Blacktail Deer Plateau. Soon the rain returned, and then we entered yet another terrible blowdown.

Not only did we have to climb over a maze of blowdown, but we also had to deal with the entire slope being a swamp-like quagmire. Instead of post-holing through the snow, we were post-holing through a swamp. We certainly should have anticipated these conditions, since we were hiking down a long, north-facing slope. Thankfully, we finally emerged from this bog, and concluded our trip at the Blacktail Creek trailhead. This trip yet *again* reminded us why off-trail travel can be fraught with so many hardships. It also helped me to greatly appreciate those 1000 miles of maintained, marked, trails!

Into the Maze

The months of May and early June are wonderful times to view large herds of bison and elk in the lower valleys of Yellowstone, because the high country is still covered in snow. Predators such as grizzlies and wolves often interact with the bison and elk at this time in an attempt to prey on calves. Once the higher elevations begin to green up, the large herds move to the high country to graze on the lush, new vegetation, as well as to escape the biting insects that are prevalent during mid-summer. Because of the lack of crowds and the fantastic wildlife viewing opportunities, I have always felt that the period between Memorial Day weekend and mid-June is the best time to visit the park.

During this period, it is possible to view hundreds of bison as the big herds migrate through the valleys. The bison herds are like a slow-moving fleet of lawn mowers. For most of the day the bison take a bite and take a step; take a bite and take a step. To view the herds at this time of year provides one with the feeling of traveling back in time, when the West was literally covered with bison. At their peak, the bison numbered over thirty million across the North American plains and mountains. By 1900, this native North American animal had been slaughtered to the very brink of extinction, with only an estimated 540 bison remaining.

Yellowstone's small herd was carefully protected, and eventually, the conservation efforts paid off. Today, the bison is no longer endangered, and Yellowstone's population of over 4000 represents the largest free-roaming herds to be found anywhere in North America. The wild herds of bison represent one of America's greatest conservation success stories.

During June of 2003 I wanted to take some photos of a large bison herd for my interpretive slide program, *The Natural Cycles of the Greater Yellowstone Ecosystem*. Hayden Valley is a great place to view large herds, but the 1 ½ hour drive from Old Faithful made it tough to capture the low-angle light after getting off work.

My solution to this dilemma was to plan an overnight trip into Cougar Creek patrol cabin. I knew that there was a strong likelihood that we would see a large number of bison, as we traversed the beautiful open sagebrush meadows of the Madison Valley. Sam Holbrook, Jim Lenertz, and my daughter, Alison, joined me for the trip. Jim was just finishing up his stint at the Ranger Museum at Norris. Each summer, the NPS invites "old-time" rangers to spend a couple of weeks staffing the Ranger Museum. Even though Jim was still involved in volunteer work in the park, he was a good pick for the museum. Since starting his NPS career back in 1967, he has observed many changes in Yellowstone. A stroke in 1987 had slowed Jim down, but nevertheless, the summer of 2003 marked his 33rd season. Sam was in his 37th season, and I was in my 30th season in the park. Jim had already observed that this expedition would consist of "three old farts" and one young lady (Alison was 23). Sam did not get off work until 6:00 p.m., and then we assembled at my quarters at Old Faithful, where Margaret and Sam's wife Dee treated us to a fine meal. By the time we reached the trailhead at Seven-Mile Bridge, the halfway point between Madison and the West Gate, it was 7:45 p.m.

I knew that we had only about two hours of daylight remaining, which should have been sufficient for a four-mile hike. However, I had failed to calculate Jim's pace--a steady, but *slow* 1 ½ miles per hour. The first 1 ½ miles of our hike consisted of traveling along the Madison River. Then we turned north through a burned forest, before entering the gorgeous open expanses of the Madison Valley. I looked at my watch and realized that we had about one hour of daylight remaining. This meant that we were most likely going to have to negotiate the last mile in darkness.

The four of us discussed our plight and decided to push on. All of us had been to the cabin before, but this was my first trip back in six years. Alison seemed to be the most concerned and suggested that we turn back and return in the morning. However, the rest of us dismissed her good judgment and we continued our trek. We climbed up over a knoll just as the late evening sun lit up the entire valley in a golden glow. To the north, the imposing, snow-covered hulk of Mount Holmes dominated our view. To the west, the sun was about to set behind the mighty summits along the Continental Divide above Hebgen Lake—Lionhead, Hilgard and Sage Peaks. To the east, the aspen and lush green forests were burnished a rich golden tint by the setting sun.

A stiff, brisk, wind was blowing in our faces, bringing with it the fresh fragrance of wildflowers coming into bloom on the valley floor—sugarbowl, leopard lily, lupine, balsam root, prairie smoke, phlox and larkspur. As we topped the knoll, there below us in the valley was just what we had hoped to view—a large herd of bull bison. There were at least 150 bison in the herd and the setting before us was reminiscent of a scene from the movie, *Dances With Wolves*. This was exactly what I had been looking for, and I took out my camera and began snapping one photo after another.

As the four of us stood atop the knoll, I tried to absorb our surroundings with my senses. I always feel an incredible sense of joy and freedom at times like this in the Yellowstone wilderness. As we continued our hike the herd of bison detected our presence and appeared quite nervous, despite the fact that we were several hundred yards away. I have always found it interesting to contrast the behavior of elk and bison near the road with those encountered in the backcountry. The bison and elk along the road appear to be almost impervious to people walking or driving by. This is probably the main reason why some people get too close, and end up being injured by the wild animal's charge. However, in the backcountry, the animals tend to easily spook at the first detection of a human passing nearby. Such was the case with this herd, as the bison began running en masse, an impressive sight. The green valley appeared to be covered by a rolling, dark-brown wave! The spectacle of seeing this large herd of bison running along the valley floor at twilight was truly a magical experience.

The magic quickly faded away, as the last rays of light disappeared behind the jagged peaks to the west. Our thoughts suddenly returned to the difficulty of following our trail. This particular trail receives little use, since it ends at Cougar Creek patrol cabin. At one time, the Cougar Creek trail was maintained an additional twelve miles beyond the cabin through dense forest, to the junction of the Mount Holmes trail. However, the trail's light use made it difficult to justify the extensive trail maintenance required through the thick woods, so it was abandoned. Lodgepole pines, with their shallow root systems, are continually blowing down across trails. With limited budgets, the trail crews of the park have a tough enough time keeping the more heavily-used trails maintained.

Because of the extremely light use of our trail, it was almost impossible to find as it coursed across the meadows. As is usually the case, bison had knocked down most of the posts containing the orange metal trail markers. Nevertheless, with four sets of eyes working overtime, we managed to stay on the faint trail for another mile, until we finally reached the edge of a dense lodgepole forest. This forest had completely burned over in the big fire season of 1988.

On my previous hike into Cougar Creek six years earlier, I had recalled following an animal trail through a boggy area that, for the most part, skirted the burned forest as it led down to Cougar Creek. However, with the daylight now completely gone, it was impossible to see any animal trails or bogs in the area. All that we saw in front of us was the impressive dense regrowth of lodgepole pine.

The fires of '88 had killed all of the mature trees here. However, since the lodgepole pine literally reproduces from fire, the area was carpeted with six to eight foot young pines. The heat from a fire actually causes the serotinous pine cones to open and release the seeds hours after the flames have passed. The ashes on the forest floor make the perfect seedbed, and presto, a new forest is born.

Typically, within ten years of a fire about thirty-five per cent of the burned, dead snags blow down. In another five years, this total doubles to seventy per cent, as the young forest takes on the appearance of a Christmas tree farm. We were hiking through this area fifteen years after the big burn, and it certainly appeared to us that *at least* seventy per cent of the dead snags were down!

Not only were they down, but they were also stacked up like giant pickup sticks, piled as tall as waist high. You know that you have encountered a bad blowdown when you find yourself crawling *under* as many of the logs as you climb over! We knew that we had no choice but to push forward through the blowdown, until we reached Cougar Creek, nearly a mile away.

The dense growth of young trees completely obscured our view. We felt like needles in a giant haystack. Consequently, the four of us stayed close together. Fortunately, we had flashlights, and we were putting them to good use. Ironically, the weather on this evening had turned out to be very nice— just the opposite from the forecast of snow. Sam and I had joked all day about how much we were going to enjoy the "patrol cabin weather." After all, using a patrol cabin during cold, inclement weather is always a treat, as you gather around the old wood stove to dry out and warm up.

"Thank goodness the forecast of cold rain and snow did not materialize," I thought to myself. Climbing over these waist-high logs was hard enough. I could only imagine our misery if the logs had been slicked down with snow and ice! As we made painstakingly slow progress, Alison appeared to be quite concerned. A former college basketball player, she was having no trouble maneuvering through the maze of deadfall. However, she was concerned about her three hiking partners. "Dad," she whispered so Sam and Jim would not hear, "you three are not exactly spring chickens. What if someone falls and breaks a leg out here in the middle of this mess?"

The words had hardly left Alison's lips when I heard Sam ponder, "You know, I just finished reading a Louis L'amour book where that Sackett guy was walking through some deadfall like this and got tangled up and broke his leg!" "Oh great!" I thought, "Now this is starting to get inside our heads." I knew that if someone did get hurt in the middle of this pile of logs and trees, it would be virtually impossible to lead a rescue party back to the same spot. We were literally *engulfed* by the extremely dense, eight-foot tall trees.

By now, it was after 11:00 p.m. and we were tiring. Sam seemed to be doing okay, but I knew from past trips that he usually had difficulty with having to lift one of his legs over logs. Jim was somehow making progress, but it was excruciatingly slow. Every now and then, we would obtain a glimpse of Mount Holmes on the horizon to the north, which kept us on course in the darkness. I began to think that we were going to have to stop and bivouac for the night. We had sleeping bags but no tent, so my biggest fear was the weather. The forecast had called for snow after midnight. We would become prime candidates for hypothermia if we stopped here, and the weather broke down on us. Therefore, we continued to push on through the maze.

Despite all of our unanticipated hardships, I was amazed at everyone's attitude. Alison was not at all concerned for herself. Rather, she was very worried about her three "senior" comrades. Jim was his usual stoic self. I have often said that if I had one dollar for every time I had heard Jim exclaim, "Aww shit!" I would be a rich man. However, on this night, Jim was keeping his troubles to himself. Each time I would ask, "Jim, how are you doing?" he would simply answer "fine."

Sam was the one who amazed me though. At an age of 70, he was tough as nails, but his extremely positive attitude caused him to handle just about any adversity. Our most difficult moment occurred when we reached the top of a small ridge, and had hoped to see the Cougar Creek valley below us. Instead, all we could see was more dense forest ahead. At this point Sam said, "You know, we didn't expect to have this difficulty, but this is what memories are made of. We'll look back on this hardship and have some good laughs over it later around the campfire."

His positive attitude lifted my spirits. I chimed in, "Well, we had hoped to see Cougar Creek below, but just imagine how Lewis and Clark felt in the Bitterroot Mountains of Montana, when they had expected to see a river leading to the Pacific Ocean, and all they saw were mountain ranges as far as the eye could see." Despite *our* hardships, I was simply trying to put them into proper *perspective*!

Finally, we came to the edge of a steep slope that we had been anticipating for the past hour. There below us, we could see the Cougar Creek valley. The quarter moon in the sky was providing just enough light to allow us to see the valley. Our spirits soared, but our progress slowed to a snail's pace, as we climbed over piles of deadfall down toward the creek. We knew that this would be the most dangerous portion of our trip so far. We were tired, the logs were piled high, and now we had to negotiate a *very* steep slope. "Everyone be extra careful here!" we kept yelling back and forth, as we worked our way down the ridge.

Once we finally made it to the bottom, we were relieved to finally be free of our prison of stacked logs, only to encounter boggy conditions. Sam promptly stepped into a watery hole, and sank one leg up to his crotch. "Sam," Alison yelled, "Are you okay?" "Yea, I'm fine," he answered. "I've never gotten anything wet before that didn't eventually dry out!" There was that marvelous attitude again. To Sam life has only one side, the sunny side.

For some reason, I seemed to have the best night vision of the group, and was the only one able to make out the faint outline of the cabin's roof in the distance. I had a hard time convincing the others that we were nearing the cabin, especially Jim. "Dang it, Jim, I can *see* the cabin up ahead. We're almost there. In fact, I stake my reputation on it!" "Well, that's sure not worth much," Jim mumbled back.

We had our lights beamed on the grassy meadow below trying to avoid stepping into any more bogs. Suddenly, Sam stopped in his tracks and exclaimed, "Hey, I see some lights right over there. There are two of them." "You mean there's someone else out here trying to find this cabin?" I queried. "Now the lights are moving," Sam added. "Those aren't lights!" squealed Alison. "Those are the eyes of a buffalo!"

Sure enough, Sam's lights had reflected in the eyes of what appeared to be a big bull buffalo, and he was too close for comfort. Lone bulls like this are typically the most dangerous. I never did see the light in the eyes, but I could see a large, dark object moving, and I was praying that it would not move in our direction! He was snorting and was obviously agitated, but fortunately for us, he moved away from us, further out into the meadow.

We reached the cabin at nearly midnight. Normally, we would have started a fire in the wood stove and enjoyed some snacks, but on this evening, everyone was so exhausted that all we did was open a couple of windows, pull out the bunks, and hit the sack.

The next morning we awoke to a bright, blue sky overhead, with frost on the meadow. The old bull bison that we had startled the night before was casually grazing right out in the "front yard" of the cabin. As usually happens, all of the previous night's hardships were soon forgotten, as we enjoyed hot chocolate, fruit, and granola bars for breakfast. After tending to several chores around the cabin, we departed and began hiking downstream along Cougar Creek. What a difference a little sunshine and daylight can make! I told Sam that rather than climb back through that hellacious maze of deadfall, I would rather swim down Cougar Creek all the way to highway 191 if necessary! No sooner had the words left my lips than did Jim mysteriously leave the meadow, and begin climbing right back up through hell again!

Sam, I, and Alison looked at each other in bewilderment. "Jim," we all shouted, "Come back down here. Don't go back through all of that deadfall!" He just ignored us and kept climbing. "I think he was paranoid about getting his boots wet," Alison opined. Jim had suffered terrific foot problems with standard boots since his stroke, and had finally ordered a custom-made pair of hiking boots at a price of $400.00.

There had been two spots that Alison, Sam and I had crossed Cougar Creek on logs, but it had not been difficult at all with the aid of a long lodgepole branch. "Even if Jim was concerned about crossing these logs, he could have easily forded the stream," I added. No matter, Jim had made up his mind, and was headed back up the same ridge we had tortured through the previous night.

Meanwhile, the rest of us followed the stream, and soon came to a major buffalo crossing. It appeared that the Park Service had wisely picked the buffalo trail to mark through the maze. What a difference it made! It took us only thirty minutes to cover the mile through the maze that had taken well over an hour the previous night!

Once on top of the ridge, we could barely pick out Jim's cowboy hat above the dense growth of young trees. "Jim, over here," Alison yelled. "We have found a maintained trail." We sat down on a log and waited for at least half an hour for Jim to work his way toward us. Once the stubborn old codger finally neared us, we could not resist playing a practical joke on Jim. "Sorry Jim," I said. "There is no maintained trail. We just lied to entice you over here so we could all be together. Which way do you think we should now head?" I asked. Jim just pointed toward the southwest. Then we all started hiking up the trail. In a few moments, I heard Jim begin to spout out a few niceties behind me. "Now Jim," I asked, "What are you whining about?" Would you rather be traveling on a maintained trail or not?"

At lunch, we stopped on top of an open knoll near where we had lost the trail on the previous night. A huge old Douglas fir tree above provided us with a cool, shady respite from the heat of the day. The old tree had somehow survived the great fire of 1988. From our lunch site, we commanded a wonderful view of Mount Holmes to the north, and the big peaks to the west above Hebgen Lake. We were serenaded by a western meadowlark, as it fritted from one branch to another. All was right in the world with the four of us on this bright and sunny June day.

We hiked back across the open expanse of the Madison Valley, and marveled at the show of flowers that we had missed in the low light the previous day. Then, as we topped our final sage-covered knoll before descending back to the Madison River, we encountered our herd of 150 bison! Except this time, they were mostly laying down, resting in the mid-afternoon sun. A few were coating themselves with dust in the bison wallows to keep the bugs off. They appeared very content--nothing like the highly-charged herd we had seen the previous evening.

Our problem though was the bison were scattered across our trail. We would either have to take a sizeable detour around the herd, or walk through the middle. Sam said that he would be willing to walk through the herd given the many times he had done so in Hayden Valley. I seconded the idea since the bison appeared to be so lazily contented. Alison quickly announced that she was going to make the wide detour. As Sam and I walked toward the biggest open area among the bison, the animals suddenly did not act so contented anymore. Several stood up and gave us a hateful glare.

"Well, it's a good thing that Alison has some sense," Jim surmised. As we began our long, wide detour around the herd, Sam recalled a narrow escape that he had seen John and Deb Dirksen have with a herd of bison in Hayden Valley several years ago. On that particular day there were about seventy-five bison standing on one hillside, and another seventy-five standing on the other. The trail coursed right along the bottom of the ravine between them.

There was no way to make a detour around this bunch. There were bison scattered all up and down the sides of the ravine, but at least the trail along the bottom was clear. Sam and his son Mike stood back as John and Deb starting walking through the ravine. Suddenly, something spooked the herd. Both groups of seventy-five bison began running down both sides of the ravine, joined up into one big herd, and began running right at John and Deb.

John always carries a hand axe with a long handle for chores around camp, and for occasional trail-clearing. He pulled out the axe and held it high over his head. Deb kneeled down behind him and began to pray. John would later say that he was simply going to take a swing at the first huge animal before it ran him over. He also said that this incident was the most frightening of all his time exploring the Yellowstone backcountry. Deb thinks it was her most frightening too, though she isn't sure since she had her eyes closed!

Just before the first big bull was about to run over John and Deb, the herd parted and ran on both sides of them. Some 150 bison stampeded within inches of John and Deb, as they stood their ground and fortunately, the animals steered around them. "I thought for sure they were goners," Sam told us.

I have heard John tell this harrowing story several times, and frankly, it made me thankful that we followed Alison's advice on this day and walked around the herd. The story provided an appropriate ending to our trip, which had brought the four of us close to a big herd of a majestic animal that has roamed the Yellowstone country for centuries. May the wild bison herds of Yellowstone continue to thrive in this wild country for centuries to come.

Widowmakers and Moose

During the summer of 2001, my daughter Caroline and her husband Dave wanted to accompany me on an overnight backpacking trip covering a good distance, preferably making a loop. Lengthy loop hikes, where you actually finish from where you began, are difficult to find in Yellowstone. In most cases, you come out several miles from where you started your hike, which is a problem, since there is no shuttle bus system that operates in the park.

Poring over a topo map, which to me is at least half the fun, I finally found something at least close to a loop trip of about twenty-two miles. We could begin from the Fawn Pass trailhead on Highway 191, about twenty miles north of the West Gate, turn up the Fan Creek trail, and head for Sportsman Lake for the night. We would return via the Specimen Creek trail, which would bring us back out on Highway 191, about four miles to the north of where we began.

Admittedly, this trip was a bit long for a two-day outing, but most of the hiking would be through fairly level terrain. I had not been through this country since the fires of 1988, and looked forward to seeing the beautiful scenery around Sportsman Lake again. During my previous trips there, I had always been fortunate to observe several moose in the area. I knew that the area all around Sportsman Lake had burned. Moose prefer old growth forests, so I wondered if we would still see moose there.

The weather on this late July day was ideal—bright, beautiful blue skies with fluffy white clouds. July is wildflower and mosquito month in the park, and we saw plenty of both. However, the mosquitoes soon became no problem, as a fierce wind blowing out of the southwest kicked up. The hike up Fan Creek was special, as the meadows were carpeted with fields of blue, red, white, and yellow wildflowers.

Once we came within three miles of Sportsman Lake, the evidence of the 1988 fires came into full view. As far as the eye could see were stands of bleached spruce and fir snags. About 80% of Yellowstone is forested and 80% of the forest consists of the lodgepole pine. Since lodgepole pines contain a serotinous pine cone that actually opens and releases seeds during a fire, this type of forest quickly regenerates. As the years have passed since the '88 fires, it has become easier to accept the role that fires play in the ecosystem. Young lodgepoles planted by the fires of '88 have already climbed to heights of ten to fifteen feet.

However, in old growth spruce and fir forests, such as we were walking through, it is a different story. Yes, there are many shrubs, flowers and bushes that are thriving in the new-found sunlight, but the new trees are slow to come back in. Seeds have to blow in from the spruce and fir that survived the fire, and in this area there were not many.

As the day progressed and the sun climbed higher, the nice coolness of the morning gave way to the heat. Before the fires, we would have been enjoying a sun-dappled trail with the shade of the big trees to keep us cool. Now, here, there was no shade to be found. However, the wind itself had a cooling affect on us.

Soon the wind velocity accelerated and trees began to fall all around us. I had been on numerous hikes before where robust winds caused trees to topple, but nothing compared to this day. As the winds grew stronger, trees began to fall at the rate of about one every thirty seconds. The insidious danger from falling trees stems from the fact that it is difficult to detect their fall, until it is too late to move out of the way.

Amazingly, the trees' plunge to the forest floor is silent. Plus, there is an abundance of background noise present what with the howling and whistling of the wind through the snags. And finally, it is tough to *see* the tree beginning to topple, unless it is directly in front of you. For these reasons, falling trees are sometimes called "widowmakers." During the huge fire season of 1988 that involved over 25,000 firefighters, only one fatality occurred, and it was the result of a falling snag.

Each time we would see or hear another widowmaker crash to the forest floor, we would stop and nervously look around, but this just made us feel like sitting ducks. There was nowhere to hide. We simply began walking at an extremely fast pace, as if this was somehow going to protect us.

After what seemed like an eternity (it was actually more like forty-five minutes), we gained a view of the meadows around Sportsman Lake, and knew that we would soon be out of danger. As we approached the lake, still walking through the burned forest, we came upon a young bull moose grazing on fresh vegetation about fifty yards north of the trail.

The enjoyment of observing the moose was suddenly halted, as to our horror, we saw a tall spruce snag begin its descent toward the unsuspecting animal from his rear. The tree appeared headed for a direct hit. Then, as abruptly as the tree had begun its descent, somehow, the young moose detected danger and bolted. However, the moose was not moving left or right away from the path of the tree; rather, it was running straight ahead.

The three of us just stood there with our mouths open. The scene unfolded as if it were in slow motion. We watched the tree's inexorable descent right over the racing form of the panic-stricken moose. Our minds quickly computed that this was going to be close. Would the moose make it? Or, would we witness the weird death of a wild animal deep in Yellowstone's wilderness? Just as the tip of the huge tree was about to crash into the back of the moose, the young bull seemed to somehow sense the contact. He suddenly shifted to overdrive and lunged forward. The tree grazed his rump, causing him to rear up as he made his final dash to safety.

After his close call, this moose moved to the safety of the meadow surrounding the lake. We promptly did the same. We realized that we had almost observed an animal die of a natural event, but it also made us even more aware of just how dangerous hiking through these trees on this day had been. "How in the world did that moose know the tree was on top of him," I asked Dave and Caroline. "Guess we'll never know," Dave responded. Then we realized that we were measuring the moose's response from our human senses, and that is a poor comparison.

Afterall, the moose has huge ears that rotate around like radar. Perhaps he detected the falling tree with those big ears. Or, maybe his eyes picked up some movement. The placement of the eyes on the sides of the heads in ungulates such as deer, elk, bison, sheep, and moose allow for outstanding peripheral vision to detect approaching predators. On the other hand, predators such as cougars, bears and wolves, in addition to humans, have eyes in the front of the head.

One of the activities that I have enjoyed with my interpretive program for kids, is to have each youngster field test their peripheral vision by extending their arms horizontally to their sides and wiggling their thumbs. The kids bring their arms in until their eyes can detect the sight of their thumbs. Then we discuss how much better the field of vision for ungulates such as elk, deer, moose and bison must be!

Once we arrived at Sportsman Lake, we observed two more moose feeding along the shore. My streak of always observing moose at this lake thereby continued. The National Park Service maintains a patrol cabin near the lake. There were several patrol cabins that nearly burned during the major fires of 1988, but here the cabin did burn, and it was a complete loss. It was easy to see why given the extensive burn all around the cabin.

The cabin was replaced, because it is an important station for patrols by backcountry rangers. The replacement cabin was pretty impressive—bigger than most of the other old, rustic patrol cabins in the park. The relatively new logs caused this cabin to appear almost out of place this deep in the backcountry. We noted that the winds had caused some trees to fall across the horse corral, smashing the railing. Luckily, none of the newly fallen trees were close enough to have damaged the cabin itself.

From Sportsman Lake there is a spectacular view of the western shoulder of Electric Peak to the east. As dusk descended upon the lake we enjoyed the alpenglow on the mountains above us, burnishing the green meadows with a gold tint. The strong winds that had raged all day had finally given way to a calm, serene evening. We carefully scanned the high mountain meadows with binoculars hoping to spot a grizzly. High country grasslands such as these represent ideal habitat for grizzlies, as they enjoy grazing and digging for roots, bulbs and rodents. However, we could only spot a few herds of elk.

The next morning broke clear and crisp, just an ideal day to wake up over eleven miles deep in the Yellowstone wilderness. There were three moose grazing around the shores of Sportsman Lake. Again, we inspected the slopes high above us but could find no bears. Electric Pass, the high mountain pass at about 9600 feet above us, seemed to call out to us to explore. The one time that I had hiked over the pass remains as one of my fondest memories of spectacular wild mountain scenery in the park. I knew that we would be hiking out via Specimen Creek to the west, but I promised myself to cross that pass on another trip in the near future.

During late June of 2003 my good friends John and Deb Dirksen offered me the golden opportunity to join them on a lengthy loop hike of the Gallatins, in which they would cross that very pass. My work schedule did not allow me to go, but their stories took me there vicariously.

John and Deb had stopped for a lunch break just below the pass. They had hoped to stop on top, but strong winds were blowing through the pass, and Deb wanted to cook up some soup on her stove. They set up their lunch stop on the lee side of the pass. As Deb prepared lunch, John relaxed and scoped the distant hills for any movement of wildlife. Suddenly, a huge black blur appeared in John's binoculars! "Oh my God, a grizzly," he yelled to Deb.

Deb looked up just as a large black hump came into view on the outline of the horizon at the top of the pass, directly in front of them. Then their alarm yielded to laughter, as the black hump turned out to be the back of a large bull moose. John and Deb had never expected to see a moose in this open country at such a high elevation. Moose were supposed to be down in the swamps and river bottoms of the low country.

One of the more humorous Yellowstone stories I have heard involving moose was told to me by the venerable interpretive ranger, Bill Lewis. Bill worked in Yellowstone from 1949 through the mid 1980s. He worked as a naturalist and later as a communications specialist in helping train the new staff each year.

One summer, Bill was giving an interpretive walk on the slopes of Mount Washburn near Canyon. His hike began from Dunraven Pass and traversed subalpine country around an elevation of 9000 feet. Along the way, he noticed some distinctive moose tracks, and pointed them out to his group. "You don't know what you are talking about," shot back a lady in the group. "Everyone knows that moose habitat is along the low lying valleys and river bottoms. A moose would *never* come way up here!"

Bill wasn't sure how to respond. Afterall, the distinctive flat hat and ranger uniform usually command more respect than is probably deserved, but it was unusual for a visitor to blatantly question the accuracy of the ranger leading the hike. Bill loved for visitors to participate, but not in this confrontational manner. "Well, sometimes they do," he gently replied to the lady's comment.

As Bill led the group still higher, he came across some obvious moose droppings, which are rather conspicuous due to their oval shape. Bill stopped the group to point out the fresh animal sign, and again the woman protested. "You can't be serious young man," she reprimanded. "Everyone knows that moose would never be up here. They live way down in the lowlands!"   "Well, sometimes you find them up here," Bill meekly responded.

Bill then led the group over a ridge and down into a small bowl-shaped ravine. Here, he found the unmistaken evidence of fresh grazing on some small shrubs by moose. As Bill pointed out this evidence, the woman could hardly restrain herself. "Ranger, this is getting to be ridiculous! There is no way a moose would be living high up here on this mountain. Everyone knows they live down in the willow bottoms."

This time however, as the lady was berating the ranger for misleading the group, a strange thing happened. Ranger Lewis watched three moose appear above the bowl-like depression to the rear of the group. Bill was the only one looking in their direction. When the lady finished her tirade about how moose would *never* visit this high terrain, Bill answered by saying, "Well, sometimes they do. Please look behind you."

Bill said that in all his years in Yellowstone, that was probably his happiest moment! Now as for me, my moose sightings have all been in the low elevations. But because of these two stories, I know that in some instances moose have appeared in the high country where you might least expect to find them!

Despite the strong call of Electric Pass, Dave, Caroline and I hiked back out via Specimen Creek. Our morning hike was delightfully cool with little or no wind--quite a change from the conditions the previous afternoon. This time the walk through the burned snags was much more relaxing and less stressful. The moose and elk probably felt the same way!

Part II

Adventures by Water

The Makeshift Log Bridge at the Clark's Fork

Clark's Fork Fury

Yellowstone Park Historian and friend Lee Whittlesey authored a book in 1995 titled *Death in Yellowstone: Accidents and Foolhardiness in the First National Park.* Lee details how easy it is for the unsuspecting visitor to find trouble in many ways—wild animals, falls, hot water, and drowning, just to mention a few. Each summer it seems that someone is hurt or killed in an accident in the wild Yellowstone ecosystem.

One of my occasional duties as a seasonal ranger at Old Faithful is to give an orientation talk to the concession employees, many of whom are working in the park for the first time. I try to instill within them a deep respect for the many dangers that exist in Yellowstone. This is very easy for me to do. I can empathize with how easy it is to get in trouble in Yellowstone, because during my first summer in the park, I came within an eyelash of becoming a statistic in Lee's book.

When Margaret and I first came to Yellowstone in 1968 to work as concession employees, we had never been west of the Mississippi River, and we were completely ignorant of the many dangers present. When you are from central Alabama, you aren't familiar with the hazards presented by grizzly bears, falling off mountains, stepping into scalding water, hypothermia, or raging rivers during snowmelt. I don't remember too much of an orientation back then; actually my mother gave me an excellent one prior to leaving. "Butch," she said, "I know you like beautiful country but just remember this land is new to you. You don't have to fear it, but you *must* respect its dangers!" "Yes Ma'am," I told her. Boy did she ever know what she was talking about!

When Margaret and I arrived in Yellowstone in June, we were immediately enthralled with the clear mountain streams that meandered through the high country meadows. They certainly bore little resemblance to the muddy red rivers we were used to in Alabama. They seemed to call out for exploration. There was a bit of Tom Sawyer in me that wanted to hop on a raft and drift through the wilderness. Part of my first paycheck went to buy a small, but sturdy, two-person rubber raft.

On our first day off, Margaret and I drove over to Norris Junction, twelve miles from where we worked at Canyon Village, and found a beautiful little stream meandering through a large meadow. The stream was only about ten feet wide, but according to our map, this stream was the Gibbon "River."

In the South, a stream of this size is called a creek. The term "river" only applies to large, wide, moving bodies of water. We soon found that small bodies of water in the park were called "lakes," such as Ribbon Lake and

Cascade Lake. Again, in the South, little bodies of water are called "ponds." A lake in the South is a very large body of water.

We put in our little raft and began to gently float down the Gibbon River. We really didn't care what terminology was used to describe this stream, because we found it to be idyllic. The stream was barely wide enough to contain our rubber boat as it quietly bounced from one grassy bank to the other, winding through the verdant meadow. We passed right by grazing elk and moose. To me, I had found the Garden of Eden.

After floating for about a mile, we reached a bridge near the campground and disembarked. A young man came to meet us. "Did you enjoy your float?" he asked. "Yes, it was beautiful." I answered. "Well, I'm a park ranger, and it's a good thing I'm off duty right now, because otherwise I would have to write you a ticket. You are in violation of park regulations." We had no idea what he was talking about but soon found out. In our haste to explore the park's streams in our newly purchased raft, we had overlooked the need to study the park's regulations.

When we did, we were surprised to learn that almost all of the park's streams were closed to boating. We found that the primary reason for this restriction was to protect and preserve wildlife and the opportunities for visitors to enjoy viewing them. In later years, I came to better understand and appreciate this important regulation.

In any event, I was hooked. If we couldn't float inside the park then we would have to find other streams outside the park. For our next day off the following week, I wanted to take a longer trip. I wanted to float a stream for several miles well away from the road.

Studying a road map of the surrounding Yellowstone country, I found just what I was looking for. Not too far from Cooke City, Montana (just outside the Northeast Entrance) flowed the Clarks Fork of the Yellowstone. According to the map, we would be able to launch our raft and float about five miles through some wild country before the river returned to the road at a picnic area.

"This is perfect," I thought. "We can float the river and have a cookout with friends at the takeout." By week's end we had made plans for seven of us to make the outing—four guys and three girls. The weather on the morning of our trip was not exactly ideal. The skies were dark and overcast with a light drizzle falling. With ponchos, raft, picnic basket and seven eager souls on board our old Chevy, we began our 2-½ hour drive to the Clark's Fork.

By the time we reached our destination, the weather had not improved. The temperature was in the 40s, and a light rain persisted. I noticed the river was well out of its banks, but the potential danger of a stream swollen by snowmelt just didn't register with this green southern boy. We enjoyed a mid-morning snack before proceeding with our plans to launch Ron, Rich and me in the raft with the rest of the group heading downstream to the picnic area to gather wood and prepare for the wiener roast.

Ron and Rich were both from Washington state, but unfortunately, they were as green and inexperienced as I was. The three of us pumped up the raft, put on our ponchos and waved to Margaret as she drove off with the rest of the gang. As the three of us dragged our raft over to the river, we were about to commit five unpardonable sins. First, we had not scouted the river or even studied topo maps for dangerous rapids. If we had, we would have discovered that this section of the river, despite its innocuous appearance at our put in and takeout, plunged through a narrow canyon and contained numerous big rapids.

Second, we were floating the river in mid-June at the peak of the snowmelt. This is why the river was out of its banks. Experienced paddlers often avoid rivers in this condition, because the powerful river flow can be unforgiving or pushy. Third, we were ill prepared for the cold weather conditions. Experienced paddlers will check the air and water temperature; if the sum of both is less than about 105 degrees F, then appropriate gear such as wet suits and/or wool clothing is necessary. Exposure to cold weather conditions can result in rapid loss of body heat, known as hypothermia, which can be life threatening. On the day of our trip, the air temperature was about 45 degrees, and the water temperature about 38 degrees for a total of only 83 degrees! Plus, it was raining. Yet we were dressed in cotton jeans, sweatshirts and ponchos!

Fourth, we had three people piled in a raft designed to hold only two. And finally, we were not even wearing life jackets. Given my background of outings on warm water lakes, I had developed the mistaken notion that life jackets were just for folks who couldn't swim. Of course, since Rich and Ron were from Washington state, I can't offer any such limp excuses for their lack of good judgment.

As we began our float there were few waves or rapids, yet I was surprised at how swiftly the current was transporting us downstream. Rich and Ron were sitting at one end of the raft, and I, with oars in hand, was at the other. Within fifteen minutes, we had floated through a long meadow leaving the road behind and had entered a forest. The waters were becoming turbulent and standing waves began to appear. I began to feel a sense of uneasiness, mainly because I did not think the three of us were stable in the small craft.

As the waves became insidiously bigger, I could tell from the expression on Ron's face that he shared my concern. Rich, on the other hand, was grinning from ear to ear. He was the kind of guy who would not hesitate to jump on a Brahma bull and ride him out laughing all the way. Ron was more of the serious, studious type. Physically, he was rather thin and frail. Rich was a free spirit who had played linebacker on his high school football team.

We were soon caught in a maelstrom of raging standing waves. There were no rocks visible because of the flooded condition of the river. As we rode the river's roller coaster into a deep hole and then back up, I knew we were going to flip over. As my end of the raft began to dip under water, I could see Ron and Rich flipping over the top of me. As they went over, Ron still had that pained, frightened expression on his face while Rich was laughing wildly.

Suddenly, I found myself being tossed around like a ping-pong ball in an icy world of darkness. I could not understand why I could not get my head above the surface. At first I thought I had come up underneath the raft, but when I began groping wildly with my arms, I realized what had happened. My large, Army-style poncho had wrapped up around my neck and head. The river was tossing me around, and I could see nothing. I might just as well have had a burlap sack tied over my head. My lungs were screaming for oxygen, but my head seemed to be under water more than above water.

With one hand I was attempting to swim in the roiling waters, while with the other hand I made a futile attempt to tear the poncho off of my head. The fact that I was a fairly strong swimmer made no difference in the swift, churning whitewater. The powerful river slammed me over and over again against submerged boulders. My lungs continued to take in water as I frantically tried to grab hold of one of the boulders.

By now I had been helpless in the grip of the river's icy waters for perhaps two minutes (which seemed like an eternity) when a thought suddenly hit me like a ton of bricks: "This river is trying to kill me!" I had never before had a close call with death, but I was having one now. "If only I could see where I was in the river," I thought. With the poncho wrapped around my head, it was impossible to know if I was tumbling in the middle of the river or near its banks. A strange feeling began to come over me that my time had come. I felt I should just quit struggling and give in to the force of the river. But that feeling was quickly interrupted by a much stronger one.

I vividly remember thinking, "By God, if this river is trying to kill me, I am not going to go down without a fight!" Drawing from my reserves, and perhaps an extra rush of adrenalin, I continued to grope for a submerged rock that I could latch onto and put an end to my terrible pummeling. Suddenly my right hand found a deep indentation in a submerged boulder. It was almost like a handle. With all my strength I held onto the boulder and pulled myself up onto the top of it, thus finally bringing my river tumbling to a halt.

I was now able to pull the despicable poncho off of my head. The river's icy waters were rushing over my back as I clung to the rock, but at least my head and shoulders were now above water. I could draw a full breath free of water, and could see the bank. There, directly in front of me about fifteen yards away and downstream, was a large root protruding from a tree. Another handle! My body was now quite numb from the frigid waters. I knew if I did not grab hold of this root, I might not get another chance to pull myself out of this raging torrent. I positioned my feet against the boulder and then lunged toward the handle, swimming with every remaining ounce of strength left in my body. I had it!

When I pulled myself out of the freezing water and onto the sandy bank, three feelings engulfed me. First, a rush of warmth swept over my body.

The air temperature was only about ten degrees warmer than the river, but strangely enough, I felt as though a tropical breeze had hit me. Second, I could feel the presence of God. It was as if He was there on the shore with me saying, "Butch, it's just not your time to go." There was no way that I could rationalize the sudden appearance of the strange "handles," first on the submerged boulder and then on the protruding tree root. Without either one appearing when they did, there is no question in my mind that I would have never made it out of the river.

The third feeling was a severe wave of nausea, which swept over my body as I coughed up river water I had swallowed. My body seemed to be signaling that it had given all it had, and the tank was about empty. I sat down on the bank and leaned against a tree. Slowly the nausea began to dissipate, and some strength began to return to my body. I looked out over the powerful river and now a fourth feeling came over me—a sense of outrage. "How could we be this careless?" I asked myself, as my eyes searched up and down the river for any signs of Ron, Rich and the raft.

All during my struggles in the river with the poncho wrapped around my head, I had been unable to catch a glimpse of what had happened to them. Given my extreme good fortune with the submerged rock handle, and then the protruding tree root, I assumed that they were downstream from me. By now I felt strong enough to begin walking along the bank. The great concern that I had for myself only moments earlier now switched to Ron and Rich, especially Ron.

Given Rich's physical strength, I just knew he could make it out, but I wasn't so sure about Ron. As I rounded a bend in the river, sure enough, there stood Rich on the shore. He appeared to be in pretty good shape, but I could tell the river had worked him over as well. "Where's Ron?" I yelled over the deafening roar of the river. "I don't know," he shouted back. When I grabbed on to this tree, Ron was still holding on to the raft heading downstream." The usual free-spirited, flippant nature of Rich was now absent in his voice and serious facial expression. I could tell he was as concerned about Ron as I was.

Neither of us had much to say as we walked downstream, straining our eyes for any sign of Ron. A dense forest of spruce and fir trees extended to the river's banks, so it was difficult to see very far downstream. As Rich led the way around another bend in the river, we almost tripped over him. There lay poor Ron stretched out on the forest floor, leaning back on his elbows. He looked as though someone had tossed him into a heavy-duty washer at the Laundromat. A sense of relief swept over the three of us, as smiles once again appeared on our faces.

"When I caught hold of this tree I tried my best to pull the raft in, but it came down to me or the raft," Ron lamented. Ordinarily the thought of losing a new raft which had taken half of my paycheck would've bothered me, but not on this day. As I listened to Ron and then Rich describe their tumultuous rides down the river, I concluded that I had actually come closest to buying the farm thanks to my bout with the poncho. Now that the three of us were safely off the river, we directed our attention to our next problem.

Ironically, all three of us had exited the river on the west bank—the side *away* from the road. We were all cold, wet, and had no way to get across the raging torrent. There were no bridges between the put-in and takeout. The road stayed on the east side of the river. We continued walking downstream, but we had no plan for getting across. I wanted to let Margaret and the others know we were okay. I was sure that by now they had seen our empty raft float by and were assuming the worst.

As we walked downstream, the river narrowed and plunged through a deep canyon. At the end of the canyon the white fury suddenly disappeared at the brink of an eight-foot waterfall. The three of us just looked at one another. We knew that if we had not gotten out of the river when we had, there was little chance we could have survived going through this canyon.

"Hey, look at how narrow these canyon walls are here," Rich shouted. "Let's lay a log across." At first I thought Rich was kidding, but as I looked at the narrowness of the canyon here I knew he wasn't. All of us were shivering and needed to get out of the elements. The canyon bluffs were no more than twenty feet apart. "Rich, I think you've got a plan," I told him, "but we've got to do more than just lay a log across." I'm sure Rich would've settled for shimmying across on a single log, but as I looked at the frothing white water below, I was more interested in building a bridge.

We were fortunate to have a dense forest close by, and we had little trouble finding fallen trees long enough to span the chasm. We stood two long logs on end and let them fall across the gorge. Rich volunteered to crawl across. Once on the other side he was able to pull the logs close together and secure them with his weight. As a result, Ron and I had the luxury of a sturdier bridge for our crossing. As I crawled across, I looked down at the frothing whitewater of the Clark's Fork and shuddered at our close brush with death.

Once across, we hiked through dense forest until we reached the road and found the girls waiting for us. Bruce was down at the river searching for us. Margaret had pulled over at a scenic pullout, and had seen Ron in the distance struggling with the raft, so they had been consumed with worry until we showed up. Once we located Bruce, we proceeded with our wiener roast despite the harrowing close call we had just had.

As we gradually warmed ourselves around the fire, we traded moments of laughter with moments of quiet contemplation. We fully understood that the three of us had come perilously close to losing our lives on the river on this day. The Clark's Fork had spared me and taught me an incredibly valuable lesson. My mother's words now loomed even bigger: "You don't have to be afraid of that wild land *but you must respect it*!" I never forgot the Clark's Fork experience, and I made a commitment to give this wild country its due respect, especially its rivers.

While I have continued to enjoy paddling streams in the Yellowstone country, I have rarely again ventured out on a river during high water. Unfortunately, there have been numerous, water-related accidents in the Yellowstone country. Lee Whittlesey actually has an entire chapter devoted to water-related fatalities in his book, *Death in Yellowstone*; the chapter is called "Danger in the Water: Deaths from Drowning." In that chapter he states, "There are more deaths in this category than any other in Yellowstone National Park...More than one hundred persons have heard Shakespeare's "dreadful noise of waters" in their ears before they drowned in Yellowstone."

After college, Ron enjoyed a successful career in government intelligence. Rich tragically died only a few years after our close call. A jack failed while he was working under a car.

Deep in the Arm

Paddling a canoe on Yellowstone Lake can be addictive. Exploring the Flat Mountain, South, and Southeast Arms is truly one of the great wilderness adventures in the contiguous forty-eight states. The lake is situated at an elevation of 7733 feet, and is the second largest natural lake in the world at such a high elevation. There just aren't too many places left where you can paddle 110 miles of pristine, undeveloped shoreline. The three arms of the lake are not only undeveloped, but their southernmost tips extend over fifteen miles deep into some of the most magnificent wilderness in the West.

However, getting there is not easy. Yellowstone Lake can be a very dangerous place to paddle a canoe for two primary reasons: First, the water is extremely cold. The lake is frozen for much of the year. Visitors arriving in the park in mid-May are usually surprised to find that Yellowstone's major lakes—Yellowstone, Shoshone, and Lewis are still frozen. Some seasons, the lakes are still frozen over as late as *mid-June*! Even when Yellowstone Lake thaws out, it is fed all summer by high mountain streams coursing down some of the highest mountains in the region. If you fall into this icy water, your survival time may only be minutes. Second, many days are windy, whipping the lake into a frothy, white-capped sea. An open canoe is no match for such conditions.

For these reasons, it is imperative that anyone paddling the lake stay right along the shore—even when the lake is as placid as a sheet of glass. The lake can be insidious. Its calm waters will lure you in and then suddenly, you find yourself among whitecaps.

In the summer of 1989, Jim Lenertz and I planned a canoe trip on Yellowstone Lake to meet John and Deb Dirksen, and Deb's Mom. Jim and I had planned to meet them at Park Point, and then proceed deep into the Southeast Arm. It was the first trip I had planned with Jim since he had suffered a serious stroke during the fall of 1987. Jim has always been a very strong and steady paddler in the bow of our canoe. He started his seasonal career in Yellowstone in 1967, and had gained quite a reputation over the years for his superb hiking, skiing, and climbing abilities.

Ironically, it was while returning from a lengthy canoe trip into the Southeast Arm of Yellowstone Lake with Hank Barnett in September of 1987, that I received the bad news from West District Interpretive Ranger Joe Halladay. Jim had suffered the stroke while playing racquetball at his home campus of Arizona Western College, where he taught Biology.

Though Jim made a remarkable recovery, at age 47, he was dealt a cruel blow in that he could no longer embark on lengthy ski and backpacking trips, but he showed no sign of cutting back on his canoeing.

When we arrived at Sedge Bay at 6:00 p.m., the winds were raging and the lake looked like the Atlantic Ocean. This was not uncommon. Our hope now was to simply wait for the winds to die down, and the lake to calm. When you plan a canoe trip on Yellowstone Lake, you simply have to accept what the lake gives you. That may involve launching much later than you had anticipated. But on this evening, the lake did not follow its normal pattern.

The winds held steady past sunset. Jim and I decided to wait until 10:00 p.m., and if the lake was still too rough, we would try again at daybreak. The winds continued to howl. Lucky for us, fellow ranger and good friend Harlan Kredit worked and resided at Fishing Bridge not too far away. Harlan is one of Yellowstone's senior interpretive rangers, and he is a treasure. His knowledge of the park's natural history is legendary, plus he has a wonderful, dry sense of humor.

Even though it was after 10:00 p.m., Harlan was still up when we arrived at his quarters. We found him working on a player piano. Parts were scattered all over the floor. Repairing old player pianos is Harlan's hobby. When we told Harlan of our trip plans and how the wind and waves had turned us back on this evening, he simply shook his head. The three of us walked out on the shore of the raging lake and watched the waves crashing in. Harlan made us feel welcome to spend the night, but expressed great concern over our safety given the lake's behavior on this day. I assured him that we would not head out at daybreak unless the winds had stopped and the waves had died down.

At first light I rose in my bunk and noted that the sound of crashing waves had stopped. "Jim," I spoke out in a low voice from across the room, "the lake is calm, let's hit it!" We grabbed some fruit and granola bars, left a thank you note on the table for Harlan, and headed out the door for my truck. We pushed off in calm waters and headed for Park Point about seven miles away. We wondered if John and Deb would still be there waiting for us. We felt pretty confident that they would understand what had happened to us. However, we had no idea what had happened to them!

The wind came up on cue at about 9:00 a.m., but it was manageable, nothing like the previous day. There was not a cloud in the sky and the warmth of the sun felt good on this cool morning. We marveled at the teeming life along the lakeshore. White pelicans, with their huge wingspans, soared over us. I've always found it amazing how they seem to fly in concert; when one bird starts flapping its wings the others do the same. When one bird begins gliding, they all become synchronized. Ospreys were commonly seen, as was a bald eagle.

One of the advantages of paddling so close to shore (besides the most important one of safety) is the fact that you can enjoy observing activities along the lakeshore. Jim and I were surprised to notice a buck mule deer standing in a steep alcove along the lake. We had no idea how it got there. Did it swim there? Did it jump down from the overhanging bank fifteen feet above it? Or was this a flying deer?

We made reasonably good time and arrived at Park Point to find John and Deb and her Mom there waiting for us. It turned out that their day had been rather unusual as well. When they arrived at Park Point the previous day and began setting up camp, Ranger Mark Marschall, one of the backcountry rangers patrolling the region, arrived by boat and politely told them that they could not camp there. Mark proceeded to explain that the previous night a grizzly had walked into the camp and chased the occupants out into the lake.

The district ranger had ordered the backcountry campsite closed indefinitely until it was clear that the bear had moved out of the area. John and Deb explained the predicament they were in. First, they were supposed to meet us for our trip, and second, the wind had kicked up the lake, making it impossible to paddle to a different campsite. Mark considered the alternatives, and then suggested that the three of them stay overnight in the Park Point patrol cabin for the evening. After detailing the proper cabin maintenance procedures, Marschall departed in the NPS patrol boat.

After relaxing on shore and enjoying lunch on the shores of Park Point, the five of us readied our canoes to continue our trip into the Southeast Arm. Just as we were about to push off, Mark Marschall arrived again in his patrol boat. This time he notified us that a pack mule had died a short distance away, and there was a deep concern that the already troublesome grizzly in the area would feed on the carcass and become habituated to this campsite. "What can you do in a situation like this?" John asked. "We dynamite the carcass," Mark answered with a big grin on his face.

We pushed off our canoes and turned to the south headed for the remote tip of the Southeast Arm. The winds so far on this day were largely absent. With clear skies, cool weather and calm waters the day was shaping up to be a paddler's dream. "Just another day in paradise," I remarked to Jim. We were all still laughing about the dead pack mule. "Do you really think they'll blow up the mule?" Jim asked. "I think Mark was pulling our collective legs," John answered. "Well, I've always wondered what they do with pack animals when they die in the backcountry," I chimed in.

About fifteen minutes later our questions were answered with a loud *boom* behind us. We turned to see a mushrooming cloud of white smoke rising above the shoreline and drifting over toward us. "Yuk, get out your umbrellas," John said, "here comes the fallout from the vaporized mule!" This was definitely a first for the four of us in Yellowstone. Watching the size of the cloud, it was easy to understand how this procedure would deny a grizzly from feeding on this carcass. There might be a few tidbits left for the ravens but little else.

Late that afternoon we reached our campsite on a small peninsula deep in the arm. The big peaks in the Absaroka range to the east, Mt. Schurz, Mt. Humphreys and Colter Peak, were all beginning to turn a golden red from the low angle rays of twilight. After dinner John and I decided to paddle over to the outlet of Trail Creek. We tied the canoe to some willow brush and attempted to climb up a steep, eroded bank. There blocking our path staring at us was a cow moose with her calf. If looks could kill we would have been dead. We slowly climbed back down in our canoe and paddled a bit further along the shore to bypass the moose. We walked through a meadow and entered a forest that had been completely burned over during the big fires of '88 the previous year.

Even though the light of day was fast disappearing, the scene before us was stunning. The black, charred trees stood in stark contrast to what was beneath them on the forest floor. As far as the eye could see was a lush carpet of white lupine. I had never seen anything before like this in Yellowstone. The flower fields of Lompoc, California had nothing on this. Typically, lupine in the northern Rockies are blue, but to find such a large area of white lupine was very unusual.

The following morning John and Deb and her Mom (comfortably seated in the middle of their seventeen-foot Coleman canoe) headed north back up the arm. I wanted to show Jim the fields of flowers, and also take some photos for my interpretive slide program. We planned to meet up again near Columbine Creek in the early afternoon. Rays of sun now dappled the fields of flowers, so conditions were perfect for taking photos. Prior to the fires of 1988, we would have been standing in the shaded understory of a dense forest. The fires had completely changed that. In addition to the white lupine, the scorched forest floor was covered by pink fireweed, blue lupine, and a variety of yellow flowers.

The scene was not only a feast for the eyes, but the sweet fragrance of the blooms was delicious as well. I could not help but think of the politicians' claims following the fires about how Yellowstone had been destroyed and the soil sterilized for decades! As we paddled up the arm, we saw similar fields of flowers in each burned area. We also noticed herds of elk grazing amidst the charred trees chowing down on what must have appeared to them as a giant salad bowl. Prior to the fires, there would have been precious little food supply for elk in this forest.

The fires had accomplished just what nature intended. After all, a nice, green, dense forest might look attractive to us humans, but from an animal's standpoint, there really isn't much there to make a living off of unless it is a squirrel or porcupine. The key to a healthy forest is diversity. Just as you would not want a fire to sweep across the landscape and burn 100% of the forest, neither would you want to see an extensive buildup of old growth forest.

Following the big fires of '88, some politicians and members of the media claimed that the entire park had gone up in flames. Actually, satellite photographs revealed that thirty-six percent of the park's acreage had burned, but half of that consisted of low or moderate intensity fire and open meadows. So in 1988, only about eighteen percent of Yellowstone's acreage experienced fires that consisted of canopy burns, where fire consumed the treetops. Fires help provide that important diversity—young trees, middle-aged trees, old trees, and yes, even dead trees. The more diverse the forest, the more abundant the food for a good variety of wildlife.

The paddling conditions on this day were again a dream. The waters were calm. It is amazing how a canoe can glide so effortlessly through the calm water. All that is required is an occasional firm stroke from the stern and bow. However, the sun was really bearing down, requiring protection with hat and sunscreen. We met up with John and Deb and her Mom at a beautiful point that protrudes out into the arm near Columbine Creek.

At this point the winds over the eons have raked the shores of the lake, resulting in a nice beach consisting of very small light-colored pebbles. Behind the beach is a lush growth of cottonwood trees. There is also a wonderful view looking down into the arm, and the outlet of the Yellowstone River. From here we reminisced over a previous trip the four of us took in this arm, one that resulted in the scariest moment John and Deb had ever encountered on Yellowstone Lake.

On that trip the roles had been reversed. Jim and I had headed up the arm to try some fishing, while John and Deb had decided to relax around camp for a while, and then explore the region around the outlet. When Jim and I reached the point near Columbine Creek, we looked back down the arm with field glasses to see if we could spot John and Deb. We did not see them, but we did notice a rather ominous thunderstorm rolling north over the Two Ocean Plateau. I told Jim that I sure hoped John and Deb were not headed over to the outlet, because they would not see this storm coming.

Suddenly, our worst fears were confirmed. I spotted their canoe just before the storm overtook them. The ensuing sheets of rain completely obliterated them from view, and moments later the storm and accompanying high winds were upon us. Jim and I headed over into the woods to take shelter. Little did we know that John and Deb at that moment were fighting for their very lives. As they told us later, the waves came within an eyelash of swamping their canoe.

John was able to maneuver their canoe into the outlet and take refuge among the willow brush. John had felt safe cutting off some of the bay in this case because the lake was calm, and there was nothing in view blowing in. Normally the sheltered nature of this end of the arm would prevent prevailing winds from stirring up big waves. Here was one more example of how treacherous and deadly Yellowstone Lake can be. That was the last time that John cut off part of a bay, but it was not the last time to get in trouble on the lake. That was still to come on our present trip.

We had originally planned to camp in the arm one more night. But after we finished dinner, we looked out across the gorgeous, calm waters, and decided to conclude the trip on this evening. We were about ten miles from Sedge Bay, and figured that we could easily cover that in three hours under these ideal conditions. There is no more beautiful time to paddle the lake, in my opinion, than the period just before and after sunset. The colors in the sky and across the water take on pastel shades similar to those found on an artist's pallet.

As we continued our journey back up the arm, we couldn't help but notice the sulphuric odor emanating from the Brimstone Basin above us to the east. Throughout the day westerly winds blow the fumes away, but during the calm evenings the smell is ubiquitous. Once the sun dropped below the horizon, the heat of the day disappeared. In fact, it became downright cold. However, the continuous physical activity of our paddling kept us warm. I was still in my shorts, but did not feel like trying to dig out my long pants and pull them on while in the canoe. John was in the same situation. In fact, he and Deb paddled strongly past us, and I noticed John, with a big smile on his face, was also still in his shorts and shirt.

The fact that Jim and I could not keep up with John and Deb, I attributed to the fact that their long, sleek seventeen-foot canoe was more streamlined in the water than my rather fat, fifteen-footer. Our pride could rationalize it that way. Nevertheless, they arrived at Sedge Bay only about two minutes ahead of Jim and me. When our canoe reached shore, Deb ran up with a frantic look on her face, "Butch," she shouted, "John is hypothermic!" "Oh Deb," I laughed, "there's nothing wrong with John."

Jim and I climbed out of our canoe, stretched our limbs, and pulled the craft onto the beach. I walked over to John and began to laugh, "John," I chuckled, "Deb thinks you have hypothermia." "Uhcha, uhcha, uhcha uncha, ahcha," replied John. Deb was right. John's stammering was showing a classic sign of the body cooling down. She knew he was in trouble when he was almost unable to step out of the canoe when they arrived on shore. We took John over to my truck to get him out of the cold night air, started the engine, and turned the heat all the way up.

Apparently, the reason John got in trouble ahead of the rest of us, though we were indeed getting chilled as well, was the fact that for the past couple of days John had not worn a shirt, and had suffered some sunburn on his upper body. On this evening he had simply lost more body heat than he had realized. The constant movement had kept him warm to an extent, but this was one more example of the insidious nature of the danger inherent in exploring Yellowstone Lake by canoe.

After this trip I realized that Jim's stroke had not diminished his paddling ability. Even though we had not planned to do so, we had ended up paddling eighteen miles all the way down the length of the Southeast Arm on one day, and all the way back out the next. This was our first and last time to do so. Afterall, this is not the recommended way to soak in the beauty of this wonderful place. It is much better to allocate at least a week to explore the lake's arm. A water surface is really a function of how much time it takes one to explore it. A powerful motorboat could cover most of Yellowstone Lake easily in one day. A paddler needs at least a week. And it is guaranteed that the week will offer up a glorious wilderness experience. Just be sure to hug the shoreline, protect yourself from the sun, and do your best to stay dry and warm!

A Cold Dark Night on
Yellowstone Lake

Most veteran paddlers on Yellowstone Lake emphasize that you have to be willing to accept the conditions the lake provides. If the wind blows all day, then you may have to do much of your paddling late in the evening or around dawn. I have followed this advice on many occasions with great success, and indeed, there is no more beautiful time to be out on Yellowstone Lake than twilight or dawn. At these times the lake's waters are often as calm as a sheet of glass. Strong southwest winds typically come up in the morning around 9:00 a.m. or so, and may blow until sunset. Canoeing under such conditions is often extremely dangerous. During the summer of 1990, I encountered those strong winds, and also discovered one downside to paddling the lake after dark.

Jim Lenertz and I had planned to launch our canoe from Grant and paddle around West Thumb into the Flat Mountain Arm, and meet up with our friends John Dirksen and Andy Caudillo, who were camping along the south shore of the arm. We got off work at Old Faithful around 4:00 p.m. and began the twenty-mile drive over to Grant. Along the way we noticed with concern that the trees were swaying back and forth, indicating that there was a strong wind blowing out of the southwest. However, when we arrived at Grant we found the waters in West Thumb to be perfectly calm. Despite our combined forty years of experience in Yellowstone, Jim and I were about to learn yet another lesson the hard way.

Over the years, Jim and I had taken many canoe trips on Yellowstone Lake, but we almost always launched from Sedge Bay and paddled along the eastern shore of the lake. This was our first time to launch from Grant. We mistakenly assumed that the strong winds we had observed on Craig Pass on the drive over from Old Faithful had dissipated. We launched our canoe at Grant and headed for the Flat Mountain Arm. The lake was tranquil as we pushed off toward Breeze Point on the other side of West Thumb.

Given the late start, we knew that we would probably not make it into the Flat Mountain Arm until after dark, but we weren't too concerned. The NPS marks the designated backcountry sites along the shores of Yellowstone Lake with bright orange metal tags mounted on posts, and Jim and I had always had good success finding them after dark. A good flashlight will usually do the trick. As an extra precaution I had instructed John to look for us as we paddled down the arm. "I'll look for your flashlight and then shine mine," he said. I told him to keep his campfire going and if we didn't make it by dark, to wait up for us at least until midnight.

Jim and I were pretty good about staying close to shore on our canoe trips on the lake, but on this afternoon we succumbed to the temptation to take a shortcut. Given the round shape of West Thumb we decided to cut off a significant portion of the bay, and head directly to Breeze Point in the placid waters. Yes, we were breaking a cardinal rule that paddlers should never paddle very far from the shores of Yellowstone Lake. However, not only were the waters calm, but we were also approaching the evening hours when the lake typically becomes quite tranquil.

As we moved farther from shore I noticed that the winds were steadily increasing. Suddenly, the situation hit me like a ton of bricks. Most of the West Thumb bay was protected from the winds by the shape of the land and dense forest. "No wonder the waters were so calm in the bay," I thought to myself in disgust. By now we had reached the point of no return. It was just as short to continue straight ahead to Breeze Point as it was to turn our canoe south and paddle directly to shore. We were about one mile away from shore in either direction.

The winds continued to increase until the situation became quite frightening. We were now paddling our seventeen-foot Grumman aluminum canoe among powerful waves with whitecaps, the biggest we had ever attempted to paddle through on Yellowstone Lake. The one thing in our favor was that the wind was directly behind us. From the stern, I had to dig my paddle into the water and use it as a rudder to prevent the big waves from hitting us broadside.

Unfortunately, this was not easy to do. The waves were coming close to crashing over the stern. I was fairly certain that from his angle in the bow, Jim did not realize just how big the waves were that kept rolling into our boat. Jim and I usually talk back and forth on our canoe trips as we discuss the various sights and sounds along the way, but on this afternoon, Jim had noticed that I had become completely silent. "Butch, is everything okay back there?" Jim asked with concern in his voice. The last thing I needed was for Jim to develop any fear that might cause him to make any unexpected moves from his spot in the bow. "Jim," I managed with my dry cottoned-mouth, "just keep paddling straight for Breeze Point, and we'll be fine."

I knew that we had a zero margin for error. One mistake from my stern position and we were dead. It was as simple as that. I was using every ounce of my strength to keep the waves from jerking the stern sideways, and capsizing us. Breeze Point appeared to be so tantalizingly close, but I knew that we were still too far away to survive the cold water if we capsized.

Finally we reached a comfort zone near the shore of Breeze Point, which only meant that we felt we could swim into shore if our canoe were to capsize. We were both shaken and Yellowstone had taught us an important lesson.

We were shocked at how quickly the winds had come up and transformed the smooth waters into whitecaps. Jim and I discussed the fact that in the process of attempting to save perhaps fifteen minutes of paddling, we had inadvertently placed ourselves at great peril. We had survived the big waves across West Thumb for two reasons: first, the wind direction had been favorable and second, the distance between the crests of the waves had also been in our favor. The key to paddling through waves is that the distance between the crests of the waves needs to be at least as long as the canoe, say sixteen feet or more. The danger of Yellowstone Lake had revealed itself on this day in a rather sinister way, and we made a vow: no more shortcuts, even if the lake showed calm waters.

Regrettably, our difficulty was not over. We did not anticipate the choppy conditions that prevailed due to the big waves reverberating off of the rocky bluffs along the shore. The very annoying choppy conditions continued all the way around Breeze Point, as the smooth waves continued to crash into the rocky bluffs, causing a rebound effect. This further slowed our progress.

By the time we finally rounded Snipe Point and paddled through Eagle Bay toward the mouth of the Flat Mountain Arm, it was dark, late and cold. There was no moon and the stars were spectacular in the clear skies, but as always, the night's clear skies allowed the heat of the day to quickly radiate away and it was cold! We entered the arm after midnight, so I wasn't sure that John and Andy would still be up. We did hope to see their campfire though.

Jim and I paddled along the south shore with our flashlight shining. "John, Andy!" we yelled. We heard no reply and we saw no glimmer of a campfire. The Flat Mountain Arm is over five miles in length, and given the pitch darkness of the evening, we were uncertain of our location. This time our flashlight did not help us locate any orange metal tags.

As the temperature dipped into the mid-twenties, and the clock neared 1:00 a.m., we were becoming physically exhausted, and if not slightly hypothermic, very stiff from the cold. We continued to shout and shine our flashlight to no avail. Suddenly, our canoe came to an abrupt halt. I thought that we had run aground on some type of sand bar, but when we shone our light straight ahead, we realized that we had apparently beached at the very end of the arm. This meant that we had paddled over two miles *past* the campsite we had been looking for!

Given the fact that we were cold, tired, and had no idea where the backcountry campsite was in the pitch black of the night, we decided to set up our tent in an emergency camp near the shore. We stumbled around in an open meadow full of uneven tufts of grass, until we finally found a spot level enough to pitch our small tent. By now, both Jim and I were shivering and could hardly wait to crawl into our sleeping bags.

Once we had our tent up I had walked over to the canoe to retrieve some gear when I heard Jim exclaim, as only Jim could, "Aw Shit!" Over the years, I have heard Jim express that phrase on many occasions, and it always meant that something had gone wrong. However, from the tone in his voice

I knew that this was perhaps more serious than, say, knocking over a cup of coffee!

I turned around to see what in the world had happened, and there was Jim sprawled on top of the tent, which was now smashed flat to the ground. The stroke that Jim had suffered a few years earlier plus the coldness of the night, caused him to lose his balance and fall directly over the top of the tent, breaking one of the tent poles and collapsing the tent.

Jim and I were using a North Face tent that we had used for many years. It was the same one we had used on the ranger-led overnight interpretive trips, as well as the one Jim used during his many backpacking demonstrations at the Madison amphitheater. We were very familiar with the fact that this tent contained an emergency sleeve for repairing a broken tent pole. The sleeve worked to perfection, and no harm was done, except to Jim's ego. By now we were pretty used to that!

There were no trees anywhere near us, so we had the dilemma of what to do with our packs that contained some food. We decided to place them in the canoe, tie a long rope to the bow, attach a rock for shallow anchor, and push the boat well off shore for the rest of the night. We then entered the tent and crawled into our sleeping bags. By now it was around 2:00 a.m. and the temperature was in the low twenties. Of all the nights I have slipped into my warm down cocoon to escape the cold, that night stands alone. I still use a goose-down sleeping bag I purchased in 1970 with the brand, "Alaska Sleeping Bag Company," which was made in Beaverton, Oregon. Oddly, the company went out of business the year after I purchased my bag. On this night, it was truly a lifesaver!

The next morning we crawled out of our tents to see just where we had ended up, and as suspected, we had beached at the western tip of the arm. As I pulled the canoe back in, I looked down on the lakeshore, and there to my surprise were grizzly tracks. "Jim," I called, "take a look at these." Upon closer examination it appeared to us that the tracks were at least a day old. Nevertheless, we would have never pitched our tent there had we known those tracks were present.

We paddled up the south shore of the arm and easily found the campsite that had been invisible in the dark. There were John and Andy waiting for us. Jim and I gave them a hard time about not waiting up for us, but they were quick to point out that they had given up at midnight as we agreed upon. This particular campsite was situated in the woods well back away from the lakeshore, so it was no surprise that we had been unable to see the embers from the campfire. For some reason, we had failed to see the campsite marker, but the dark night had provided no margin for error for locating it.

Since this unpleasant experience I have taken other trips on Yellowstone Lake during the evening, and have never again had a problem finding our designated campsite. However, there was something unique about that night—the pitch dark and cold that simply thwarted our attempts to find our campsite.

When a backcountry traveler obtains a backcountry use permit, it represents an agreement between the NPS and the visitor that the party will camp at the designated campsite that has been reserved on the permit. Occasionally, especially under extenuating circumstances, it may not be possible to reach or use that campsite. I never like to stray from my reserved designated backcountry campsite and for good reason. The park's permit system preserves a quality wilderness experience while minimizing impact on the resource. Also, the sites typically contain bear poles for hanging one's food (a major benefit), and in many cases a fire pit, where it is legal to build and enjoy a campfire. However, on one cold, dark, night on Yellowstone Lake, we simply had to make the best of unpleasant circumstances.

The Swimming Ghost

During May of 2001, I was hiking up Daly Creek with Sam Holbrook and John and Deb Dirksen. There was still a substantial amount of snow scattered up and down the valley. I have always enjoyed spring hikes with snow on the ground, because I find the animal tracks to be fascinating. Such tracks offer the hiker the opportunity to unravel wildlife activities and movements in a way that just cannot be accomplished later on in the season.

On our trip we did not see any of the park's big three predators--the grizzly bear, mountain lion or gray wolf. However, fresh tracks of all three species were spotted in the snow. The sense of wildness that one feels when sharing the backcountry with these magnificent creatures that are literally at the top of the food chain in Yellowstone is incredible, especially when you see the evidence of their recent activity but not the animals themselves.

The following summer I took a course at the Yellowstone Institute called "The Ghost of the Rockies," taught by Dr. Toni Ruth. Dr. Ruth calls the mountain lion, or cougar, the ghost of the Rockies, because it is so elusive. Her research team has spent agonizing hours in some of the most rugged terrain in Yellowstone to document their movements and activities.

On one of our field trips, Dr. Ruth led us to a narrow passage next to a cliff above the Lamar River that ungulates such as mule deer traverse. She showed us where mountain lions crouch above the pass waiting for

unsuspecting deer to pass below; however, the ensuing attacks are not as easy as one might think. Dr. Ruth described how on one occasion a cougar had jumped down on the back of a buck mule deer. The big buck immediately threw back his head with its full set of antlers and impaled the cougar against the cliff.

Dr. Ruth and her research team make up a minority of people in Yellowstone who can count many observations of mountain lions, because most visitors will never see one. You may see their tracks but don't hold your breath waiting to see these majestic animals. They truly are ghosts.

The cougar, like the wolf, was persecuted during the early years of the park. Early park officials divided animals into two categories: "good" or "bad." The good animals were mostly the ungulates—deer, elk, moose, and bison, and of course, bears were also popular; the bad animals were the predators, because after all, they went around trying to eat the good animals. It took many decades before biologists began to truly understand the relationships between predators and prey. I have always been amazed by the foresight demonstrated in the early 1900s by our conservationist president, Teddy Roosevelt, who expressed concern that the lions were being killed off in the park. He wrote the park and requested that they be "left alone."

Today, the lion numbers somewhere around fifteen to twenty animals and they are found mostly in the north end of the park. Until 1995, my only encounter with a lion was a possible glimpse of one scampering up Little Saddle Mountain in the upper Lamar Valley. But during the summer of 1995 my luck changed.

I was with a group of four paddlers that had launched our canoes in the West Thumb of Yellowstone Lake. We were eventually headed for the South Arm. Jim Lenertz and I were paddling one canoe, and Tom Gerrity and Denny Ruggerie of Great Falls, Montana were in the other. Tom and I go back many years to my days in the Air Force at Malmstrom in Great Falls, and we have enjoyed numerous backcountry trips in Yellowstone.

Jim and I had concluded our workdays for the weekend at 5:00 p.m., so we managed to launch our canoes around 7:00 p.m. Unlike our last trip in the West Thumb, we found little wind and calm waters. We had 2 ½ hours of daylight to reach our first campsite.

As we neared Breeze Point I noticed a light brown-colored animal in the distance easing into the water, and swimming out into the lake. The animal was headed for Pumice Point, about a one-mile swim across open water. "What animal would be taking such a swim?" I wondered. It is not uncommon to see a moose out for a swim. I once watched a moose swim across McBride Lake up in the Slough Creek Valley of Yellowstone. Moose love the water and are great swimmers, but they are very dark in color, almost black. This animal just did not have the color of a moose.

I had frequently observed elk and bison swimming across a river, but this animal was headed for a one-mile swim across the ice-cold waters of Yellowstone Lake. I did once watch an elk take a rather unusual swim out into Buffalo Lake near the west boundary. The big cow waded out until it was deep enough to swim, then actually turned over on its back and performed what I would have to call the "elk backstroke!" It was a hot day and there were mosquitoes out. I just assumed that particular elk was looking for some relief.

The sun had already set over Yellowstone Lake, so the lighting was growing dim. All that was visible was the animal's head above the water. It just did not look like the head of an elk.

Jim and I were about 100 yards ahead of Tom and Denny, so the animal had not yet come into view for them. I told Jim that whatever this animal was, I felt confident that we could paddle our canoe faster than it could swim. We really started to dig our paddles into the water. From my vantage point in the stern of our canoe, I was impressed at how quickly we started to close the gap between the animal and us. Then I noticed the rounded ears on the head. As we came closer there was no mistaking the animal's identity any longer. "Jim," I exclaimed, "can you believe it? It's a mountain lion!" Jim had started his career as a seasonal ranger way back in 1967, and in all of his years of exploring the backcountry, he had never seen a mountain lion either.

Jim and I were equally dumbfounded, because we had always figured that the most likely setting to see a lion in the wild in Yellowstone would be in rugged terrain. The absolute last place anyone would expect to see a lion would be swimming across Yellowstone Lake. After all, didn't cats hate water? I suddenly realized that I needed to get a photo of this unbelievable sight, but my camera was packed in my airtight dry-bag, stowed behind my seat. I put down my paddle and started digging through the clothing in the dry- bag looking for the camera. During my search for my camera the canoe continued to glide toward the cat. When I finally located it I heard Jim yell,

"Damn it, Bach! Turn this boat around!" Our momentum had indeed carried us close to the swimming lion—much too close. We dug our paddles in to slow our momentum, but we still came within about ten feet of the lion. The lion turned its head toward us (Jim thought the big cat was going to jump into the boat), and then attempted to growl at us. But in the process it swallowed some water and started to cough and wheeze. "Jim," I yelled, "back paddle, back paddle, we are too close!" I really felt guilty allowing us to get so close.

After we had backed away the cat turned back toward the shore at Breeze Point. By now Tom and Denny were approaching the scene and would enjoy a great view of the cat swimming back to the shore. Tom, an excellent photographer, snapped some nice shots of the lion. I had taken a couple of close-ups and now took one of the cat with West Thumb Geyser Basin in the distance. We all watched as the cat swam back to the shore and climbed up on the bank. It then gave us a long stare, turned, and disappeared into the dense forest.

The four of us paddled our canoes over to the shore and examined the cat's tracks, which the sandy beaches had nicely preserved. We found the point where the cat had first come out of the woods, and walked across the sandy beaches of Breeze Point to enter the lake. We also followed the tracks back into the forest. By now it was approaching twilight, so we took some photos of the tracks before it was too dark. Our adrenalin flow was finally slowing down and we sat down on the shore to simply soak in the surrounding views from the point. In my mind I tried to figure out why a mountain lion would try to swim across Yellowstone Lake. Beyond the lakeshore were miles of dense forest. It was hard to imagine many deer in the vicinity for this cougar to prey upon, so the cougar may have been taking a desperate swim to find better habitat. In one way I felt guilty that our canoe party had come along and disturbed the natural activity of this animal, but on the other hand, I wondered if the cat would have survived such a long swim in icy waters.

During the winter months, mountain lion habitat is pretty much limited to the lower elevations of the Northern Range, where many ungulates gather to feed. However, during the summer they might disperse widely. The NPS maintains an observation form for sighting rare animals, such as mountain lions, so when I returned from the trip I submitted the details. Some folks were taken back and somewhat skeptical when we told them that we saw the lion swimming in Yellowstone Lake. Longtime Fishing Bridge ranger Harlan Kredit jokingly told me to let him know the next time we spotted an elephant swimming in the lake. However, our photos were more than convincing. In subsequent years, I have on many occasions observed tracks of lions in Yellowstone, but I have not had the good fortune of again viewing the ghost of the Rockies.

The Eagle and the Osprey

The rivers and lakes of the Greater Yellowstone Ecosystem teem with an abundance and variety of wildlife. I have always found that one of the best ways to truly renew your senses is to simply get out of your vehicle, walk over to a stream bank or lake shore, sit down, and just allow your senses of observation to absorb the surroundings. Within thirty minutes it is almost guaranteed that something of interest will come into view, especially early and late in the day.

During July of 1994, I paddled out to a campsite on Jackson Lake in Grand Teton National Park with my wife, Margaret and friends John and Deb Dirksen. From a safety standpoint, Jackson Lake is safer to paddle than Shoshone Lake or Yellowstone Lake, because the waters are not as frigid during mid- to late summer. It would be nice if a few portions of Jackson Lake were made off limits to powerboats. Two wonderful sections of Jackson Lake to paddle that really should be hand-propelled only are Moran Bay and the north end where the Snake River enters.

We had finished dinner and were enjoying watching the sunset over the Tetons, when we were treated to a dramatic battle between an osprey and an eagle. The episode began with a sight I had been treated to many times in the Yellowstone country. An osprey circled overhead, then dove into the lake right out in front of us, and emerged tightly clutching a nice-sized fish in its powerful talons. The osprey began to bank to the left as it gained altitude to head for a tree.

Suddenly, without warning, a bald eagle approached from high above the osprey. The eagle gathered in its wings, launched a high-speed dive right at the osprey, and swiped the fish away. I turned my binoculars to the osprey to see what its next move would be. At first the osprey appeared to be banking back toward the lake to search for another fish to catch, but then it seemed to change its mind in mid-flight. The osprey turned toward the eagle. Apparently the osprey was going to attempt to take back its fish!

The osprey stayed behind the eagle climbing above it until it was basically in the same position the eagle had been in before it stole the fish. The osprey made the same exact maneuver that the eagle had made, closing in its wings and launching into a high-speed dive right toward the eagle. As the osprey approached the eagle we were all cheering in support of the osprey. What could be more equitable than for this osprey to retrieve its catch?

However, just as the osprey was about to snatch the fish back, the eagle made an incredible mid-air maneuver. How the eagle knew just at the right moment that the osprey was directly above and behind it I'll never know, but

The eagle executed a 360-degree roll. The eagle had turned 180 degrees just as the osprey raced past, causing it to clutch nothing but air in its talons. I felt as though I was attending an air show watching skilled F-16 or F-18 pilots execute tight maneuvers in a dogfight. The question was now whether the osprey would return and make another run at the eagle. The osprey seemed to ponder it momentarily but then turned back toward the lake looking for another fish to catch. Apparently, after witnessing the nifty mid-air maneuver by the eagle, the osprey had concluded that it would be easier to simply catch another fish rather than try to recover its fish from the talons of the eagle! The air-to-air combat had been thrilling! I turned to John and said, "The Blue Angels and the Thunderbirds don't have anything on these guys." "You're right," John said. "But I wouldn't be surprised if some of our best pilots have studied the maneuvers that birds of prey make."

The Little Titanic

Over the years Jim Lenertz has been my most trusted companion for taking canoe trips on Yellowstone Lake. However, after his stroke in 1987, I thought our long trips had come to an end. The thought of no longer being able to take an extended backpack or canoe trip with my long-time backcountry companion was tough to accept. Then I came up with a possible solution—bringing a used powerboat into the park to transport Jim and me, and others on the lake. I recalled a canoe trip that Jim and I were on once in the Southeast Arm, where we passed a small motorboat occupied by two elderly gentlemen who were fishing. "Bach," Jim mused, "that's you and me one of these days." I laughed at the time, but now it appeared that "one of these days" might have arrived.

I checked with my friend and fellow paddler, Tom Gerrity, from Great Falls, who had joined Jim and me on many canoe trips in Yellowstone, and Tom agreed to go fifty-fifty with me to buy a second-hand boat to use in the park. I managed to find a *very* used fiberglass boat and motor for use on Yellowstone Lake. However, as it turned out, no one had bothered to ask Jim if he was ready to cease hiking, backpacking, and especially paddling. In fact, Jim resumed hiking and backpacking, though moving a bit slower and covering less ground. However, Jim's paddling ability seemed to be just as strong as ever, so our lengthy canoe trips continued.

I probably should have sold the powerboat immediately. However, Tom was enjoying getting some good use out of it, so I thought I would give it a try as well. Philosophically, as a purist wilderness paddler, I almost felt like a traitor taking the boat out on Yellowstone Lake. However, the beginning of the end arrived on a beautiful Saturday morning. I thought it would be a nice day to take my wife Margaret, daughter Alison, and friends Bill (a fellow seasonal interpretive ranger) and Nancy Millar, their son, John and daughter Michelle, out for a picnic at Breeze Point. Since the mountain lion sighting here, this spot held a special place in my heart.

We all piled in my trusty old 1978 Dodge pickup and with boat and trailer in tow, we headed for the boat dock near Grant campground. With seven of us we had quite a few supplies stored in the boat—fishing gear, gas cans, chairs, coolers, life jackets, and numerous other items. As we were transferring our gear from the truck into the boat, we noticed a family packing for an extensive backcountry canoe trip. The canoe appeared to be terribly overloaded. The family consisted of a Mom and Dad, and two small daughters. Having that many in the seventeen-foot canoe was bad enough, but in the middle of the canoe they had piled all of their gear, and it was stacked high above the gunwales, causing the boat to appear very top-heavy and unstable.

I could not help but think of the many times Jim and I had run into rough conditions on the lake, requiring both of us to get down on our knees to lower the center of gravity as we paddled and fought through the waves. This family would have no chance if they ran into rough waters out on the lake. Margaret was *really* concerned. "Butch," she appealed, "you have *got* to go over to that family, tell them you're an off-duty ranger with lots of experience on this lake, and warn them against going out overloaded!" "Okay," I agreed. "But first let's go ahead and get our boat in the water, and get the truck and trailer parked."

I proceeded to back the boat into the water, released it from the trailer, and then drove my truck and trailer over into a parking spot. As I was about to get out of my truck to walk over to the boat, I noticed in my side rear view mirror the image of Margaret running toward me with her arms frantically waving. As she got closer I could hear her shouts, "The boat is sinking, the boat is sinking!" Then it dawned on me. I had forgotten to screw in the boat's drain plug in the bottom of the stern! The drain plug is normally left unplugged when the boat is not in use, so any rainwater drains out of the boat.

By the time I reached the boat it was half full of water, and all of our gear was floating within the boat. I realized that if I did not act quickly, the boat would soon be situated on the bottom of the bay at Grant. I jumped into the boat but to locate the drain plug, I had to begin tossing our gear out of the boat. I did not have time to pick up chairs, coolers, etc. and place them on the dock. Rather, I was slinging gear out on the dock right and left.

The dock is a fairly popular area for the campers at Grant Campground to visit, and out of the corner of my eye, I realized that a fairly sizeable crowd had gathered to observe my little calamity. In an instant I began to imagine what they were thinking. I probably appeared to be a cross between "Clark Griswold Goes Camping" and the "Beverly Hillbillies Go Boating!" After all, the sixteen-year-old truck and the thirty-two-year-old boat combined with Tennessee license plates made for a pretty humorous appearance. The family of four who were about to depart in their heavily overloaded canoe had also stopped packing to enjoy watching all of the action.

Once I had thrown out our gear all over the dock, I managed to locate the drain plug and screw it in, promptly stopping any further water from flowing into the boat. Now, as I stood knee-deep in the water in the boat, we had a large-scale bailing operation to carry out. Once we got the boat bailed out and the gear back in, Margaret again reminded me that I needed to go talk to the folks in the overloaded canoe, who were now about ready to push off.

I looked at their canoe. I had never seen anyone pile so much gear so high in the middle of a canoe. I walked over and spoke to the father. "Sir, have you ever taken a canoe trip out on Yellowstone Lake?" He appeared to be rather bothered by my question, but just shook his head to mean no. "Well, I'm an off-duty ranger and I have a lot of experience canoeing on this lake. You need to be careful to keep your center of gravity low and stay very close to shore at all times. The water is very cold." It is difficult to describe the man's reaction. His facial expression was somewhere between a look of disbelief and one of laughter. He kind of rolled his eyes and without saying a word, pushed off.

His reaction was understandable, though. Considering what I had just done with *my* boat, I was giving *this* man advice? Despite my substantial experience in a canoe, I had precious little in a powerboat (as I had just demonstrated to all the onlookers). I had put on quite a show and had heard lots of laughter. I'm sure that in the eyes of that father I had zero credibility when it came to instructing him on how to go boating on the lake! Anyway, they must have readjusted their gear once they paddled around the bend, for there was no way they could have made much headway the way their canoe had been loaded.

When we returned from our outing, I noticed that several folks had come down to the dock to watch us take our boat out. I guess word had gotten around that we could be pretty entertaining. Well, we didn't disappoint them. This time I encountered difficulty in getting the boat lined up straight on the trailer, and finally had to wade out waist-deep in the water to get the boat loaded correctly. Bill walked over to the onlookers who seemed to be sympathetically following our every action and said, "You know, this man has canoed a million miles but he's kind of new to powerboats."

Even though we had a nice trip on this day in the boat, it soon became obvious to me that I really didn't belong in a powerboat. Once Jim demonstrated that he could still handle his role of paddling in the bow of a canoe, I really had little interest in going out on Yellowstone Lake in a powerboat. Tom did continue to enjoy using the boat up in Montana until one fateful day on Flathead Lake. Tom had taken his wife Nora and little daughter Meghan out for a ride on the lake, and Meghan wanted to go out once more after dinner. Tom told her to go put the fishing rods in the boat, and he would come over and start it up.

Meghan came running back to the campsite with a wild expression on her face yelling, "Daddy, Daddy, the boat has sunk, the boat has sunk!" On more than a few occasions little Meghan had played a trick on her Dad. But Tom could tell by her wild-eyed expression that this was no joke! He ran over to the dock to see what she was so excited about, and there in about ten feet of water lay the boat on the *bottom* of the bay! As it turned out, a crack had formed where the motor was mounted, and as other boats would enter and exit the marina, small waves would wash up over the crack, each time letting in a bit more water. Eventually, the rear of the boat became filled with water and down she went. Under Nora's orders the boat was pulled out of the lake, and taken straight to the landfill in Great Falls, where a bulldozer flattened and buried it.

Tom now has his seventeen-foot Old Town; I have my fifteen-foot Coleman; and that is all we need to get around on Yellowstone Lake. Our misadventure with the "Little Titanic" only reinforced the fact that we are first and foremost wilderness paddlers, not power boaters.

Wolves on the Prowl

The Howl of the Wolf

On many evenings, while camped deep in the Yellowstone wilderness, I have gazed out at the night sky and lamented the fact the howl of the wolf was missing. This keystone species at the top of Yellowstone's food chain did not disappear on its own--humans eliminated it. I never expected to see the wolf reintroduced to Yellowstone in my lifetime, but I had underestimated the determination of citizens all across the country. After wolves were restored to the Yellowstone ecosystem in 1995, I began to anxiously look and listen for wolves whenever I ventured out in the backcountry. It did not take long for me to see wolves in such places as Lamar Valley, the Blacktail Deer Plateau and in the Lower Geyser Basin, but I had yet to hear the howl of the wolf.

I envied those who shared with me their stories of hearing wolves howl in Yellowstone. Sooner or later, I figured my time would come. The omnipresent yips, barks and howls of the coyote were still commonly heard. Where was the howl of the wolf? By the summer of 2003 I was still waiting. Ironically, my friends John and Deb Dirksen, who spend a lot more time in Yellowstone's backcountry than I, were in the same boat. John and Deb had also seen wolves in the wild on several occasions, but too had not heard the distinct deep-throated howls. I had always figured it would be the other way around. That is, wolves would be frequently heard, but rarely seen. In fact it was just the opposite. In August 2003 this would change. We would finally hear wolves, and it would occur in a remote section of Yellowstone's backcountry.

Twice I had tried to reach the summit of Eagle Peak, Yellowstone's highest mountain, and both times I had failed. During the summer of 2003 I teamed up with John, Deb and Hank Barnett to try again. This time our plan was to canoe down the Southeast Arm of Yellowstone Lake, stash our canoes, and attempt to reach the summit via the Trappers Creek drainage.

Hank was visiting from Tennessee, and we had just completed a strenuous backpacking trip up Pebble Creek, and over Bliss Pass the previous week. Our feet were still aching so the idea of using our upper bodies to paddle over thirty miles, rather than walking the distance, was well received by the four of us.

We launched our two canoes at Sedge Bay in the Southeast Arm at 8:30 p.m. on a gorgeous early August evening. The winds had blown for most of the day so the lake was just now settling down to decent paddling conditions. I have always considered an evening canoe trip on Yellowstone Lake to be one of the premier wilderness experiences to be enjoyed in the park. As we paddled down the arm the low angle rays of the sun lit up the Absaroka peaks to our east. The amazing sight of the Grand Tetons loomed to our south some sixty miles away, a testimony to the fact that we were paddling on a lake situated high up on a volcanic plateau. Indeed, at an elevation of 7733 feet, Yellowstone Lake is some 1300 feet higher than the valley floor of Jackson Hole and the base of the Grand Tetons.

Soon the sun set over the Promontory and twilight conditions prevailed. The lake's choppy conditions finally gave way to the glassy surface that constitutes a paddler's dream. Then a three-quarter moon rose over the lake, and provided ample lighting for the next several hours. By the time we reached Columbine Point at the ten-mile mark, we were overdue for a break. The choppy conditions earlier had slowed our progress, and it was now approaching midnight.

As soon as we stepped out on the shore we began to shiver. The constant movement of paddling had helped to keep our bodies warm, but now it was time to layer up. Deb was especially cold because she had been using a double-bladed paddle, and quite a bit of water had dripped in her lap.

After our break we were dismayed to watch our source of light, the moon, disappear behind the Two Ocean Plateau. The dark of the night now completely enveloped us. The cold clear night was spectacular and we were treated to several shooting stars. The Milky Way was so brilliant that it almost appeared close enough to touch. However, in the darkness we did not detect just how low the water level was in the southern tip of the Southeast Arm, and we managed to get stuck in some mudflats near the mouth of Beaverdam Creek.

Once again, everyone became chilled when the repetitive motion of paddling ceased. Deb was approaching hypothermia, so we knew that we needed to get off this mud bar and find our campsite. During our struggles to find more water than mud, we were continually treated to more spectacular shooting stars, but no one commented on them—a sure sign that we were all quite cold and fatigued!

When we finally managed to steer our canoes back into open water and paddle to shore, Deb was almost unable to get out of the canoe. By now it was 2:30 a.m. Over six hours of continuous paddling with cold water dripping in her lap had taken a toll. We managed to pull our canoes on shore to our campsite, quickly store the food, pitch our tents, unroll our bags, and crawl in.

John is usually quite the stickler when it comes to setting up a camp, taking care to pitch his tent in the ideal spot where it is level, smooth, free from any falling snags, yet protected from the sun by the shade of trees. But on this night nothing much mattered, other than crawling in our bags and warming up. After John and Deb were in their tent and Hank and I were in ours, we heard John mumble, "Well, this isn't the greatest camp I ever set up!" Hank and I chuckled as we drifted off to sleep.

At 6:00 a.m. the next morning a loud voice exclaiming, "Time to get up!" awakened Hank and me. Whatever physical problems Deb had suffered the previous evening were obviously over. John may be the meticulous camp organizer, but Deb was the trip's navigator, and she knew we had to get an early start if we were to have any chance of accomplishing our trip goals.

After pulling our canoes behind a dense stand of trees, we hoisted our backpacks and began the hiking phase of the trip. After fording Beaverdam Creek we found a beautiful meadow with a sitting log overlooking the wild and majestic Upper Yellowstone River. Deb announced that this would be our breakfast stop. By now the sun was beginning to warm up the day. We shed our packs and relaxed against some large trees on the edge of the meadow, anxiously watching Deb prepare Egg McMuffins.

Then, without warning it hit--the unmistakable sound of wolf howls! I had heard this sound many times on tapes. This was clearly *not* the common high-pitched note of yipping coyotes. Rather, we were listening to low, deep-throated, long howls that could only be from wolves. Adding to the enchanting sound was the harmonizing effect achieved by several different wolves howling at different pitches. The hair on my neck stood up. No one said a word. We all just looked at each other wide-eyed and cupped our ears to increase the volume. Here we were about twenty miles deep in Yellowstone's wilderness, hearing the howl of the wolf for the first time. I couldn't think of a more appropriate or wilder place in Yellowstone to finally be introduced to the howl of the wolf!

After breakfast we continued our hike down the Thorofare Trail. I have always been amazed how a cold night on the high Yellowstone Plateau can quickly give way to such a warm day. We were now hiking through an extensive burn from the fires of 1988, and there was practically no shade to escape the hot rays of the sun. The tough hike over Bliss Pass the previous week had taken a toll on me, and my pack seemed unusually heavy. Hank motioned for everyone to stop. "Listen, I hear the wolves again," he whispered. Our excitement turned to laughter. "Hank," I laughed, "that's just the wind blowing through these burned snags." "Well, it sounded just like those wolves we heard this morning," he added. Actually, the wind did produce an interesting cacophony of tunes, as it whistled through the snags above us.

We stopped to rest and cool down at a stream crossing where a couple of live trees did provide some shade. Suddenly a party of several backpackers appeared. We were somewhat taken back by their dress. One fellow was decked out in spandex, like a bike racer, and another fellow looked like he was on an African safari. A member of the group began to ridicule John for carrying an axe. As long as I have known John he has carried a hand axe while hiking. He uses it for many things—clearing limbs that have fallen across the trail, chopping firewood where fires are permitted, extending a helping "handle" to others when crossing streams, hammering in tent stakes, smashing containers to compact trash, you name it. I've even seen John shave with the darn thing—the axe is that sharp.

Since the axe is always carried in his free hand, John often performs curls with it to strengthen his biceps. He even has a homemade leather sheath protecting the blade. The axe is just part of John's personality. I guess there is also a measure of self-defense John derives from having it with him, even when he is in the tent.

One thing I have learned from my travels with John, you don't mess with his axe. If you borrow it you had better take good care of it. So when the one fellow started in on John's axe, I knew the conversation was going to head downhill. Now normally, John is just about the nicest, friendliest guy you could meet along the trail. But I could tell that running into this particular group bothered John, because he kept referring to "Spandex Man" and "Safari Boy" the rest of the trip. It made for some good laughs.

By the time we reached our camp near Trapper's Creek, we had hiked about eight miles and I was physically beat. The short night's sleep, along with my aching feet were taking a toll. After we set up camp and rested for a spell, we decided to explore Trapper's Creek to determine a route up Eagle Peak the following day. I had not hiked through this country since the year before the big fires of 1988. The extent of the fire's effects here stunned me.

This country was primarily spruce and fir, and few trees were coming back. As we explored the terrain around Trapper's Creek we found a jungle of burned snags piled up, making for an arduous journey to Eagle Peak. As a result we opted for climbing nearby Colter Peak instead.

The following morning we hoisted our backpacks containing food on the bear pole, donned our daypacks, and began climbing the south slope of Colter Peak. As we gained elevation, I simply could not believe how much of this region had burned extensively during the fires of '88. Of course, like most folks who enjoy hiking in Yellowstone, I had studied topo maps depicting where the big fires burned. I knew that despite all of the negative publicity, only about eighteen percent of Yellowstone's acreage had experienced a severe canopy burn. In addition, most of the burned lodgepole forest has regenerated nicely. However, this hike up Colter Peak changed my outlook on forest fires.

Most of the spruce and fir forest here was now gone. I could remember our naturalist training sessions during the 1970s and most of the 1980s, when Research Biologist Don Despain explained that Yellowstone's forest desperately needed to burn. But each spring and summer season was so wet, that practically nothing burned. However, now the cycle had turned. Since the early 1990s, the Yellowstone region has remained in a drought. In fact, due to the extreme fire conditions, our backcountry permits did not allow campfires on this trip. Each summer consisted of more fires, smoke and haze and backcountry restrictions.

Ironically, only a few weeks after this very trip, a huge fire burned along the east shore of Yellowstone Lake, destroying several vehicles that had been parked at Sedge Bay and at the Thorofare trailhead.

While I could appreciate the role forest fires played in the natural ecosystem, I had grown weary of them. I did not enjoy hiking through the hot, dry dusty burned areas that had previously consisted of cool, shady forests. I did not like having to constantly climb over fallen snags when exploring off-trail areas. As far as I was concerned, Yellowstone had experienced enough fires to last another century. Of course, I knew down deep that Yellowstone didn't give a hoot about how I or anyone else felt. Natural events would continue to occur on Mother/Father Nature's own schedule in Yellowstone.

As we climbed higher on the slopes of Colter Peak, we came across some impressive petrified logs embedded in the volcanic lava rock. The views of the entire southeast region of the park opened up before us. We felt as though we were hang gliding over the Southeast Arm, since it was almost directly below us. At around 2:10 p.m. we witnessed a rather stunning event. Although we were underneath a clear, sunny sky, we were taking note of a thunderstorm passing over the main body of Yellowstone Lake about fifteen miles to the north.

Suddenly a spectacular lightning bolt sprang out of the dark cloud, and struck Frank Island, causing trees to burst into flames. As I watched the forest erupt into flames three thoughts went through my head. First, I knew that Frank Island was an old growth forest, so given the extreme fire conditions, this brand new fire would most likely really take off. Second, I found it comforting to know that this fire was already 100% contained, since Frank Island (two miles long and a mile wide) was in the middle of Yellowstone Lake, and finally, in a selfish way, I was pleased that at least this fire would not impact future backcountry travelers, since there are no trails on the island. This fire, which came to be called the Frank Fire, would provide incredible visual effects for the rest of our trip.

The summit of Colter Peak is 10,684 feet according to the topo map. We were able to reach an elevation of 10,200 feet on the southeast shoulder before being blocked from reaching the summit by a vertical wall of volcanic rock. Nevertheless, the view from this spot was spectacular. The huge peaks just a few miles away to the east-southeast—Mount Schurz, Mount Humphreys, Eagle Peak, Turret Mountain and The Trident—formed an impressive panorama. Looking over at Eagle Peak I was convinced that there was no way the view from atop that summit, the park's highest, could possibly match what we were looking at from near the top of Colter. In addition to viewing these peaks, we could see most of Yellowstone Lake and the Upper Yellowstone River valley below us.

Over the years I have become more interested in soaking in Yellowstone's wild backcountry and less goal-oriented. I knew that to some backcountry travelers, climbing to the top of Yellowstone's highest peak was an important goal. Despite its very remote location, even the Yellowstone Institute offered a course during the summer of 2003 which included a hike and climb to its summit. I had attempted the summit three times and though Hank Barnett and I came so close in 1987, I still had not made it to the top. "Guys, the heck with Eagle Peak," I spouted out loud. "How could anything top this view?" The rest of the gang agreed with me. As far as we were concerned, we were in a mountain paradise, and did not want to come down off the peak anytime soon.

To add to the enjoyment we found bunches of raspberries growing on the talus slopes. We followed bighorn sheep trails, and found plenty of sheep tracks and droppings; however, we did not spot any sheep. We spent most of the afternoon relaxing in the grassy meadows above 10,000 feet, just soaking in the views and the warmth of the sun. Eventually we headed back down to camp, but the several hours spent on the slopes of Colter had truly been a magnificent time in our lives! That evening at our camp near Trapper's Creek, Deb prepared a feast of red beans and rice, with sausage and potato and cheese soup.

The next morning we headed back north along the Thorofare Trail, where we encountered backcountry rangers Brad Ross and Lisa Coleman. We discussed the status of the Frank Fire, and then we asked them how often the howls of wolves were heard along the Upper Yellowstone. Brad told us they heard the wolves almost every day. What had been a rare event for the four of us was apparently a daily occurrence for these Thorofare rangers.

When we reached the lake and our canoes, we decided to paddle out to near the mouth of the Upper Yellowstone River, and spend the remaining daylight hours. As we paddled out into the Arm, we could not believe the huge clouds of smoke billowing up from the Frank Island Fire. We found a delightful spot on shore to relax, soak in the lovely scenery, and enjoy our dinner.

On this evening Deb prepared pizza and glazed sweet potatoes. While waiting for dinner we were treated to a magical experience in an exquisite setting. First, a bald eagle flew into our midst, perching on a tree limb directly overhead. We studied the eagle with our binoculars for at least half an hour. I was amazed at how the eagle would constantly rotate his head 360 degrees, surveying his majestic domain. Next, several beaver swam right up to shore, and practically put on a parade, as they swam back and forth in front of us. We wondered if these beaver were just curious and had never seen a human before. Then a spectacular thunderstorm rolled across the Upper Yellowstone River valley only about five miles to the south of us.

The storm completely engulfed Colter Peak. The brilliant lightning strikes and deafening claps of thunder provided a wonderful play on our senses. "Well, it's a darn good thing we aren't up on Colter today," I mused to Hank. "We would be running for our lives if we were," he replied.

Then, as if on cue, the stunning climax to our evening occurred—the stirring howl of wolves again! We cupped our ears and tried to separate the claps of thunder from the harmonious chorus of wolf howls. Yes, I had heard this sound before on tape. But here I was on a magnificent evening in one of the wildest and most spectacular regions of Yellowstone's backcountry listening to the sound of wild wolves! Perhaps the backcountry rangers down here become accustomed to hearing this on a daily basis, I don't know. But the four of us were enthralled. The unique loveliness of this evening only accentuated the experience.

At around 8:30 p.m. we begrudgingly left our magical place and began paddling back up the arm toward our last campsite, seven miles to the north near the outlet of Columbine Creek. A full moon was rising over the plateau and would provide ample lighting for our journey back up the arm.

By the time we neared Columbine Creek we had a tough time spotting the small orange marker, which denoted the designated backcountry campsite. I paddled while Hank shined his flashlight into the dark woods along shore. Finally, we spotted the sign and pulled our canoes up on shore. The first thing we noticed was that the bear pole was down. This proved to be quite a pain, as we had to search a while in the dark looking for a decent tree limb that would support our food bags.

Even though we had already enjoyed a wonderful dinner, the evening paddle up the arm had caused us to work up a good appetite. Due to fire restrictions we knew that we could not enjoy a campfire on this our last evening. But the forces of nature had provided one for us. Almost directly across from our campsite the Frank Fire on Frank Island was raging. One tree after another would suddenly become engulfed in flames. Even though it was now around midnight, Deb cooked up some popcorn on her stove. We then sat on the shores of Yellowstone Lake to view the late evening presentation while munching popcorn. Through binoculars the torching of the trees was something to behold. "Burn another one," Deb exclaimed after watching yet another tree go up in flames. "I can't believe I said that," Deb chuckled.

When I finally retired for the evening in my dome tent, I found myself physically fatigued, but mentally stimulated. I listened carefully for more wolf howls, but they did not occur. The gentle murmur of ripples on the shore of Yellowstone Lake was all I could hear. No matter. My mind and spirit were full.

We got a very early start the next morning to make sure that we would make it out before the winds kicked up. We stopped at Clear Creek where Deb cooked up a breakfast of biscuits and gravy. We could no longer see any flames on Frank Island, but smoke was continuing to billow.

The trip had been an extraordinary one for us. Eight years after wolves had been restored, I had finally heard the howl of the wolf in Yellowstone's backcountry.

Part III

Winter

A Winter Primer

During the winter of 1973 I had the privilege of taking an eighteen-day ski trip through Yellowstone's wilderness. The trip proved to be one of my greatest adventures in Yellowstone, but it is a good thing that I first garnered some winter experience from some other trips. After having hiked and backpacked Yellowstone during the summer and fall for three years, Margaret and I moved to Great Falls, Montana in 1970, where I was stationed at Malmstrom Air Force Base. I could not wait to venture out into the winter wilderness. While my summer and fall experience had grown to be extensive, I knew *nothing* about winter travel.

It was time to learn. My good friend and hiking partner, Rod Busby, lived nearby in Pullman, Washington, where he was attending Washington State University. Rod had grown up on a farm and had experienced severe winters, but had never ventured out on a winter wilderness trip. All of my winters had been spent in Alabama, so my experience to date was limited to a December backpacking trip Rod and I had once taken through Great Smoky Mountains National Park. While we did have to endure temperatures of minus ten degrees on the trip, we never encountered snow deeper than five inches.

Ski touring was apparently still in its infancy, because most winter wilderness excursions were by snowshoe. The Air Force base rented snowshoes so I checked out two pair for a weekend trip in February 1971 for Rod and me. The plan was to drive up to Glacier National Park, and snowshoe twelve miles into Arrow Lake Patrol Cabin for the night. I had just finished reading Jack London's *Call of the Wild,* and the thought of spending a night in a snowbound log cabin deep in the winter wilderness was enchanting. I could easily imagine us sitting around a crackling fire in the wood stove, while the snow flew and the wind howled outside.

All of my clothing was Air Force issue. I had an arctic coat that was so thick I probably could have been comfortable in minus sixty degrees! I also had some "snow bunny" boots that were thickly insulated with wool. With my coat and boots I figured I would be impervious to anything that Montana could throw at me. Unfortunately, the concept of wearing layers of clothes was not yet in my realm of knowledge. Despite his winters in Washington, Rod was not up to speed on the need to wear layers of clothing for such a trip either.

I told Rod of my great Air Force clothing and recommended that he obtain something similar for the trip. He promptly informed me that he had found a superb double-breasted, knee-length wool overcoat at a Salvation Army thrift shop. He also purchased some insulated rubber boots at a garage sale, and we were set for the trip.

The winter of 1971 was a humdinger in Montana. Snow accumulations through western Montana were way above normal, and temperatures were frigid. Rod and I drove to West Glacier, where we found an old motel to spend the night. We were rather surprised to find snow depths exceeding three feet. The snow and ice around the motel created some problems, as we had difficulty getting the door to our room open. Once we pried it open, we found it impossible to get the door completely shut. It just so happens that this defective door would work out in our favor later. The town was completely deserted, except for the truck drivers in the coffee shop waiting for U.S. Highway 2 to reopen. Heavy snows had closed this scenic road that skirts the park's south boundary. February was obviously not the peak of the tourist season.

The next morning broke beautifully clear and very cold. The thermometer on my backpack registered negative twenty degrees! We drove on into the west side of Glacier and went into the ranger station to check out the key to the Arrow Lake Cabin. There Rod and I were pleasantly surprised to find ranger Bob Maury. Rod and I had gotten to know Bob well during our summers working at Canyon Village in Yellowstone. He had often advised us on our backpacking trips there. I knew that Bob was very experienced in taking long cross-country ski patrols while he had been stationed in Yellowstone. He had recently transferred to Glacier.

"Well, it sure is gratifying to see familiar faces here in the winter time," Bob cheerfully offered. "I know you guys are experienced old hands when it comes to backcountry travel. You wouldn't believe some of the inexperienced people who come in here thinking they are prepared to venture out into the winter wilderness," he added. Bob's comments made me feel uneasy. While I felt very experienced at backcountry travel in the summer, I was just hoping that we had properly prepared for this our inaugural trip in the winter.

"Well, let me go get you the cabin key then I'll perform our customary check to make sure you guys will make the trip in good order," Bob said. "I'm sure you two have everything you need." When Bob returned with the key, he looked down at Rod's rubber boots and frowned. "Is this what you are going to wear on your snowshoes?" he asked. "Well, uh, yes sir," Rod answered. "I knew a man who lost part of his foot wearing boots like those," Bob replied.

My Air Force snow bunny boots were probably more than I would ever need at the North Pole, but Rod's boots appeared to be a thinly insulated pair that you would find in most discount stores. Rod's face appeared quite grim when Bob offered the comment. "Oh well, you fellows are just going in for the night," Bob volunteered to break the uncomfortable silence. "Let's see now, what kind of shovel do you two have?" "Shovel?" I sheepishly repeated. "You know, a shovel to dig your way into the cabin. The cabin will be buried under six feet of snow. You fellows are the first to go into

Arrow Lake this winter," Bob added. "Uh, we don't have a shovel," I said. I'm sure that at this point Bob knew that we were not experienced winter travelers. Yet, he was too nice to verbally scold us, as I'm sure many rangers would have. "Well, that's okay. I have one you can borrow." Bob disappeared into the next room and returned with a compact, aluminum snow shovel, perfect for packing in and digging our way into the cabin. "Now, what kind of snowshoe repair kit do you have?" "Uh, repair kit?" I managed to say. "Yes, what would you do if you got half-way to the cabin, and the bindings on your snowshoes broke?" Bob asked.

Rod and I had no answer. We just stood there like two young, puppies, waiting for Bob to say something. "Well, that's okay. I have a kit you can borrow." Bob again walked back into his office and returned with a small kit complete with pliers, wire, tape and leather that would allow us to mend a broken snowshoe. "Alright, last but not least where is your rope?" "Rope?" We again sheepishly replied. "Yes, rope!" Bob repeated emphatically. "What if one of you guys falls through a snow crevasse out there! How would you be able to perform a rescue?" It was obvious that all of our goodwill with our summer experiences in Yellowstone was now down the drain. Bob, as nice as he was, was beginning to show concern about the safety and well being of these two obvious greenhorns.

"Well, I guess you can borrow my rope too!" Bob added, and again disappeared back to his office. Rod and I just looked at each other in embarrassment, as he returned with several yards of light-duty climbing rope. He showed us how every five feet were marked and each of us should attach the rope to our belts while on the snow, in the event of an avalanche or stepping into a snow crevasse. "The rope is no guarantee of your safety, but it's sure a damn sight better than nothing," Bob said. I was feeling very antsy and frankly completely humiliated. I just wanted to get out of that ranger station and hit the trail.

"One last thing," Bob added as we thanked him and turned for the door. "You will cross a couple of avalanche chutes. Exercise extreme caution. Look above for any wind movement and snow swirling. If you see any then don't cross." Bob then shook our hands and wished us luck.

We had expected to walk into the ranger station, check out the cabin key, and be gone in five minutes. Instead, we had basically attended what turned out to be a fairly lengthy snowshoe safety and equipment course. We had spent *a full hour* in the ranger station due to our lack of knowledge and preparation on snow shoeing in the wilderness. We were already behind schedule, and then found out that due to the heavy snow, the road was not open all the way to the other end of Lake McDonald to Kelley's Camp. That added another four miles to our trip into Arrow Lake. By the time we parked our vehicle and hit the trail, it was 10:00 a.m.

By the time we reached Kelley's Camp it was noon, and we were a full two hours behind our expected schedule. The weather was gorgeous though. Deep blue skies contrasted with the brilliant white snow-covered lake and snow-capped peaks in the distance. Although the temperatures were rather cold, snowshoeing in the sun soon taught me the lessons of dressing in layers. I was burning up in the Air Force arctic coat, so I took it off and hung it on my backpack. All I had on underneath was a short-sleeved shirt, but as long we kept moving in the bright sunlight, I was comfortable.

Our trek up Howe Ridge went smoothly until we reached the first avalanche chute. In Yellowstone, the trails are marked with orange metal tags high on the trees, which really helps during the winter. However, Glacier had no such markings, at least on this trail. As long as we were going through the trees we could easily make out the trail, but when we came to this open area, we could not find where the trail re-entered the forest on the other side. It was obvious that no one had been on this trail for a long time. No tracks were visible.

It took us quite a while to traverse the old chute, because it was littered with large and very rough chunks of snow. Once we completed the crossing it took us an hour to finally locate the trail. We would see a small opening in the trees and start down it, only to find a dead end. We had to do this several times before we found an opening that led to the actual trail.

At this point our late start finally caught up with us. Darkness settled into the forest, but the full moon was providing quite a bit of help—as long as we were in the forest and could see the trail's natural contours. When we came to the second chute though, we were in trouble. Not only did we have significant trouble finding a way across the chute, but it was also impossible to see where the trail continued on the other side.

Continuing on was now out of the question, since we could not locate the trail in the darkness. By now it was 8:00 p.m. and we were exhausted. We were thinking that we would simply camp in the snow for the night, since we had brought along a small canvas tent for just such an event. However, we were hungry and dehydrated and decided it was time for dinner. We had originally hoped to be eating our dinner around a wood stove in the cabin, but since that plan was now out the window, we opted for our trusty SVEA gas stove (a European brand popular with backpackers then). The night air had now dipped to about minus fifteen degrees. All the sweating I had done in the heavy coat now came back to haunt me. Even with the big coat on I was shivering badly.

Rod and I gathered around the little stove and attempted to light it. The stove would not light. Of course, I had never tried to light the SVEA in weather this cold. The stove was cantankerous enough at *plus* thirty degrees, requiring quite a bit of fuel to prime it. At minus fifteen, the priming technique was not working. This original SVEA did not include a pump that most backpacking stoves now contain.

My only solution was to just keep adding fuel to the primer. Suddenly the darn thing caught and a big flame blew out. Rod and I jumped back from the flame. I'll never forget thinking to myself at the moment, "Why are you running from *flames* when you are so *cold?*" Other than a few singed hairs on our eyebrows, we survived the flameup, but the stove was barely chugging along like my old '64 Chevy II when it was in need of a tune-up. The best we could do was heat up some soup until it was barely lukewarm. Still, the warm soup helped immensely as we had become quite dehydrated. The temperature of the night air had now dipped to minus twenty degrees and I was shivering badly. The big arctic coat could not compensate for my damp body as a result of my earlier, heavy perspiration. Rod's feet were now starting to freeze up. As long as we were moving on top of the wooden snowshoes his feet were fine, but just as Bob Maury had predicted, the boots were not adequate for standing around in the frigid snow.

We now had a decision to make. The option of going for the cabin had been taken away now that it was dark, and we held no hope of finding the trail on the other side of the one-hundred-yard-wide chute. Therefore, we could either bivouac on the side of Howe Ridge for the night, or we could follow our tracks eight miles back to the car and drive back to the motel for the night. In retrospect, we would have probably done just fine had we pitched the old canvas tent, and simply crawled in our bags. Over the years, as my winter experience increased, I have always been amazed at how warm and comfortable you can be inside a tent with a good sleeping bag.

However, neither Rod nor I had ever camped in the winter, and as we stood there shivering badly, we were not confident that we would ever warm up if we camped out. So we opted for the long return to the trailhead. It was nearing 9:00 p.m. We had been snowshoeing mostly nonstop for *eleven* hours. However, with a full moon and a packed trail going *downhill* we figured that we could make the trip out in half the time it took us to get to this point. That would put us at the car by 2:30 a.m.

As we turned and headed back, I felt disappointed that we had not made it to the cabin, but I was also amazed to find just how different taking a winter trip into the backcountry could be. I naively assumed that we would just strap on our snowshoes, and march right up the trail to the cabin. I never dreamed that we would not even be able to find the trail!

As expected, we were making excellent time now that we were snowshoeing over our packed trail. The moonlight was plentiful and what a difference going downhill on a packed trail made. The two most difficult aspects of our return trip were dehydration and sheer exhaustion. Our water was long gone and the stupid stove would not work in the frigid temperatures, so our only option was to scoop up the dry, powdery snow and let it melt in our mouths. At times I would stop to rest on my ski poles, and actually nod off to sleep! I would shake myself back awake and continue moving.

Rod and I checked on each other. We knew that the worst possible thing we could do would be to fall over and go to sleep, so we did our best to try to talk to each other. This was difficult since we were both physically spent.

At 2:30 a.m. Rod and I made it back to the trailhead and my car. Just as we had thought we had covered the eight miles back in exactly half the time it took us to trudge uphill through the deep snow. We had now been snowshoeing nonstop for *16 ½ hours!* When I opened the car and sat down in the seat, I just about passed out. "Well, you can't stop now," I thought to myself. The night air was terribly cold. All I could think of was trying to warm up, getting something to drink, and going to sleep.

I began to slowly drive the car back down the snow-covered road. Snow was piled six feet deep on either side. I almost hit an elk that was walking down the middle of the road, which in the moonlight, almost appeared to be a tunnel. Rod immediately nodded off. I guess I did too, because I awoke to find my car careening off the side of the large snow berm. I forced myself to keep my eyes open. As we pulled into the little town of West Glacier, I could see that the little coffee shop was still open, and it was full of truck drivers. They were all still waiting for Highway 2 to open.

I pulled up outside and woke up Rod. "Rod," I murmured. "I am absolutely exhausted. Would you please go inside and order me the largest strawberry milkshake they can make!" "That sounds great to me too," Rod said, as he opened the door and headed back out into the cold night air. Here it was twenty degrees below zero, and I was absolutely craving a milkshake. My body was not only dehydrated, but it was longing for some nourishment.

The heat of the car had taken away my shivering. Now all I wanted was a milkshake and a warm bed. Suddenly, I realized how dumb it seemed to be requesting a milkshake on one of the coldest nights of the year at a Montana coffee shop in the middle of the night. I leaned over and watched as Rod walked into the coffee shop.

When Rod opened the door and walked in, every head in the shop turned and stared at the enigmatic figure standing in the doorway. Rod's winter garb obtained from the Salvation Army thrift store was adequate for backcountry travel, but it was not exactly common dress for a coffee shop in the little town of West Glacier, Montana! The big double-breasted wool coat was bad enough, but Rod had strapped a hand axe on his belt. Over the years, carrying a little hand axe had become a tradition for our backcountry trips, and we always took one along for cutting firewood.

Rod also had a winter hat that looked identical to one of those Russian military fur hats. All that was missing was the red star in the middle. Every eye in the joint was glued on Rod—from the truck drivers to the waitresses, as he walked up to the counter to make his order. I could practically read his lips as he said, "Let me have two large strawberry milkshakes—*to go!*" Suddenly the entire café erupted. The waitresses and truck drivers were slapping their knees and guffawing.

All the attention and commotion did not faze Rod as he calmly waited at the counter for his two milkshakes. When he walked out the door the shop's clientele was still erupting. I guess it had been many a year since a figure wearing Rod's garb had appeared in the middle of the coldest night of Montana's winter to order *milkshakes!*

I have to say that strawberry milkshake was the best one I ever drank. I just guzzled it straight down and then we drove a couple more miles to the old motel. We knew from our previous night's experience that no one would be staying at the motel, and we knew of one room that we could simply walk into without a key. We hit the beds and did not move until 11:00 a.m. the next morning.

After paying for our room, we knew that we had one more unpleasant thing to do, and that was to return all of the borrowed gear to Bob Maury at the ranger station. I was hoping that Bob would be off and we could just leave the gear with someone else, but as soon as we opened the door there stood Bob behind the counter. "Well what are you two doing here?" Bob inquired. "You are supposed to be at the cabin!" I guess Bob had not lost all of his hope for us. He really had expected us to make it to the cabin. When we explained what had happened, he seemed surprised that we would hike out. "You mean you didn't even try to bivouac for the night?" he asked incredulously. By the same token he did seem quite impressed that we were able to cover such a distance without stopping. "Well, sorry you didn't make it. Come back and try again."

Rod and I never returned for another winter trip in Glacier. It was the last time that I saw Bob Maury. In future years, I had the good fortune of being able to make several ski trips into Yellowstone's backcountry, often staying in the park's patrol cabins. I would usually find entries made by Bob from his long winter ski patrols. I learned that Bob died in March of 1995. I will always consider him one of Yellowstone's great rangers. He was tough as nails, but he was also very friendly and helpful—especially to a couple of greenhorns who were learning the hard way just what winter wilderness travel was all about.

Skiing into Shoshone Geyser Basin

Ski Touring—Eighteen Days
Through Yellowstone

Exploring Yellowstone's winter wilderness is an incredible adventure. In recent years the winter use of Yellowstone has generated great controversy regarding what constitutes the appropriate use of snowmobiles along the snow-covered roads. However, the backcountry, which is wild enough in the summer, is truly a bastion of wildness in winter. The following is an account of a wonderful journey I made on skis through the Yellowstone backcountry, which appeared in the winter issue of *Backpacker* magazine in 1975.

Every dyed-in-the-wool backpacker has experienced the feeling that pervades the mind and body just prior to embarking on a lengthy trip. The two- and three-day backpacking trips are great, but when you are about to enter the wilderness for two weeks plus, well, it's just an exceptional sensation. Such were my feelings of excitement as I stood in the doorway of a rustic log cabin at Old Faithful, in Yellowstone National Park, admiring the winter beauty of a cold February morning.

After months of planning meals and eyeballing topo maps (which is at least half the fun), Brian Severin, Steve Veltrie and I were finally ready for an eighteen-day ski tour that would take us deep into Yellowstone's winter wilderness. Brian and Steve were adding a few finishing strokes of wax to their skis. In the distance a tremendous cloud of steam began to mushroom above the trees, signaling another eruption of Old Faithful. The minus fourteen-degree air only magnified the loveliness of the surrounding thermal features in the Upper Geyser Basin, where extreme heat and cold combine to produce unique scenes. The deep blue sky was filled with tiny ice crystals that were the result of geysers erupting throughout the basin; they had the appearance of a million miniature prisms.

Soon our packs were donned and we were gliding toward the trailhead, located only a few hundred yards from the cabin. It appeared that my dream was about to finally come true. Although I had explored Yellowstone's vast backcountry many times during the summer, I had made only a few brief visits to the grand old park during the winter. For several years I had anticipated making a lengthy cross-country ski tour there, but for lack of time and available companions, the trip had remained only that, a dream.

Finally, though, I managed to find the time (twenty days) and the companions "crazy" enough to go with me. First, I met Brian Severin, a rugged backpacker and cross-country skier from Great Falls, Montana, who completely shared my enthusiasm for the trip. Two other backpacking friends were eager to go but could not arrange the time; through them, however, I met Steve Veltrie of Spokane, Washington, a rock and ice enthusiast who seemed to spend half the year on the slopes of Mount Rainier. I felt quite satisfied with the experience of our threesome, and trip plans were quickly under way.

Because the Yellowstone country produces some of the nation's coldest winter weather (the record is minus sixty-six degrees with no chill factor), we had to be ready for anything. Our plans were to make a semicircular tour of the park's backcountry, starting at Old Faithful in the southwest, and concluding at Gardiner, Montana, on the northern boundary. The distance to be covered measured about 150 miles, for which we had allotted eighteen days. We knew that weather conditions would be the determining factor in the actual distance we would cover, but as it turned out we never imagined that we would encounter such extreme circumstances.

According to park records, December and January are mostly stormy with plenty of snowfall; also, the days are quite short. The best time for making the trip would be from mid-February to mid-March, when the days are longer and chances for sunshine greater.

Our biggest problem was loading our packs for eighteen days. We would cross only one plowed road during the entire trip—the northeast entrance road in Lamar Valley (the other roads are open to over-the-snow vehicles.) We left a cache of steak, potatoes, beans and wine at the Lamar Ranger Station on the Cooke City Road, but we would not get there until the fifteenth day. With no other possibilities for caches, we were forced to go 100% freeze-dried. Even so, what with food, clothing and camp gear for fifteen days, our packs weighed in at fifty-five pounds. They would certainly be a deterrent to any "hot-dogging" on my wooden Tronder skis!

A bright spot among the plans was being given permission to stay in a few backcountry National Park Service patrol cabins. Several of them date back many decades to the early days of the park.

Our itinerary would take us past the best the backcountry has to offer. We would visit the geyser basins at Shoshone and Heart Lakes, skirt Yellowstone Lake and the Absaroka Mountains, and pass through the Black Canyon of the Yellowstone River, into which several species of animals descend every winter in search of food.

With high spirits, perfect snow conditions, and the luxury of a packed trail, we covered the first four miles to Lone Star Geyser with ease. We knew that the geyser performed about every three hours, and decided to take a midmorning break in the hope of seeing it in action. But it did not cooperate, and we witnessed merely a few bursts of water and steam.

There are many hot pools, springs and fumaroles in the vicinity of Lone Star. Although we knew about the danger involved in skiing across these thin-crusted areas, we had no idea how difficult and time-consuming it would be. In many places the underlying heat made just enough snow melt to botch up our skis. Having to stop to break off chunks of ice and rewax the skis became a necessary chore that slowed our progress considerably.

We entered deep, untracked snow as we began the long, slow climb up to Grants Pass at an elevation of over 8000 feet on the Continental Divide. Ski touring was reduced to "ski-shoeing." We did not reach the pass until shortly after darkness had settled into the woods. After stomping out a flat spot with our skies, we pitched the three-man Frostline tent (sewn by my wife Margaret from a kit), slipped into our sleeping bags, and ate a hearty meal of beef and potatoes. Then we were content to soak in the silence and drift off to sleep. It felt great to be back in the wilderness.

The following morning broke clear and cold, with the thermometer reading eight degrees below zero. Brian started things off right with steaming stewed apricots, granola and hot cocoa. We decided that our evening destination would be Shoshone Lake and Geyser Basin, and hoped that there would be enough daylight left to explore the basin.

Almost immediately after breaking camp, we became lost, at least as far as following a trail was concerned. At our elevation, and in dense lodgepole pines, most of the trail markers were covered by snow. We set a compass course on the topo map and eventually managed to find the trail and Shoshone Creek, which we knew would lead us directly into the geyser basin. But we committed a blunder by following the trail along the creek into a steep-walled canyon rather than ascending the ridge above it.

Before we knew it we were somewhat trapped on a hill that sloped down sharply to become perpendicular 100 feet above the creek. The snow was beginning to slough around us, and ideal avalanche conditions seemed to prevail. Our avalanche cords would be of little value if we fell here! Behind us, portions of our track were already starting to move, and it was impossible to continue forward because the slope was becoming even steeper. The only choice was to ascend the hill above in a zigzag fashion.

As I turned to start up, I heard a shout and turned to see Brian falling backward and sinking into the deep snow. Apparently he had been standing directly on top of a small tree, and his movement had caused the loose snow underneath to give way. To our amazement he managed to arrest his fall quickly and escape a plunge into the creek. We decided that this one big scare was enough for the entire trip.

Once out of the canyon we were shocked to hear the abominable sound of snowmobiles along the Old Faithful-Lake road, despite the fact that we were over eight miles deep into the wilderness. By 3:00 p.m. we emerged from heavy timber to see column after column of steam rising ahead. We crossed Shoshone Creek via a precarious snow bridge and entered beautiful Shoshone Geyser Basin. After camp was set, we spent the remaining hours of daylight exploring and admiring our own private thermal area. We had expected to find some wildlife, attracted by less wintry conditions created by heat below ground, but spotted only a few coyote tracks.

It was very cold the following morning; the thermometer read fourteen degrees below zero. The geyser basin was completely enshrouded by a hanging fog from the thermal activity, which prevented the sun from warming things up. I had placed my boots beneath my sleeping bag to prevent them from freezing. To emerge from our warm cocoons and begin breaking camp required some strong words and willpower.

Steve led the way out of the basin and soon we were skiing on the ice of Shoshone Lake. We had decided to ski directly across it, Heart Lake, and a portion of Yellowstone Lake, because the terrain would be flat enough for easy skiing, the snow would be well set from wind packing, and we would save several miles. We had fully anticipated, however, the potential danger of skiing across a frozen lake—especially in Yellowstone where thermal features abound. Even a cold spring beneath the ice can cause a "blow hole" or thin spot. In 1960 two rangers died in a tragic mishap while crossing Jackson Lake in Grand Teton National Park after the ice beneath them collapsed, apparently weakened by a nearby hot spring. A similar tragedy involving a snowmobiler occurred on Holter Lake, near Great Falls, Montana.

We attached avalanche cords to our waists as safety precautions, and allowed a safe distance between us. If anyone went through, the other two would immediately pull him out, place him in a bag, and build a fire. Fortunately, that was never necessary. Once out on Shoshone Lake, we emerged from the fog of the geyser basin to an intensely blue sky.

The seemingly interminable white expanse was awe-inspiring. Mount Sheridan (10,308 feet) and the Red Mountains stood out prominently in the distance, while clouds of steam from the Shoshone Geyser Basin rose up behind us. We found skiing conditions ideal and were making good time. My feet, however, refused to respond to the strenuous activity, and became quite numb. The others waited while I took off my boots and attempted to warm them. Several minutes passed with little success. Then Steve, a true friend indeed, offered to let me place my feet against his bare stomach to restore circulation. This trick worked and once we were moving again my feet stayed warm.

Our most frustrating problem this day was psychological; we had to stare for hours at our destination on the east shore without seeming to get any closer to it (the lake measures over seven miles from the west shore to the east shore). After lunch, progress was slowed considerably by changing snow conditions. As usually happens in the early afternoon, rising temperatures made the snow rather sloppy, which created a sinking sensation. To avoid this we had planned to do all of our skiing between daybreak and 2:00 p.m. But we had to pay the penalty for a lengthy breakfast and tardiness in breaking camp on that cold, foggy morning.

Finally, we reached the east shore and managed to locate one of the two cabins we would use during our trip. We dug through five feet of snow to enter the cozy structure and promptly decided to spend a rest day there, washing and drying our clothes and selves, relaxing and day skiing. Late that afternoon a warm front moved in, and a heavy snow began to fall. We had no idea that this snowstorm was to continue, more or less, for thirteen days!

Two days later, having left the shelter of the cabin, we skied under miserable conditions through a driving snow. A foot of new snow had fallen during the previous twenty-four hours, which also slowed us down. After skirting Lewis Lake and crossing the desolate, unpacked south entrance road, we trudged three miles along the Heart Lake trail to make camp in a protective young grove of lodgepole pines. We had covered only eight miles for the day.

The following morning held some promise; the sky was merely overcast. The snow had finally stopped falling, at least for the time being. Shortly after breaking camp we encountered a large cow moose standing belly deep in the snow among the dense trees. It surprised me until I remembered we were nearing Heart Lake Geyser Basin, which extends northwest 1-½ miles from the lake, and would provide some respite for animals from the harsh winter conditions. Soon we came upon the first of several groups of hot springs. From there we had a beautiful view of the frozen white expanse of Heart Lake, 700 feet below, with Mount Sheridan and Mount Hancock looming up in the darkened sky.

We decided to leave the trail and descend to the lake via the groups of hot springs along Witch Creek. Some of the most exciting scenery of the entire trip rewarded us; group after group of colorful hot pools, springs and brooks marked the way down. Several pools were quite large, deep and colored an intense emerald or milky blue. Steam rising from some pools had completely coated nearby trees with ice, transforming them into the "ghost trees" that are unique to Yellowstone.

Additionally, the thermal features had created amazing warm-season sights. The sides of many hot pools and runoff channels were lined with a growth of succulent green plants, and a sprinkling of yellow monkey flowers; verdant mats of algae coated the channel beds. The entire basin was almost free of snow, so we attached our skis to our packs and explored the area thoroughly on foot. Brian said he felt like John Colter, the first frontiersman to explore Yellowstone in 1807. Indeed, we were alone, deep in the wilderness, with Heart Lake and its entire geyser basin all to ourselves. For all we knew we were walking in Colter's very footsteps.

Just before reaching the lake we spotted a group of seven elk, two of them large bulls; one of the bulls appeared to be in very poor condition. In fact, he seemed to be too weak to even hold up his head, which contained a big rack of antlers. It was obvious that this old bull was not going to survive the winter. Our first feelings were those of remorse. We almost wished we could bring it some food. But then we stepped back and were able to see the bigger picture here. Even in the Bible, the book of Ecclesiastes makes it clear that there is a season for life and a season for death. What might be considered "bad" for this elk was literally a gift of life for other predators and scavengers. In fact, we noticed coyote tracks were abundant in the area.

Nothing is wasted in a wild, natural ecosystem. All nutrients are either consumed and/or recycled back to the earth.

We had planned to spend two nights at the Heart Lake patrol cabin, so we might explore the geyser basin, and then head east toward Yellowstone Lake. As we neared the cabin ferocious winds bearing the day's first snowflakes began to sweep across the lake. Our brief spell of decent weather had ended.

We awoke on March 1, our sixth day out, to a howling blizzard. The thermometer read a balmy thirty-eight degrees F., and the white stuff was really coming down. We were truly disappointed because we had planned to devote the entire day to exploring and photographing the area. By midafternoon conditions were unchanged. The snow was so wet that it was almost rain—just the type of weather you would expect in Yellowstone in May, but not the first of March! After feeling very sorry for ourselves, we finally agreed that when in the wilderness we might as well accept it on its terms and try to enjoy it. So, with winds raging up to forty-five miles per hour, visibility perhaps 200 yards, and a heavy wet snow dumping down, we skied over to the geyser basin, hoping to catch an eruption of Rustic Geyser.

After half an hour there, Steve decided to appreciate the wilderness back in the cabin. Brian and I stayed on to watch the geyser erupt a few times. The water surged to a height of twenty feet, and lasted approximately fifteen seconds. A few moments after the second eruption, a tremendous gust of wind swept over the geyser basin at about fifty miles per hour. Bracing myself, I looked up at Mount Sheridan's mighty slopes, which could now be seen through the clouds, and marveled at the raw power of nature. Trees swayed and groaned in the wind, and snow flew from their branches.

Just then I turned and noticed a large, dark-colored animal loping into an isolated but thick group of trees along the lakeshore, only 100 yards from where I was standing. From its size and gait I guessed it might be a gray wolf—a species once thought to be extinct in Yellowstone. A few recent sightings had raised hopes that the animal was making a comeback.

Excited, I called Brian over and told him what I had just seen. I thought the animal was well enough "trapped" in the trees so that we could get a really fine look when it emerged. We skied down to the shore and confirmed from the fresh tracks that the animal was indeed a wolf. Some of the tracks were imprinted in mud (the result of underlying heat), and the baskets of my ski poles, which measured almost five inches in diameter, scarcely reached across them. The sly creature eluded us, however, by slinking behind a small snow bank to return to the heavy timber. We spent the next forty-five minutes tracing the animal's tracks, and reconstructing a fascinating predator-prey scene.

Apparently, the wolf had crept up on a snowshoe hare beneath a tree, from which it flushed the hare into the open, and eventually chased it into the bunch of trees. It was then that I had spotted it. Although not certain, we think the wolf became aware of our presence and abandoned its chase. From our vantage point near Rustic Geyser, we could have witnessed the entire chase scene had we only been looking in the right direction. Still, even that brief glimpse was electrifying, and the afternoon provided the trip's best wilderness vibes.

That night in the cabin the winds continued to roar across Heart Lake. The old patrol cabin is situated near the north shore of the lake, and on this evening was catching the brunt of the winds coming out of the south. During the middle of the night the incessant noise from the winds had made it rather difficult to sleep.

I had already heard several trees falling in the forest and other mysterious sounds, when suddenly the front door to the cabin blew wide open and snow flew right into our beds. All three of us sat up in our beds in a dazed shock. For a brief moment I felt that I had been transformed into the movie, "The Thing" (the original version), where the monster appears in the doorway of a hangar in the arctic in the middle of the night. Once my mind cleared and I realized that "The Thing" was not standing in the doorway of the Heart Lake patrol cabin, I quickly jumped up and pushed the door shut.

The next morning we got up at 5:30 to find the blizzard still howling, and the temperature at thirty-six degrees. The snow was glop—we would have to wait still another day. When I gazed out the front door I found the answer to at least one of the mysterious sounds I had heard during the night—the winds had actually blown the cabin's pit toilet over!

With visibility almost zero, conditions were intolerable for skiing, so we spent most of the day playing cards and baking corn bread in the wood stove. We knew that if we did not move out the following morning, we might be unable to complete the trip as planned. That night the temperature dropped to eighteen degrees giving us new hope.

We awoke on March 3rd to find the same blowing snow, but it was still eighteen degrees and the glop was gone. We left before sunrise with Steve leading the way across Heart Lake. Visibility was absolutely zero, so we had to follow our compass. The wind was raging terribly. If not for my hooded parka my face would probably have been frostbitten, for the wind chill factor reduced the temperature to minus twelve degrees. After sunrise visibility remained close to zero because of the blizzard.

We were traveling through a whiteout. Everything blended into one; there was no sky, no ground. I felt as though I was superimposed on a white screen. Even Brian and Steve, only a few feet away, continually disappeared from view. I could fully believe the old pioneer stories about people getting lost during a blizzard between the house and the barn. Our avalanche cords kept the three of us together, as we groped our way across the lake.

Despite the weather we managed to make decent time because the wind had packed the snow. By 10:00 a.m. we had crossed Heart Lake and were only six miles from the south arm of Yellowstone Lake. Disaster, however, struck in the forest in the form of deep, heavy snow. It was so deep and soft that we sank with every stride to the tops of our gaiters and occasionally even to our knees.

We lost the trail. Then, to cap it all off, we turned south down the Heart River instead of east up Outlet Creek. We had simply confused the drainages. By the time we discovered our error and returned to Outlet Creek, we had lost two valuable hours, and it was rapidly becoming impossible to make any headway in the snow. So we surrendered to Mother/Father Nature. Because our timetable did not grant us the luxury of waiting out the weather for better conditions, we returned to the Heart Lake cabin to make new plans.

The trip back across the lake was more of the same—windy whiteout, with the addition of scares from ice settling. We would be moving along, suddenly sink a couple of inches, and hear a sound like a muffled rifle shot beneath our skis. That night we were all a bit down in spirits. Our original plans were shot, the temperature had returned to a warm thirty degrees, and it was still snowing heavily. The following day it snowed and snowed and snowed. We measured the fall at an astounding three inches per hour!

March 5th started as another snowy, windy day. Our plans now were to return to the south entrance road, ski north on it to the West Thumb of Yellowstone Lake and west to Old Faithful, catch a park snow coach to Mammoth, drive to the Lamar Ranger Station, and there resume our original itinerary. We left the cabin at sunrise and encountered the miserable skiing conditions we had anticipated. I broke a ski pole and toe plate during the first mile. The groups of hot springs bore no resemblance to their appearance five days earlier; we could hardly believe the accumulation of snow. It had fallen too rapidly to be melted by thermal heat. By late afternoon we had trudged seven miles and made camp in the snowy woods.

The next morning the snow was falling as heavily as ever. Our exciting trip had been reduced to a slow, agonizing effort. Breaking a trail was extremely tiring; we had to switch lead positions every fifteen minutes. We had hoped to find the south entrance road packed by a NPS snowcat for travel by snowmobiles and snow coaches, but it was untouched, and trudging down it was no different from bucking the trail through the timber. At this point our party of three had a major disagreement. Since the road was no different from the trail, we had a discussion on the best strategy to make our way back to Old Faithful. I wanted to retrace our route to Shoshone Lake to Lone Star to Old Faithful. At least we knew we had a cabin to stay in at the lake. Steve wanted to follow the south entrance road to Grant with the hope that we would be able catch a ride on a snow coach over to Old Faithful. Brian simply did not care which route we took. Steve and I refused to budge on our positions so finally Brian said that he would flip his ski pole high up into the air and whichever way the basket pointed when it landed would get his vote. It landed pointing toward Grant. Well, at least I wasn't worried about getting lost, but I was not too optimistic that we would meet anyone on the road in these horrendous conditions. The road had not been groomed and the snow appeared to be too deep for snowmobiles to travel (we later learned that the roads had been closed due to the heavy snow accumulation).

That afternoon we finally reached Grant and to our delight found an NPS snowcat operating there. The driver, long-time Yellowstone Ranger Paul Miller, said he was heading for Old Faithful early the next morning, and offered us a ride if we would help him shovel snow off some cabins. We were elated to be spared twenty miles of road skiing. In retrospect, Steve's position had turned out to be the best after all.

The snow finally stopped falling when we arrived at Old Faithful. We learned that it had snowed *ten feet* in eight days! Many of the cabins were practically buried. That evening we talked with several well-wishers in the Old Faithful Snow Lodge lounge who were surprised we had made it back under such terrible conditions. "Thought we'd find your bones come spring," one laughed. We could laugh too.

March 8th was spent riding a snow coach to Mammoth, digging out our car and driving to the food cache at the Lamar Ranger Station. Steve decided that he had seen enough snow to last the rest of the winter, and headed back to Washington rather than complete the northern portion of the trip. Brian and I were eager to continue our trip toward the north entrance to visit the Black Canyon of the Yellowstone River, where we would surely see many forms of wildlife. We made camp near the Lamar River and enjoyed an evening serenade from a chorus of coyotes. We awoke March 9th to beautiful clear weather and a temperature of eight degrees. If only we could have had twelve other mornings just like it; it was our first blue sky in thirteen days.

A small herd of buffalo was spotted grazing only a few hundred yards away from our camp. The trip into the Black Canyon was fantastic. The snow was well crusted, and we could really ski for the first time since heading to Lone Star Geyser. White mountains stood out against the deep blue sky. We stopped for lunch by a delightful stream, and four bull elk ran up a gully right past us, apparently unaware of our presence.

After lunch we began our descent into the canyon, and entered a completely new world. Rather than bucking snow at an elevation of 8000 feet, we were now approaching 5800 feet with little snow at all. We attached our skies to our packs and began hiking. The change felt great. We went from the middle of winter to almost the beginning of spring. What a delight to have huge Douglas firs towering over us, rather than trudging through dense lodgepole pines.

Our final camp was to be our most beautiful. We pitched our tent on a ridge overlooking Crevice Lake and the Black Canyon. Just before retiring I noticed a yellow glow slowly creeping up the cliff above us. Brian and I watched in awe as a huge golden moon began to rise above the head of the canyon, spilling rays upon the shimmering waters of the Yellowstone River. "This is what it's all about," Brian said reverently. He was right.

Later, most of the night, we enjoyed the yips and barks of coyotes echoing through the canyon. On our last day we would continue through the Black Canyon and cover eight miles to reach Gardiner. It was a wonderful journey. The excitement began as soon as we emerged from the tent and found three coyotes on Crevice Lake. One was rather large and required a long look through the field glasses. The recent heavy snows in the high country had crusted, evidently forcing many animals to compete for food in the canyon. There was not enough food to go around; we spotted several winterkills and the coyotes were making short work of them.

Near Knowles Falls we spotted two bighorn rams, one with a full curl of horns. Shortly thereafter, we confronted thirty elk right on the trail. The big bull leading the group ran right up to us, surveyed the situation and decided to lead his harem up a steep, rocky ridge. I felt like a terrible intruder, especially when I noticed that one small cow had a badly injured leg. Rather than follow the herd she jumped into the Yellowstone River, and barely made it to the opposite shore. She was a pitiful sight and I knew she would not last the night with coyotes in the immediate area. Within the next few miles we spotted nine more bighorn sheep, a pronghorn antelope and two mule deer.

We took our lunch break on the banks of the river. With the temperature now in the fifties and the constant singing and chirping of birds—a large flock of cedar waxwings had descended into the canyon and were really rejoicing—it felt like spring. Everything was so alive and vibrant that it was hard to believe we had been snowbound only a few days earlier. An occasional pair of mallards raced along only inches above the river.

After lunch we emerged from the timbered canyon into open country, resembling an Arizona desert. In the summer this stretch is hot, dry and drab, but now it was gorgeous. We spotted a herd of some 350 elk on the sage-covered slopes above us, only a quarter-mile away. In the distance the white expanse of Electric Peak was impressive. From our lowly vantage point it looked Himalayan. Three bald eagles soared over the Yellowstone River. I followed their free flight through my binoculars and truly appreciated John Denver's words in *Rocky Mountain High*: "It's a poorer man who has never seen an eagle fly."

Soon we were approaching the north boundary at Gardiner. Our eighteen- day trip was nearing an end, and thoughts about the journey raced through my head. The wildlife show on this day had been simply spectacular. But so had the winterbound geyser basins, and the wolf, and the moonrise. Oddly, the ten feet of snow and the hardships did not seem to occupy much space in my memory. From the Gardiner bridge we took a long last look back up the Yellowstone River to the wilderness from which we had just emerged. "Yellowstone," I thought. "It truly is a world apart."

Afterword

Today, Yellowstone's winter wilderness is every bit as wild and potentially dangerous as it was when we made our trip in 1973. I never again was able to line up such a lengthy ski trip into Yellowstone's backcountry. I have often fantasized about what the trip would have been like if we had encountered decent weather, but the experience of dealing with ten feet of snow in eight days was truly a unique, memorable experience. I did not realize at the time that the wolf sighting was monumental. The park's literature did state that occasional sightings occurred. However, looking back I wish that I had documented the sighting with a photo of the tracks in the mud. Obviously, seeing a wolf in the backcountry today would not be such a rare event!

The NPS patrol cabins are no longer available to visitors during the winter. However, the U.S. Forest Service does rent out many of its backcountry patrol cabins around the northern Rockies. Controversy continues over what constitutes appropriate use of the park during winter. I will never forget the intrusion of hearing the whine of snowmobiles eight miles into the wilderness. In his book *Reflections from the North Country*, Sig Olson wrote, "Silence is one of the most important parts of a wilderness experience; without it the land is nothing more than rocks, trees and water."

Part IV

Geologic Wonders

The Canyon

Within Yellowstone's 3472 square miles of unique natural beauty and diversity, there is one section of the park that simply stands a cut above all else—the Grand Canyon of the Yellowstone River. My sister Alice worked for the Yellowstone Park Company at Canyon Village in 1959, and returned home to Alabama with a scrapbook full of superb photos. Her many snapshots of the Canyon were stunning, but nothing would prepare me for seeing it for the first time in 1968, when Margaret and I also worked there for the YP Company.

The Yellowstone River plunges 109 feet at the Upper Falls, and then less than a half mile downstream, plummets another 308 feet into a colorful chasm almost 1000 feet deep. There is simply no way that a photograph can do justice to the Canyon. First, most cameras do not capture the very rich tints of red and yellow, and second, the slow-motion beauty of the Lower Falls can only be truly appreciated in person.

The Canyon takes on a rich appearance both early and late in the day, and also during cloudy and even inclement weather. During the middle part of the day, when most people visit the Canyon, the sun is directly overhead and tends to wash out the brilliant colors.

The first time that Margaret and I walked up to the edge of the Canyon, we took a deep gasp. We also noticed that other visitors around us were reverently whispering, as though standing in the halls of a great cathedral. The yellow walls of the Canyon provided clear evidence to me where the name Yellowstone came from. Surprisingly, I was wrong and it took quite a few years before I learned that the name Yellowstone probably came from yellow-colored rocks that Native American Indians and fur trappers observed along the banks of a river near present-day Billings, Montana.

A French term "Roche Jaune," meaning yellow rock, was used on maps prior to 1800. So the name "Yellowstone" was probably being used to describe the river long before the interior of what is now the national park was even discovered by European-Americans.

Other great canyons in the West such as the Grand Canyon of the Colorado River, Hells Canyon of the Snake, the Black Canyon of the Gunnison, Santa Elena Canyon of the Rio Grande and Yosemite Valley are certainly all spectacular. But only the Grand Canyon of the Yellowstone exhibits the incredible variation of colors.

Few photographers come even close to adequately capturing the rich, diverse colors of the Canyon on film. An artist stands a better chance. My wife Margaret, whose rendition of the Lower Falls graces this book's cover (and in my biased opinion does justice in capturing those colors), has always felt that the one artist who came the closest to capturing the colors of the Canyon was Thomas Moran. Moran was one of the greatest artists of all time, and his paintings played an important role in convincing the U.S. Congress to establish Yellowstone as the world's first national park in 1872.

According to Ferdinand Hayden of the noted Hayden Survey of Yellowstone, even Moran had his doubts about being able to do justice to the Canyon: "Mr. Thomas Moran, a celebrated artist, and noted for his skill as a colorist, exclaimed, with a kind of regretful enthusiasm, that these beautiful tints were beyond the reach of human art."

Hayden described the Canyon this way: "… no language can do justice to the wonderful grandeur and beauty of the canyon below the Lower Falls; the very nearly vertical walls, slightly sloping down to the water's edge on either side, so that from the summit the river appears like a thread of silver foaming over its rocky bottom; the variegated colors of the sides, yellow, red, brown, white, all intermixed and shading into each other; the Gothic columns of every form, standing out from the sides of the walls with greater and more striking colors than ever adorned a work of human art."

Over the years the Yellowstone River has carved this deep gorge through volcanic rock that has been altered by hydrothermal activity. Consequently, the rock was soft and easily eroded. However, at the head of the canyon, the rock had not been altered, so it resisted the processes of erosion. The result is one of the most magnificent falls in North America taking a sheer drop into one of the most colorful canyons to be found anywhere. The yellow tints are due to oxides of sulphur; the red tints are the result of oxides of iron.

The Canyon's moods are constantly changing with the time of day, season and weather conditions. During the two seasons that Margaret and I worked there, we had a favorite saying as soon as our shift was up: "Let's go down to the Canyon!" We did this with our friends late in the afternoon, at night under a full moon, and during all types of weather. When we had the late shift we would often go down to watch the early rays of the sun light up the Lower Falls. We found that the Canyon was most special when the low angle of light provided rich coloration.

The twilight time of day just after sunset was probably our favorite. By then the Canyon was deserted and seemed to exude a spirit of its own. After work we would often walk down the short trail to Lookout Point on the north rim, sit back and soak in the full beauty of the Canyon with all of our senses. An evening spent watching the Yellowstone River plunge over the brink of the Lower Falls in its slow motion fashion, with no one else around, can be mesmerizing, almost hypnotic. Other times, we would continue a bit further, and walk past Lookout Point down to Red Rock Point, where few people bother to visit.

Here the senses are pleasantly bombarded. The thunderous roar of the Lower Falls directly in front of you is deafening. We would typically visit this spot with three or four friends, but there was no sense in even attempting to carry on a conversation. The spray of the falls occasionally would drift over us and provide a soothing, coolness to our skin on warm evenings— nature's air conditioner at work. A fragrant pine scent permeated the air. However, it is the utilization of the sense of sight that truly presents the greatest challenge.

Where should I focus my eyes while sitting at Red Rock Point? The choices are simply too numerous and somewhat overwhelming. The brink of the Lower Falls demands my attention, as the mighty Yellowstone River slowly eases up to the edge of the precipice, and then bursts into a frothy white curtain. During early summer an estimated 64,000 gallons of water per second flow over the rim.

But wait! The curtain of water is not all white. There is a strange green "v" extending down the fall from the brink. As the Yellowstone River approaches the brink of the falls the water has a natural green tint. That color is preserved by a deep notch at the brink that prevents the water from breaking up into spray at this particular point.

Following the long, slow drop of the river with my eyes from the brink to the bottom of the canyon is somewhat spellbinding. As the water forcefully pounds into the canyon, it rebounds upward in an enormous explosion of white spray. The sight is reminiscent of an eruption of a huge fountain geyser, such as Great Fountain in the Lower Geyser Basin.

It is difficult to pull my eyes away from the falls but I finally succeed. Now I am gazing at the walls of the Canyon and studying the rich tints of red and yellow. Amazingly, I notice a set of animal tracks on the steep canyon walls. I wonder how any animal could successfully traverse such steep terrain. Some obviously do, but perhaps others fall. The flight of a soaring osprey soon captures my attention. Sometimes the osprey disappears from view, but at other times I will observe the osprey settling into its nest perched precariously high on the tip of a pinnacle along the canyon walls.

I notice curious steam vents billowing out from near the shore of the river. There is actually thermal activity here, and it serves as a reminder of the forces that helped create the color, and allow for the deep erosion to occur. My eyes now follow the course of the river downstream, and I study the ferocious rapids. Floating through the Canyon is strictly prohibited, though some paddlers have lowered their boats into the river here and given it a try. Some had to be rescued. All who were caught have received hefty fines.

Eventually, I look high along the rims of the Canyon and notice the contrast presented by the lush green forest that extends right up to the edge of the white, yellow and red colored walls. Now my imagination begins to take over. I wonder who the first human being was that walked up on this Canyon. Was it a Native American Indian? A trapper? I find myself wishing that I could go back in time and become a bug on a tree to hear their response when they casually walked through the forest to the edge of this 1000-foot chasm. If they were in a hurry to reach a destination, they may not have been as appreciative of the beauty that I am presently feeling at this moment. In fact, some early four-letter words were perhaps muttered! I find it delightful to ponder what must have happened.

I glance at my watch and cannot believe that a full hour has passed while I have been sitting in the Canyon under its spell. My spirit has been renewed, revivified. I feel a sense of exhilaration as I finally pull myself away, and begin the short hike back to Canyon Village. I smile, knowing that in only a few more days, my friends and I will be back to again fill our senses.

Undoubtedly, the way to truly experience the Canyon is to walk the trails that travel along the north and south rims. The viewpoints at Inspiration Point, Grandview Point, Lookout Point, and the brinks of the Lower and Upper Falls on the north rim and Artist Point on the south rim, all provide spectacular views, and are especially rewarding early and late in the day when fewer visitors are present. However, only by leaving these congested viewpoints and walking some or all of the almost five miles of trails along the Canyon's rims, will you fully appreciate the intimate wonder of its treasures.

I have always thought it amazing that two such large falls are situated so close to each other. During my first summer with the NPS in 1974, an unusual event involving a small airplane occurred at the brink of the Upper Falls. Some off-duty military pilots had rented a Cessna and were in the process of flying up the Canyon very close to the river, when suddenly they saw the 308-foot Lower Falls straight ahead. They pulled up on the stick and cleared the brink, but apparently they had no idea that less than a half-mile upstream, hidden around the bend, was another big falls. By the time the Upper Falls came into view it was too late to gain sufficient altitude, though the pilot duly tried. He almost made it but the wheels caught the tip of a boulder, and the plane crashed right into the brink of the Upper Falls.

Miraculously, the plane lodged on a boulder near the south edge of the brink, and did not tumble down to the bottom of the falls. The men survived the crash with their most serious injury being a broken bone or two, but reportedly they lost their military flying privileges for pulling such a dangerous stunt.

So much attention is given to the Lower and Upper Falls, that few people are even aware of Crystal Falls, a 129-foot drop of Cascade Creek. The South Rim trail takes you right past this delightful waterfall. Just upstream from its brink, a footbridge crosses Cascade Creek, where the lovely water ouzel or dipper is often spotted. The first time I ever saw this bird was at this particular spot, and I thought that I had observed the poor thing committing suicide!

The little gray-colored bird fluttered along just inches above the water and rested on a boulder. Then it took a nosedive right down into the water and disappeared. I assumed the bird was dead for certain. However, about thirty seconds later it emerged from the water, and seemed no worse for wear. I eventually discovered that what I had observed was the normal behavior for this little bird that feeds on aquatic insects.

During our two summers at Canyon Village, Margaret and I experienced the Canyon every way imaginable. We hiked along its rims. We hiked past Glacial Boulder, a huge rock left perched in the woods along the north rim as the result of glaciers moving through the area several thousand years ago. Along this trail you can gain a view of Silver Cord Cascade, which at a height of 1000 feet, is considered to be the park's tallest. We climbed the nearby peaks—Mount Washburn, Observation Peak and Dunraven Peak--to obtain a bird's eye view of the Canyon in order to fully appreciate its size and length.

We climbed down to the bottom of the Canyon to get a feel for its depth. In those days the Uncle Tom's Trail actually provided access to the bottom of the Lower Falls and the Canyon itself; however, in subsequent years the trail continually washed out from snowslides. Today, for the safety and protection of visitors as well as the Canyon itself, the Uncle Tom's Trail does not extend all the way to the bottom of the canyon.

I once took a backpacking trip to the bottom of the Canyon at Seven-Mile Hole. While the scenery along this trail is fascinating, especially the colorful thermal features, the bottom of the Canyon here is not quite as colorful and spectacular as it is upstream. It was a great trip, except for the 1000-foot climb back out!

During our two summers at Canyon Village, the Grand Canyon of the Yellowstone River truly exerted a hold on us, almost a spell. I will never forget the mid-September day in 1969 when it was time for Margaret and me to leave. As we drove past the Artist Point road and then entered Hayden Valley, we actually began to shed tears. I was about to enter the Air Force. Our nation was engaged in a war in Vietnam. We wondered when or if we would ever visit this magical place again.

Little did we know that five years later we would return to Yellowstone, and I would begin a seasonal career with the Park Service. Even though we have been stationed at Old Faithful for most of my tour of duty in the park, we go to Canyon often. We find one of our secret spots along the Canyon Rim trail where few people walk, and we sit and gaze out at the majesty of this place, just like we did during the summers of 1968 and 1969. Margaret takes along her sketchpad and attempts to capture the scene in colored pencil or watercolor. I just sit and look out over the Canyon, marveling at its beauty. It is a place we find ourselves drawn to again and again. It is a place like no other.

Grand Geyser in Eruption

The Duty Called GP

Perhaps the most revered duty of an interpretive ranger at Old Faithful is "GP" (short for geyser prediction). Early each morning some lucky ranger draws the duty to go out into the steamy, ethereal setting of the Upper Geyser Basin to post the day's first predictions for the big geysers: Old Faithful, Castle, Grand, Daisy and Riverside. I recall having some friends, Terry and Becky Holcomb, visiting with Margaret and me at Old Faithful. We had an early breakfast together and then I announced that I had to "go on GP." Terry gave me a strange look and asked, "What is that?" After I explained it Terry chuckled and said, "Butch, do you realize that you are probably the only human being on planet earth this morning who has this duty?"

To be honest, I had never thought of it that way and over the years I have never forgotten Terry's words. Not only do I ensure that I do not take GP for granted, but when I am helping mentor the new interpretive rangers each year, I make sure they understand the uniqueness and rareness of this special duty as well.

Geyser predicting is sort of like flying by the seat of your pants. First you study the geyser logbook to see what times the geysers erupted last and also to determine the most recent intervals. Then you head out into the basin to closely examine the geysers themselves.

For example, when active, Daisy may erupt somewhere between two to three hours. In order to make the day's first prediction, unless you are lucky enough to see it erupting, you must study all of the evidence surrounding the geyser. Is the water in the runoff channel still running? If not, is the water in the runoff channel still warm? Are the surrounding pools full or drained? Are the two cones around Daisy splashing? By studying these signs you can make a pretty decent prediction for the day's first eruption.

Similar clues exist at the other geysers. For example, Riverside's main vent will typically overflow for 1 ½ to 2 hours before erupting. Grand, the basin's largest, predictable geyser, usually begins a fascinating cycle involving Grand's main pool and nearby Turban Geyser about five hours after the previous eruption. After studying these clues and the trends from recent eruptions, you suck in your stomach, and post a prediction on the sign in front of the geyser. You then call these predictions in to the Old Faithful Visitor Center. The predictions are also posted at the Old Faithful Inn, Old Faithful Lodge, Old Faithful Snow Lodge, and other visitor centers throughout the park.

As we like to point out on our geyser prediction board at the Old Faithful Visitor Center, "Remember, we *predict* the geysers, we don't schedule them!" Sometimes, despite your best efforts, a geyser will prove that it is indeed a natural phenomena, and not part of an amusement attraction at Disney World.

For example, Castle Geyser is often very predictable and regular, erupting about every twelve hours. It is a spectacular geyser in that the eruption lasts an entire hour. The water phase lasts for about twenty minutes and gradually gives way to a forty-minute noisy and powerful steam phase. Many visitors tell us they enjoy the steam phase even more than the water phase. So it is not uncommon for a large crowd to gather as the predicted eruption time approaches.

However, every now and then Castle will have a "minor" eruption overnight that we may not be aware of. A minor eruption only lasts for about five minutes and tends to delay the normal major eruption for several hours. When this happens the ranger on duty has to go out and explain rather red-faced to a large group of people why our predicted eruption is not taking place.

I have learned the hard way over the years to avoid using the words "always" and "never" when describing geyser activity, and instead use the word "may." To many geyser enthusiasts, Grand Geyser is the "King" of the geysers, since it ranks as the tallest, active geyser in the world. When I first began working at Old Faithful, I somehow got the impression that whenever waves appeared on the pool of Grand Geyser's main vent, an eruption was imminent. To reinforce this theory, I had observed the waves several times leading up to an eruption, so I thought it was indeed foolproof.

Grand's intervals may vary anywhere from six to seventeen hours or more, and we simply try to predict the eruptions to within plus or minus two hours. So any additional information to pinpoint the eruption was very useful, and I thought I had it.

One day I was on roving duty at Grand as the eruption time was nearing. There happens to be an interesting feature called Turban Geyser right next to Grand Geyser. For several hours leading up to an eruption of Grand, Turban begins erupting about every twenty minutes. When Grand finally erupts, it usually plays in concert with Turban. The problem is, Turban Geyser erupts about three to six feet high, and Grand's eruptions may go as high as 200 feet, so there is more than a rather subtle difference between the two geysers!

I was standing in front of about 200 people at Grand, when I saw the waves on the pool—the foolproof indicator! I stood up on the benches so everyone could see and hear me. "Folks, waves on the pool! Waves on the pool! Hold on to your hats. Here goes Grand!" I exclaimed. Then Turban plopped up about three feet as it typically does during its eruption, and Grand's pool dropped, which indicated we had at least another twenty-minute cycle to wait through before Grand would have another opportunity to erupt. If I could have, I would have crawled underneath the boardwalk and hid from the crowd. Instead, I had some tall explaining to do. Needless to say, I learned a valuable lesson about geysers on that day!

Another geyser that occasionally makes a fool of us is the mighty Beehive. When Beehive erupts out of its eight-inch diameter vent the water may reach a height of 180 feet. The eruptions are noisy and powerful and they last about five minutes. When active Beehive may erupt about once every twelve to twenty hours. We rarely attempt to predict Beehive's eruptions; however, this geyser has an "indicator" that is sometimes quite reliable. There is a small opening about six feet away from Beehive's cone that is called "Beehive's Indicator." When the indicator begins to splash up about three to six feet, Beehive usually follows with its major eruption within twenty minutes.

Sometimes the indicator will give every sign that it is indeed foolproof. But at some point the indicator will fail. When reliable, we always announce the indicator to visitors in the visitor center, and we also call the Inn and Lodge so they can let their guests know that one of the largest geysers in the world is about to erupt.

One day after making the announcement I headed out to the viewpoint to await the eruption and talk with the visitors. Twenty minutes went by but the geyser did not erupt. Then thirty minutes and forty minutes passed with still no eruption! At the forty-five-minute mark I had to explain, red-faced, that the indicator had failed on this day. Again, the geysers run the show, not the National Park Service!

At 7:00 a.m. there are precious few people in the basin. Most people on vacation get up at 8:00 a.m., eat breakfast at 9:00 a.m., and hit the trails or roads at 10:00 a.m. Pity. That's because most of Yellowstone's magic is observed early and late in the day, when the low angle of light burnishes the basins and ridges with a rich glow. The early mornings in the basin are typically very steamy. Every little spring, geyser, or vent seems to be gushing forth steam, providing the appearance of a "valley of 10,000 smokes!"

Early morning also provides the best opportunity to see animals wandering through the basin. Bison, elk, moose, sandhill crane, Canada geese and coyotes are the most common forms of wildlife observed, though an occasional wolf, bear and fox may be sighted.

If all goes well, by 9:30 the geyser predictor will have visited all four major geysers and posted predictions. Upon returning to the visitor center the "GPer" then downloads overnight data recorded on sensing devices into a computer. These devices tell us exactly when geysers such as Grand and Castle erupted during the middle of the night. Yes, we've gotten high-tech at Old Faithful, and this information proves extremely helpful for those geysers that have long intervals and significant variation between eruptions

Of course, Old Faithful is the easiest geyser to predict. Not only does it erupt frequently (about every ninety minutes on average), but we also have a web cam record each eruption, and we can check it on the computer to determine the last eruption.

The formula for predicting old Faithful is pretty simple. It is the only geyser we predict by timing its duration. A short duration of less than 2 ½ minutes may result in an interval of about sixty-five minutes; a duration longer than 2 ½ minutes may produce a ninety-minute interval. Using this technique, we can usually predict Old Faithful's next eruption to within ten minutes about ninety percent of the time.

I once received a call at the visitor center from a lady from California who was planning to visit Yellowstone the following week. "What will be Old Faithful's prediction next Thursday?" she asked. I tried to explain to her that we could only predict Old Faithful one eruption at a time. "I'm sorry," she said, "you must not have understood my question; what is Old Faithful's prediction for next Thursday?" Again, I attempted to explain how we predicted Old Faithful and suggested that she could just give us a call the afternoon of her visit. "So in other words Old Faithful is not predictable or faithful?" she asked.

I decided to try a different approach. I asked her what time she planned to arrive at Old Faithful next Thursday. "About 4:00 p.m.," she answered. "Well, then the prediction for Old Faithful next Thursday afternoon is 4:00 p.m. plus or minus *one hour*," I explained. "Well, what took you so long to answer my simple question?" she asked. "That's all I wanted to know. Thank you!" she added and hung up the phone, very pleased with my answer.

The point is, you never have to wait long to see Old Faithful, so I was able to be a bit creative with the prediction. Its frequency and predictability are two of four reasons why Old Faithful is the world's most famous geyser. The other two are its size (it is one of the world's five tallest geysers), and the fact that it just hasn't changed much over the years, even when large earthquakes have shaken the area.

During the hours that the Old Faithful Visitor Center is open, the interpretive staff records data associated with each eruption of Old Faithful Geyser—the time of eruption, interval, duration and height. There is a large lodgepole pine tree located between the visitor center observation window and the geyser that we use to gauge the height of each eruption. The tree is affectionately known as the "geyser tree." If the water reaches the top of the tree, we know the eruption's height is about 150 feet, well above the average height of around 130 feet. Lodgepole pine trees have a shallow root system and frequently blow over. If this particular tree ever blows over, the staff at Old Faithful will have to invent another handy way to measure the height of each eruption.

Supposedly, Old Faithful was once measured at 184 feet, making it one of the tallest geysers in the world. The tallest eruption that I have ever observed occurred at 3:36 p.m. on July 3, 2000. The eruption was so much higher than the top of the geyser tree we didn't know what to record in the logbook. So we pulled up the photo recorded by the web cam. That didn't help much either, since the photo showed that the top of the eruption extended well out of the frame at the top of the photo. It was at least twenty feet higher than the top of the tree, so we conservatively estimated a height of 170-175 feet! A lot of visitors take Old Faithful for granted, but this magnificent natural marvel is not the most famous geyser in the world for nothing!

Geyser predicting is sort of an art and science. You have some sound data, but there is also some guesswork involved. Just as with predicting the weather, Mother/Father Nature will always have the last say on just how accurate the "Gper" turns out to be. But there is no question in my mind that there is not a more pleasant duty in the world than GP.

Earthquake!

Yellowstone is earthquake country. Over 2000 earthquakes are recorded on seismographs each year, and up to 200 may occur on a single day! Only those earthquakes which register 3.0 or higher on the Richter scale can typically be felt by humans. Yellowstone's volcanic plateau has been compared to a lubricated fault zone. Pressures from plate movement of tectonic plates are being released almost constantly in small, gradual doses. Large releases are not that common, contrasted, for example, to the San Andreas Fault in California, where earthquakes are less frequent but tend to be fairly sizeable when they occur.

In 1959, though, one of the biggest earthquakes ever recorded in the West occurred in Yellowstone on the night of August 17th, at 11:37 p.m. The quake registered 7.5 on the Richter scale, and its epicenter was just outside the west entrance at Hebgen Lake. This quake resulted in significant loss of life and tremendous damage to roads and buildings. Even though I was only twelve years old at the time, I remember it as though it was yesterday. That is because my sister, Alice, was working at Canyon Village that summer. I was sitting in the den the next day with my Mom when the news bulletin flashed across the radio. My Mom and Dad frantically tried in vain for hours to place a call to Yellowstone to find out if Alice was safe.

Given the fact that Yellowstone employs over 2000 people, and on any given day there are tens of thousands of visitors vacationing in the park, there were many more people calling in than circuits could handle. To further complicate matters for my Mom and Dad, Alice was in the backcountry camped out on Mount Washburn the night of the earthquake. She has told me of her experience many times and I share it with visitors when discussing earthquakes in the park.

At the time of the quake Alice was actually curled up in a sleeping bag around a campfire. She said that she was laying on her side, propping up her head with her hand, when suddenly the ground shook, knocking away her hand, and almost rolling her over in the sleeping bag. At first Alice thought that a big bear had rumbled into camp and grabbed hold of her sleeping bag. That helps demonstrate what campers worry about the most when camping out in Yellowstone's backcountry!

A second major tremor hit a few seconds later, and the group knew that a major earthquake had occurred. However, until they returned to Canyon Village the next day, they had no idea just how big this quake had been and how much damage had occurred. Visitors were checking out and leaving the park in fear of more quakes. Most park employees were evacuated and terminated early for the season. Alice told us that before she left, you could feel tremors shaking through the buildings. When Alice finally managed to get through to us, we were so relieved to hear that she was safe.

Bill Lewis worked as a seasonal interpretive ranger and communications specialist in Yellowstone from 1949 to 1989. Bill tells the story of what happened in the Upper Geyser Basin on the night of August 17th, when tremendous changes in the plumbing system of the geysers caused many springs to become geysers. After the first tremors were felt through the basin, Dr. George Marler, the park geologist, knew that remarkable changes were already underway. On the evening of August 17th there was a full moon, and the Upper Geyser Basin at Old Faithful was wonderfully illuminated. Bill later commented that the basin took on the appearance of a huge sponge that was being squeezed, causing water to spurt up all over the place where geysers had never been observed.

Of particular interest in the basin was Economic Geyser, located just down the trail from Grand Geyser. Economic had not erupted for several years, but on the morning following the earthquake, Bill observed scalding water surging up into a large lodgepole pine tree. The boiling water killed all the branches halfway up the tree.

Today, as we approach a half-century since the earthquake, Economic Geyser provides one of the most fascinating interpretive stories to be found anywhere in Yellowstone. Economic Geyser has erupted a few times since the 1959 earthquake, but it has mostly been dormant. For the careful observer there exists a series of clues, that when connected, solves a mystery of nature.

Economic Geyser is one of my favorite places to stop when I am leading interpretive walks in the Upper Geyser Basin. Today, the geyser's pool is colored a dark orange color due to the cyanobacteria that thrives in warm water. However, such bacteria cannot live above 167 degrees F. This provides clear evidence that the geyser is currently dormant (of course, that is always subject to change). A geyser must have superheated water, that is, water heated above the boiling point, about 199 degrees F. at Old Faithful.

Behind the geyser is a very large lodgepole pine tree. Halfway up the tree the branches are all dead. Next to this tree are located about forty smaller trees, each measuring about twenty-five feet in height. As I like to point out to the group, here is a place where you can use your senses of observation to piece together a series of clues that conveys a story.

The first question: Is Economic Geyser active or dormant? The color of the pool clearly reveals that it is dormant. Question number two: What do you notice that is unusual about the large tree behind Economic Geyser? Answer: The branches are all dead halfway up the tree. Question three: What do you suppose killed the branches? Answer: The geyser suddenly had a large eruption. Question four: What do you think caused Economic to suddenly have such a large eruption? Answer: An earthquake. A big earthquake. The earthquake of 1959. Last question: How did the forty smaller trees next to the large tree get there? Answer: The scalding water from the eruption of Economic Geyser in 1959 hit the pinecones, causing them to open, and the seeds to be released.

Such cones are referred to as serotinous pinecones. These are the cones that open during a forest fire and reseed a burned-over area. However, in the case of the tree at Economic Geyser, the serotinous cones were heated not from a forest fire, but from the hot water of an erupting geyser. So the chain of events which began with an earthquake, led to the eruption of a geyser, led to the opening of pine cones and releasing of seeds, and ultimately led to a grove of forty young lodgepole pine trees next to the geyser.

Interestingly enough, the big fires of 1988 swept right past Economic Geyser and up the forested ridge behind it, burning just about every tree on the ridge. Every tree, that is, but the "Economic Geyser Tree." Miraculously, this tree was spared, allowing this fascinating natural mystery to be solved by hundreds of visitors each summer.

For some reason earthquakes are rarely felt in the Old Faithful area. However, this is not true of other areas in the park. We have a seismograph in the Old Faithful Visitor Center, and we often get calls from people in other locations in the park wanting to know if the shake they felt was recorded on our seismograph.

A couple of years ago I received a call from a law enforcement ranger at Madison. He wanted me to check our seismograph to see if we had recorded an earthquake the previous night around midnight. I checked it out, and sure enough, there was a distinct squiggly mark on the paper that indicated a local earthquake had occurred close to midnight. When I called the ranger back to give him the information his response was, "Well, that explains it!" "Explains what?" I asked.

The ranger proceeded to tell me how the previous night he had broken up a dispute between two campers at Madison campground. One man was camped in a truck camper and the other man was camped in a motorhome. The man in the truck had walked over to the motorhome camped next to him, knocked on the door, and complained that someone was sneaking over and shaking his truck. The man in the motorhome vehemently denied it and the two went back to bed. A few minutes later the tables were turned. This time the man in the motorhome walked over and accused the man in the truck of sneaking over and shaking his motorhome!

The two men began having strong words and were near fisticuffs when the campground ranger came by to investigate. Both men were certain that the other had been guilty of playing this prank. The ranger told the two men that they were disturbing other campers and to go to bed and to not come out of their camping vehicles again that evening. Well, as the seismograph revealed, it was Mother/Father Nature who was shaking these men's camping units!

I often felt tremors while working at Canyon, Norris and Mammoth. I was once leading an interpretive walk in the Back Basin at Norris and had taken a stop in the forest before heading down the steps to take a look at

Steamboat Geyser. Suddenly the trees to the west of our group began to shake and rumble as though a wave were rolling through the forest from west to east. When it reached us we were almost knocked off our feet. The best analogy I can use is that it was like we were standing on a very large carpet, and someone picked up the end of the carpet and shook it causing a ripple to pass under our feet!

On June 30th, 1975, I was working inside the Mammoth Visitor Center, now known as the Albright Visitor Center, when suddenly the building began to shake. We had a seismograph in the building so I walked back to it and was amazed to see the needle dancing all over the paper confirming that we were experiencing a major earthquake. It was time to evacuate this old stone building!

This particular earthquake was a fairly major one, in that it recorded 6.1 on the Richter scale. There were visitors standing on the metal observation platform at Inspiration Point overlooking the Grand Canyon of the Yellowstone River when this quake occurred. The terrain underneath the metal steps and deck suddenly rolled away, and the people had to climb back to safety on the reeling set of stairs, now with nothing but space under them! It was a close call but no one was injured. As a result of this rockslide caused by the earthquake, the overlook at Inspiration Point today does not extend as far away from the canyon's edge.

The University of Utah has an earthquake center and closely tracks quakes in the Yellowstone country. Some researchers are attempting to determine if changes in geyser activity might actually predict major earthquakes. Yellowstone always has and will continue to "shake and bake."

Geyser Gazing

What is it about hot, steamy, water gushing a hundred feet out of the ground that causes grown men and women to cry? I don't necessarily mean bawling. But I do mean tears welling up in the eyes. Other emotions evoked include hair standing up on the neck, chills running up and down the spine, wide grins from ear to ear, jumping for joy, uncontrollable laughter, and shouts of elation to name just a few.

The old ranger Jim Lenertz used to ask this very question in his evening interpretive slide program at Old Faithful. "After all," he would point out, "any decent-sized fire department can produce higher, longer, bigger, gushes of water!" Just when Jim had his audience hanging on the ends of their seats waiting for the answer he provided it: "It is unique! It is natural!" Jim made a great point. Geysers are indeed rare natural phenomena. There are only a few hundred known geysers on planet earth, and Yellowstone has at least fifty-five per cent of them. Most of these, some 180, are concentrated in the Upper Geyser Basin, an area that measures only two miles in length, and ½ mile in width.

Of course, not everyone displays the above-mentioned emotions when viewing an erupting geyser. If you don't experience such emotions then you are not a geyser gazer. A general definition of a geyser gazer is someone who spends the majority of their free time while in Yellowstone observing geysers and keeping notes on their ever-changing behavior. I am always amazed at how some people can casually walk by an erupting geyser without so much as stopping to look at it. But that is the nature of visitation in Yellowstone, and all national parks for that matter.

Not all visitors have a deep appreciation for the park's resources. What if all of Yellowstone's three million visitors were geyser gazers? The answer is simple—the resource could not come close to handling the visitation. I suppose the park would have to implement some type of lottery system as to who gets to walk through the Upper Geyser Basin.

That being said, I still find it frustrating when I see visitors not taking the time to slow down and soak in the experience of observing a geyser. I recall one day I was working the desk at Old Faithful Visitor Center, where I was observing and timing an Old Faithful geyser eruption. The geyser was peaking at its full height of over 140 feet when, out of the corner of my eye I noticed a man and a little boy running up, then stopping next to me at the window in the visitor center, which is about 100 yards from the geyser.

The man turned on a video camcorder for a few seconds and then turned to race back toward the parking lot. "Daddy," the little boy (he appeared to be about seven years old) protested, "I want to watch Old Faithful erupt!"

"I've got it on tape," shouted the Dad. "We can watch it when we get home. Come on, we've got to beat the traffic!"

That saddened me. If the Dad didn't care about watching the geyser that was one thing, but to deprive his little boy of viewing in person an eruption of the world's most famous geyser was another. The funny thing is, this man and his son may have driven 2000 miles to get to Yellowstone, only to limit their experience at Old Faithful to viewing a video back home. Why even take the trip? Why not stay home and just order a video on Yellowstone and comfortably "tour" the park without ever leaving the comfort of your den?

When I first worked for the Yellowstone Park Company at Canyon in 1968 and 1969, I didn't know much about geysers. I was enthralled with the backcountry. I particularly enjoyed hiking and backpacking to visit many of the park's waterfalls. However, when I began working as an interpretive ranger in 1974, I was stationed at Norris Geyser Basin. Obviously, our primary duty was to interpret the basin as well as to monitor its features.

For our first few weeks, Margaret and I actually resided in the little apartment inside the rustic museum right in the middle of the basin. It was easy to become very intimate with the basin and its geysers. I became fascinated watching such erupting geysers as Echinus, Ledge, Harding, Bear Den, Porkchop, Vixen, and Constant. It was during this summer that I got to know and became good friends with Park Geologist Rick Hutchinson.

Anyone who ever spent much time around Rick could not help but absorb his incredible enthusiasm for geysers, and since Rick had such a strong interest in the ever-changing features at Norris, I was able to spend a lot of time with him in the field. Also, Bill Lewis, the ranger who was responsible for training, coaching, auditing and evaluating our interpretive programs, was himself a geyser gazer. Bill spent a great deal of time in the basins, and I will always be indebted to him for the wealth of knowledge and passion regarding the geysers that he shared with me. Bill served as a ranger in Yellowstone for twenty-nine seasons, and during the winters he was a Professor of Communications at the University of Vermont. Bill's book, *Interpreting for Park Visitors*, is still considered to be a prime resource for all park interpreters.

There was also another greenhorn, first season interpretive ranger at Norris in 1974—Scott Bryan. Scott was into the geysers the way I was into the park's backcountry, and his considerable knowledge and enthusiasm also heavily influenced me. Scott eventually authored *The Geysers of Yellowstone*, which became the geyser gazers' primary source of information. Looking back at that summer I have to chuckle at the lack of sophistication we had in collecting data on geysers.

For much of the summer Scott and I reveled in the many late afternoon eruptions of Ledge Geyser. Ledge was distinctive in that its powerful eruptions would propel water over 200 feet at a forty-five-degree angle. Its regularity that summer was amazing. We were telling our visitors that its intervals were running twenty-four to twenty-six hours. So when it erupted early one morning, we became confused. Had its interval dramatically changed? Then it dawned on us. Perhaps the interval was more like twelve to thirteen hours, and we were just missing the middle of the night eruptions! We set up a little pile of sticks in the runoff channel to test our hypothesis, and presto, they were washed away the next morning. The interval was actually half what we thought it had been. Needless to say we were rather red-faced over that one. Today's sophisticated geyser gazers would never make such an error.

Rick Hutchinson, Bill Lewis and Scott Bryan were truly hard-core geyser gazers. But back in 1974, there weren't that many. The largest geyser in the world, Steamboat, is located at Norris. When Steamboat erupts, the height of the water phase is "almost beyond belief" as Scott says in his book, with water gushing close to 400 feet high! I really didn't have much hope for seeing an eruption in 1974, since its last major eruption had occurred in 1969. However, each time I walked by I would stop for several minutes and just imagine what it would be like to witness a close-up view of a major eruption.

Bill Lewis had studied Steamboat for years and had been fortunate enough to actually witness twelve eruptions firsthand! I feel certain that Bill has seen Steamboat more than any other person. Scott and I grilled him for any clues, any indicators, any predictors. But Bill said he had been unable to come up with any.

Today's geyser gazers are constantly observing geysers to uncover such indicators and when they do the information is invaluable. While there are some very nice high-tech gadgets that pick up overnight eruptions—and this is indeed very helpful--there is just no substitute for a set of human eyes watching and studying all of the intricacies that a geyser displays leading up to an eruption.

When I was transferred to Old Faithful in 1976, it was not because I was a geyser gazer. Rather, it was to help lead the two-day overnight interpretive backpack trips, and also to help provide some expertise in the backcountry permit office, then located in the Old Faithful Visitor Center. However, I immediately fell in love with the Upper Geyser Basin. Actually, prior to 1972, I had a rather negative view of the Old Faithful area. Each time I would visit I was turned off by the gridlock of traffic through the basin. The main road went right through the basin, passing directly by Morning Glory Pool, and Riverside, Grotto, Castle, and Old Faithful Geysers.

When Old Faithful would erupt, or for that matter any of the other geysers in view, the traffic would stop and become grid-locked. Somehow, walking around the geysers amidst the constant noise and fumes of the traffic did not appeal to me. Norris was just the opposite. There was no road through the basin. You had to park your vehicle and walk into the basin.

When I arrived at Old Faithful in 1976 I found an entirely different experience. The NPS had taken the road out of the basin at the end of the 1972 season, converting access to walking trails. The new road completely bypassed the basin. While the walk into Old Faithful Geyser was short, only a few hundred yards, you now had to walk one to three miles (roundtrip) to see any of the other major geysers in the basin. This road reroute was one of the best things the NPS has ever done in the park. It restored a quality visitor experience to the most unique collection of geysers in the world and, more importantly, significantly reduced damage to the thermal features. On the old road when the traffic would stop, many visitors would get out of their cars and "play basketball" with the hot springs and geysers, throwing rocks, coins and other objects into them. These rocks would settle down into the features' vents and mineralize, thus restricting the flow of hot water feeding them.   Unfortunately, vandalism still occurs today, but is not as severe as when the road was present.

The Upper Geyser Basin is a complex collection of hot springs and geysers. My mentors in 1976 were Rick Hutchinson, Sam Holbrook, Bill Lewis and Jim Lenertz. Also, Scott Bryan had transferred to Old Faithful and was obviously a valuable resource. Yet still, there were only a handful of geyser gazers. Two wonderful, retired, elderly gentlemen began to change that. Herb Warren and John Railey would spend most of the summer months observing geysers and collecting valuable data for our geyser logbooks. Our ranger staff, as well as the staff at the Old Faithful Inn, who placed engraved nameplates on their rooms, loved these two.

Soon others began to join Herb and John and the geyser gazers began to number in the dozens. One gazer, John Weigel, watched 500 consecutive eruptions of Riverside Geyser, no small feat, since it erupts every five to seven hours. Needless to say, our staff referred to him as "Mr. Riverside."

Today's geyser gazers invest untold numbers of hours observing and collecting data on the geysers. The data they provide to the NPS are invaluable. Most of the gazers are members of GOSA, the Geyser Observation Study Association, founded in 1983 to further the study and understanding of geysers.

Visitors often ask me to name my favorite geyser. I always tell them that this is a tough question, because each geyser is different and has its own personality. If you hear someone say, "If you have seen one geyser you have seen them all," tell that person that he or she is mistaken. First of all, there are two types of geysers: the cone type and the fountain type. A cone geyser has a constriction in the plumbing system at the surface so, the geyser erupts like water coming out of a giant hose nozzle. Old Faithful is a good example of a cone geyser.

A fountain geyser, on the other, hand has its constriction below a pool of water, resulting in a series of surges, splashes and bursts of water. Great Fountain and Grand are two good examples of these geysers. I would say that the geysers that give me the most chills, goose bumps, and yes, even cause a tear or two to well up are (in alphabetical order): Beehive, Castle, Fan and Mortar, Grand, Great Fountain, and Old Faithful. Daisy and Riverside are great too. One thing is for sure, geyser gazing can become addictive. You will know when you are hooked. When you experience that second burst of Grand, a super burst at Great Fountain, the jet-like roar of Beehive gushing out of its eight-inch-diameter vent, a vociferous steam phase of Castle, a soaking from the spray at Fan and Mortar, or an early morning or late evening eruption of Old Faithful, chances are you will feel the goose bumps go up. And, you *will* be back.

The Day a Giant Awakened

Although it is said that Yellowstone may have some 600 geysers—at least fifty-five per cent of the world's total—there may be long periods of dormancy for some of the big ones. Such was the case during the decades of the 1960s and most of the 1970s with Giant Geyser, one of Yellowstone's largest and premier geysers. Reaching heights of over 200 feet and lasting over an hour, Giant would expel over one million gallons of water before spellbound visitors.

When I transferred to Old Faithful in 1976 I held out little hope for seeing Giant erupt. I placed the colossal geyser in the same category as Steamboat Geyser up at Norris, another huge geyser that is usually inactive. I worked there all summer without seeing it, and I figured that there was no way I was going to see Giant perform. After all, it had only erupted once since 1955! However, even when dormant, Giant was still an imposing sight. You could not help but be impressed by the massive cone that had built up over thousands of years, and had partially collapsed inward. The size of the cone provided irrefutable evidence that Giant was active for long periods of time, because the mineral the cone is made of builds up at the rate of only about one inch per fifty to one hundred years! The mineral is mostly silicon dioxide, or siliceous sinter, also known as geyserite. It is basically the same mineral you find in sand or glass. So a lot of splashing water had to occur over a long period of time to build such a large cone.

Another thing that always impressed me about Giant was the fact that the cauldron of water inside the cone was always boiling at a furious rate. Given that the water temperature at the surface was superheated, or above boiling, it was obvious that the only ingredient Giant was lacking in order to erupt was a constriction in the plumbing system. Perhaps the last eruption of Giant back in 1963 had blown out the constriction, or maybe one of the frequent earthquakes in the Yellowstone region had widened the constriction below. It was anyone's guess.

Nevertheless, each week when I was out in the basin on geyser prediction duty, I would walk past Giant on my way down to post the prediction sign at Grand or Riverside. I would usually walk over to the impressive feature and stop and just look at the big cone and listen to its rumble. I would often fantasize over what it would be like to see this geyser take off while I was standing right there in front of it with no one else around. I knew that in the unlikely event this ever happened, the first person I would call on my portable radio would be Rick Hutchinson, the Park Geologist. Given his enthusiasm for geysers Rick would probably "fly" over to the basin from his quarters about a mile away.

Caroline and Rick Hutchinson at Giant Geyser in 1978

So it was with great skepticism one summer day in 1978 while on duty at the front desk of the Old Faithful Visitor Center, that I responded to a visitor who told me that he had just observed an eruption of Giant Geyser. It is not unusual for visitors to get turned around a bit in the Upper Geyser Basin and mistake the names of the geysers. "You mean *Grand* Geyser don't you?" I asked. "No, I mean Giant!" he insisted. "I'll bet you saw Grotto Geyser which is close to Giant," I proposed.

By now the visitor was obviously becoming annoyed with me. "Well, the sign said *Giant!*" the man stated emphatically. Several other rangers overhearing the conversation were obviously convinced, and the rush was on. Unfortunately, by the time I arrived, Giant had just concluded erupting. But there was no mistaking the fact that it had indeed erupted for the first time in well over a decade.

The gushing hot water had flowed out in all directions leaving behind some trenches in the soil that had built up since the last eruption. Of course, Rick was on the scene soon after we arrived, and he was investigating each and every piece of evidence that the geyser had produced. I found the aftermath of the eruption rather fascinating. For one thing, I was amazed by how much debris was thrown out of the geyser during the eruption. There were large stones, old signs, logs and sticks scattered about. The only way this debris could have gotten in the geyser to begin with was to be thrown in.

Throwing rocks, coins, sticks or any foreign object into a thermal feature is strictly prohibited. This type of vandalism can destroy a hot spring or geyser, because the foreign matter becomes mineralized and clogs up the vent. Fortunately, in the case of Giant, the rubbish never became cemented down in the vent, because the geyser was in a state of constant boil. So to me it really was like a giant deciding it was time to wake up and clear his throat! Margaret brought little Caroline over and showed her the many large rocks which had been expelled during Giant's eruption.

After Giant played in 1978, its eruptions began to occur more frequently, and Margaret and I finally were fortunate enough to see a full eruption in August of 1991. Having now seen it several times I can fully agree with Scott Bryan's description of Giant in his book, *The Geysers of Yellowstone*, "When in eruption there is nothing quite like it. A huge tower of water is thrown far into the air. To see Giant play is, and will probably remain, one of the rarest geyser-gazing treats."

Rick Hutchinson measuring temperature
at Steamboat Geyser August 23, 1978

Memories of Rick Hutchinson

Yellowstone is considered to be a paradise for anyone interested in geology. Each summer professors of geology bring their students from all over the world to study the wonders of Yellowstone's fire and ice geologic stories. For twenty-five years, Yellowstone National Park had the good fortune of being served by a man whose legendary status will only grow over time. Rick Hutchinson began working in Yellowstone in 1970 as a Park Naturalist. Later, he became the park's Geothermal Specialist, and eventually the Park Geologist. I had the privilege of knowing Rick over those years, and I never met another person who was more passionate about the resources of Yellowstone.

Rick was a tough, wiry, little guy who wore a shaggy beard that could never hide his constant, toothy grin. Rick always seemed to be happy and I think that was because he was living and working in a place that he absolutely loved. There was no such thing as a day off or a holiday for Rick as long as he was inside Yellowstone National Park. When other employees would sometimes talk about plans for retirement, Rick would counter by asking, "Retire? Retire? Why would anyone working here ever want to retire?"

Rick possessed several unique characteristics that caused him to be so special to his fellow employees, to visitors and to his professional colleagues. Everyone seemed to love Rick because he dearly loved his fellow human beings. He always thoroughly enjoyed revealing the mysteries of Yellowstone's geology to anyone who would listen to him. Even though his job was predominately monitoring and researching geologic features, Rick would frequently come over to the busy Old Faithful Visitor Center to assist our interpretive staff.

As Yellowstone's Park Geologist, Rick became somewhat of a celebrity. He was frequently interviewed for television documentaries, books and magazine articles. However, Rick never let his "fame" go to his head. His outgoing and friendly nature endeared him to his many friends

Rick's sense of humor was renowned, and he had unusual ways of achieving his objectives. For example, in 1978 my family and I pulled into the Old Faithful housing area on a cold May night to begin another summer season. We lived in a trailer next door to Rick, but on this night we found that our trailer was still occupied by a member of the winter staff. I walked over and knocked on Rick's door and told him of our problem and he quickly invited us in.

I was not prepared for what I saw in his living room. Rick had been eating cans of soup all winter long, and had built a great pyramid with the

183

empty cans that covered most of his living room floor, extending all the way to the ceiling. "Rick," Margaret exclaimed, "What in the world is this?" "It's my seismograph," Rick proudly proclaimed with a wide grin. Given the frequency of earthquakes in Yellowstone, what a brilliant method to detect them. A bit unorthodox, but very efficient!

Rick would constantly catch you off guard with his remarkable sense of humor. I remember one summer I was attending a potluck and we were sitting around a campfire. I heard Rick saying out loud to himself, "3011, 3012, 3013." I asked Rick what he was counting. "I'm counting every mosquito whose life comes to an end on my body this summer," he replied.

One moment that will always stand out regarding Rick's unique sense of humor involved a lengthy search and rescue mission that he was involved in. Rick was always quick to volunteer in such events and was also a member of the Old Faithful fire brigade. A young fellow by the name of Chuck had disappeared into the vast wilderness of the Mirror Plateau while on a hiking and fishing trip. Days went by and concern grew over the hiker's mysterious disappearance.

Rangers and volunteers had spread out over a large area but had come up with absolutely no clues as to his whereabouts. Hikers becoming lost in Yellowstone are not that rare, but even though the park is big, the vegetation is typically not dense enough to prevent a healthy person from finding his/her way out. Basically, all you have to do is follow water. One small stream leads to another bigger stream, and eventually you will run into a trail or road. However, something had obviously gone terribly wrong with Chuck.

Chuck had made the mistake of wandering down into some of the most rugged and inaccessible canyons to be found anywhere in the park. He was in the vicinity of the confluence of Broad and Shallow Creeks on the Mirror Plateau. Here the canyon walls are sheer and rise over 1000 feet, so it is not feasible to follow a stream out of the wilderness.

Somehow Rick had managed to climb down into the inhospitable terrain to see if Chuck was there. Not only is this area all but impassable, but it also contains some unusual geologic features. So when Rick came around a bend in the stream down in the bottom of the canyon, and to his delight saw Chuck sitting on a rock appearing very exhausted, dazed and confused, what do you suppose Rick had to say? According to other members of the rescue party Rick walked up *behind* the lost hiker and said, "Hello Chuck. Did you know that you are sitting in one of the most unique geologic areas in all of Yellowstone?" I'm not sure that Chuck shared Rick's enthusiasm for the area's geology at that precise moment, but I don't know of any other story that better exemplified Rick's undying passion for Yellowstone's resources than this one!

Rick's incredible fervor for the geysers was not only unmatched but also quite contagious. The largest geyser in the world, Steamboat, is located at Norris Geyser Basin some thirty miles from Old Faithful. Steamboat is completely unpredictable, and eruption intervals may range anywhere from a few days to fifty years! During the summer of 1978, no one was expecting much from the colossal geyser. Its last eruption had occurred over nine years earlier in March of 1969. But on the morning of August 23, 1978 at around 8:30 a.m., Rick's radio beamed out the news: Steamboat was erupting! Margaret and our daughter Caroline had just finished breakfast when Rick came to the door shouting, "Margaret, Caroline, get in my truck, Steamboat is erupting, Steamboat is erupting!"

Caroline was only four years old but she knew something special was happening. Rick radioed me but I was on the desk at the Old Faithful Visitor Center and could not leave. "Show Margaret and Caroline a good time," I said with envy.

Margaret and Caroline piled into Rick's old pickup truck and with caution lights flashing, sped off to Norris Geyser Basin. Margaret said that when they arrived in the Norris parking lot, the ground was rumbling, and the roar was deafening. Steamboat's water phase, which can last anywhere from three to twenty minutes, had ended, but the powerful steam phase was playing in all its glory. According to Margaret, she felt like she was standing behind a 747 jet taking off, and it was impossible to carry on a conversation.

They ran down the boardwalk to the geyser and were amazed to find large rocks that had been expelled during the eruption. Then, to Margaret's shock, Rick left the boardwalk and headed straight out to the vent with thermometer in hand. He was determined to get some temperature readings at the vent during the peak of the steam phase. Margaret was busy photographing Rick as he pranced around the vent during Steamboat's performance. The combination of experiencing Steamboat's mighty steam phase, and being with one of the world's foremost geyser enthusiasts produced an unforgettable memory for both Margaret and Caroline.

The fact that Rick was able to share Steamboat with little Caroline made it all the better, for he absolutely loved kids. Whenever Rick would see kids waiting for the eruption of a geyser, he would go over to them and explain just how a geyser worked. I saw him do this on many occasions at Great Fountain Geyser, which always appeared to me to be one of Rick's favorites.

Great Fountain typically overflows for about an hour before it erupts. While waiting for the eruption to build, Rick would round up the kids, and then he would reach down and scoop up some water in the palms of his hands. Somehow he would squeeze his palms together and cause a thin stream of water to squirt up over two feet out of his hands. How he was able to accomplish that, I'll never know, but the kids loved it.

Rick had an incredible knowledge of the park's geysers and hot springs, but what truly impressed me was his unparalleled zeal for exploring thermal basins in the backcountry. There are thermal features scattered all over Yellowstone's vast wilderness, and Rick seemed determined to find, document and monitor each one. He was especially interested in thermal features near the park boundary, because he wanted to be prepared to monitor any changes in activity if, heaven forbid, geothermal drilling ever occurred outside the park.

One of the most unusual projects Rick ever embarked on was the creation of an asbestos "hot boat." He used it to sail out on some of Yellowstone's thermal springs to explore their mysterious depths. The little square boat appeared to be quite stable, and had an open "window" in the middle of the floor for observing and retrieving objects out of the pool. The boat was named the "Little Dipper," and was used primarily on Morning Glory Pool to retrieve objects wedged in the vent that vandals had thrown in over the years, and on Grand Prismatic Pool to uncover secrets in this, the largest of Yellowstone's pools.

Grand Prismatic Spring measures 250 feet by 380 feet. For years Rick had wanted to determine the depth of this spring, and with his hot boat the opportunity was at hand. Watching Rick paddle the little boat out amidst the rising steam of the pool was an eerie sight. In the center of the pool the temperature was over 170 degrees Fahrenheit, so there was no need to carry along a life jacket in case you fell out! Rick was able to determine that the pool was indeed the deepest in the park when he measured the depth at the vent to be over 125 feet.

Rick also discovered skeletons of bison along the bottom. From the middle of the pool he told me that you could see the spectacular "dragon's teeth" formations along the walls of the pool, similar to huge stalagmites in a cave. He also said that the ultramarine blue color was the most intense he had ever seen. He asked me on more than one occasion to accompany him when he was out on the pool, but I just could not reconcile the risk of paddling a boat in 170 degree water. One winter a snowplow ran over the Little Dipper buried under the snow and destroyed it. The boat was never replaced.

Even though Rick usually traveled the backcountry alone, I had the privilege of taking several extended trips with him, two of which stand out as being especially memorable. I had been to two different regions in the park's backcountry that Rick had not visited, and I was anxious for Rick to see them. One was a remote thermal basin in Hayden Valley, and the other was the backbone of the rugged Absaroka Mountains along the park's east boundary. Rick knew that I always attempted to take a lengthy backpacking trip on my last weekend before I had to leave the park and head back to my winter teaching job. Therefore, he would go out of his way to accommodate my requests to accompany me on these trips.

We had planned for an early departure on the Hayden Valley trip, since it was about eleven miles in to the Mary Mountain patrol cabin. However, when Rick showed up at my doorstep, he looked like death warmed over. His face was pale and he looked haggard and tired. Margaret was particularly concerned by his appearance and inquired to know what was wrong. Rick said that he must have eaten something that disagreed with him, because he had been up with diarrhea most of the night.

I immediately stepped in and told him to just forget the trip and go home and get some rest. Rick would not hear of it. "I know how much these trips on your last lieu days of the summer mean to you, Butch, and I intend to go with you," he said. "But Rick," Margaret chimed in, "What are you going to do if you have diarrhea out there on the trail?" "I'll just eat some buffalo hair," he quickly answered in a typical vintage Rick comment.

Our hike across Hayden Valley could not have been more beautiful. The weather was almost perfect though it was a bit warm. Rick, however, was miserable. Every time we would stop to take a break, he would just slink down on the ground and close his eyes. We arrived at the patrol cabin at about 4:00 p.m. Rick went straight into the cabin, crawled into a sleeping bag, and was not heard from again until the next morning. I asked Rick if he felt like eating anything for supper and I only heard a soft grunt from the curled up hump in the bag that I interpreted to mean "no."

I felt sorry for Rick because I knew that he had unselfishly come on this long hike only for my benefit. I was hopeful that he would feel better the next day, when I hoped to show him the thermal area that Jim Lenertz, Tom Caples, Tom Gerrity and I had come upon during the mid 1970s.

That evening I sat on a log near the edge of Mary Lake and soaked in the total feeling of solitude. A thunderstorm rolled over the lake with loud rumbles of thunder, but the rain skirted around us. A big buck mule deer waded out into the lake, took a sip of water, raised its stately head, and looked over its domain, seemingly oblivious to my presence. I tried to stay out of the cabin until it was time to retire for the evening in order to allow Rick to get some rest.

The next morning Rick was his old self, eating a good breakfast and expressing his eager desire to see the thermal area. He apologized for being such a "poor companion" the previous evening, but I assured him that I certainly understood. Besides, we would make up for it on this day.

When we entered the thermal area Rick was in his paradise, and the setting was truly magical. The morning was quite cool and a fog hung low over the basin. A few hundred yards away was a large herd of bison, grazing in the lush, green grasses of Hayden Valley. Beyond them in the distance, the big peaks of the Washburn Range cut a sharp edge on the horizon, and helped frame the entire scene. A small stream had obviously cut a narrow canyon through this little thermal valley, and as we carefully walked through it, we were amazed by what we found.

A portion of the canyon was undercut and took on the appearance of a cave. Inside the cave were buffalo carcasses piled one on top of another. The carcasses were large with the impressive skulls intact. We counted *seven* of them. Given the fact that we were over nine miles from the nearest road as the crow flies, I was amazed at this unusual sight. "Rick," I almost whispered, "What in the world could have piled these buffalo up?" I asked. "A big grizzly," was Rick's reply.

We shook our heads in awe as we imagined a huge grizzly pulling each bison carcass into the cave and into a pile. We surmised that this must have been one really big, hungry, greedy grizzly bear that would have gone to this much trouble to protect his cache of food.

My other memorable trip with Rick was along the Absaroka Ridge the next summer. It was a trip that I not so fondly came to refer to as "Rick's Revenge." During September of 1975, Al Duff and I had taken an extensive trip along this ridge, and I had recalled some fascinating deposits of andesite and basalt with unique patterns that I knew Rick would like to see. Rick and I met early in the morning, positioned one vehicle near Sylvan Pass and drove outside the East Entrance to begin our hike on the Eagle Creek trail.

We backpacked about twelve miles before leaving the trail and beginning our long, 3000-foot climb up to the top of the Absaroka ridge. On this day, my body simply ran out of fuel about halfway up the ridge, but there were no level areas in which to pitch a tent. We had no choice but to push on.

We considered a stop to cook dinner but hated to not take advantage of the waning daylight. So we decided to push on with the hope of finding a level spot and then prepare dinner. This turned out to be a big mistake for me. Rick, on the other hand, seemed to be floating on a cloud. I could barely keep up with him.

Just before dark we found a spot just big enough to pitch a tent. By now though, I was in the same shape that Rick had been in on the Hayden Valley trip the previous summer. This time it was I who crawled into a sleeping bag while Rick cooked up dinner. The next day, we managed to complete our climb to the top of the ridge, and reach the park boundary. "There's your pond," Rick quipped, referring to the Southeast Arm of Yellowstone Lake, knowing my fondness for it.

We hiked over the summits of Atkins Peak and Plenty Coups Peak at elevations close to 11,000 feet. It felt as though we were literally walking on top of the world. On this clear day the views in all directions were fabulous. As late afternoon approached, we found a relatively level patch of terrain in a saddle north of Plenty Coups Peak suitable for pitching our tent for the night. At this high elevation we were in an alpine setting with only a few scrub trees around.

After pitching our tent we took a short stroll and were shocked to see what appeared to be a very large site that had been rototilled in preparation for planting a garden. Grizzlies! We felt the disturbed soil, and noticed that it was soft and damp, indicating the grizzly diggings had been done in the last few hours. During late summer grizzlies are often seen digging in the high country, turning over rocks looking for insects and grubs. They particularly like to eat Army cutworm moths, which are very rich in nutrients. The last thing you ever want to do is to camp near fresh grizzly sign.

Rick and I looked at each other and realized that with darkness settling in, there was absolutely nothing we could do about our predicament. That didn't stop me from asking though, "Rick, what are we going to do?" "Well, I'm just going to crawl in my sleeping bag, ask the Lord to protect us tonight, and go to sleep," he replied. That sounded like the best plan to me as well, and it worked. Both of us slept like babies all night, when we should have been on pins and needles!

The next day we continued our hike along the high ridge and park boundary, eventually turning northwest, and hiking over Top Notch Peak, before finishing our trip near Sylvan Pass. I had looked forward to making a physical trip all summer, but this one had just about gotten the best of me. Rick had demonstrated to me his physical prowess. His strength and stamina on this trip were amazing.

Rick reminded me of those early explorers of Yellowstone, the way he would go out for days at a time by himself and traverse large tracts of wilderness, usually off-trail, as he investigated remote thermal areas. And Rick did this year round. He was particularly adept on skis. Given his small size, he could stay on top of the snow, even in less than favorable conditions. Rick did not always show a great deal of concern for his safety while exploring the backcountry. He traveled the wilderness like a trapper, refusing to make any artificial noises to alert bears. He was in tune with his surroundings, and he wanted to soak it all in.

Rick thoroughly explored remote thermal basins. Such places can be extremely dangerous due to the potential for breaking through the thin crust into scalding water. However, I was never really concerned for Rick's safety in such areas. He seemed to possess an uncanny knack for choosing safe routes through such areas, plus I don't think he weighed more than 140 pounds.

On the other hand, I was always concerned that Rick would one day have a bad encounter with a grizzly. Hiking quietly and alone increased the odds of that happening. Rick saw lots of bears on his travels, but he never told me of a close encounter with one.

I never dreamed that Rick would run into trouble in the snow, because he truly loved the winter and was an expert cross-country skier. But it was a weird set of circumstances, perhaps involving recent forest fires on the slopes of the Red Mountains, that contributed to the avalanche that killed Rick and a volunteer while on a ski trip to the Heart Lake thermal basin in March of 1997.

Rick died in a land that he cherished, performing a duty that he loved. As a friend, I felt cheated that Rick was taken away from Yellowstone just shy of the age of fifty. Yellowstone lost a treasured, irreplaceable resource. However, deep in my heart I know that Rick lived more in his fifty years than most of us could hope to live in 150. I'm sorry to say that I took Rick for granted. To me Yellowstone and Rick were synonymous. I will always treasure the memories of our many travels and experiences together.

The Totem Forest

Frankly, I was not going to include anything about the Totem Forest in this book. But then *Backpacker* magazine ran a "The Secret's Out" feature article about this thermal basin in its April, 2004 issue, so I decided to add my two cents worth. Former Park Geologist Rick Hutchinson apparently was the first person to document this remote basin on the Mirror Plateau in 1976. Some park officials had observed some unusual thermal formations from an airplane, and had passed this information along to Rick. When Rick succeeded in reaching this area on the ground, he documented a place with dozens of extinct thermal cones, similar to the cones in Monument Geyser Basin near Norris.

When Rick published information about it from a scientific standpoint, he referred to the small basin (about the size of a football field) as "The Totem Forest." The basin is extremely difficult to reach. There is no trail that goes anywhere near the place, so most of the travel is off-trail using map and compass and probably a GPS.

Rick once told me about visiting this area by himself in mid-November, when the temperature dipped to minus twenty-two degrees. But Rick really did not attempt to publicize or promote the Totem Forest, probably because he recognized that the area was very difficult to reach, terribly dangerous to traverse, and the old thermal cones were extremely fragile.

However, during the late nineties, following Rick's tragic death in the avalanche near Heart Lake, there occurred an increase in publicity about the place. First, a description of the area was written up by the few who succeeded in reaching the area and publicized mainly to Yellowstone aficionados who are members of GOSA (the Geyser Observation and Study Association). However, a report on this basin, complete with photos, soon appeared on the Internet, and the news was most definitely out. The web report struck a chord in many Yellowstone hikers and backpackers, as the area was described as having been visited by only 500 people, fewer than the number who had scaled Mount Everest, the world's tallest mountain!

Having covered most of Yellowstone's backcountry, I decided to give it a try. John and Deb Dirksen, William McMillan and I tried to locate the Totem Forest by traveling cross-country from Ribbon Lake along the south rim of the Grand Canyon of the Yellowstone. This attempt was a complete failure, as we came nowhere close to the basin. Before our second attempt, I interviewed friend and Yellowstone Park Historian Lee Whittlesey, whom I knew had visited the basin. Lee provided us with invaluable tips on how to successfully negotiate a route into it.

So during a cross-country trip of the Mirror Plateau with my daughter Alison, John and Deb, Alan Martin and Hank Barnett, we successfully completed a side trip to the basin. Having been there I will never go back, and I would never recommend that anyone visit the place.

There are several reasons why I have this opinion. First, if you are really interested in thermal features, this place comes up fairly empty. There are very few active thermal features here; most of the few dozen thermal cones are completely dormant and dry. Anyone interested in visiting a backcountry thermal basin in Yellowstone would find a far more interesting and beautiful collection of features at either Heart Lake Geyser Basin or Shoshone Lake Geyser Basin. Both of these basins (easily accessible by trail) are located deep in the park's backcountry, and are replete with an abundance and variety of active thermal features. Before embarking on our journey, my friend Mike Keller, Old Faithful Inn Manager and a very knowledgeable thermal enthusiast, ridiculed me for taking the trip. "Why do you want to go to all that trouble just to see a bunch of old cones?" he asked. "You can see traffic cones in most of the parking lots around here!"

Second, the hike to the Totem Forest is one of the most dangerous backcountry trips anyone can make in the park. Our group found this out the hard way. At the time of our trip the closest backcountry campsite was at Josephs Coat Hot Spring Basin. There is no trail even to this basin, and the thin-crusted terrain here makes it extremely dangerous.

On the day of our trip we ran into a party of eight backpackers at the campsite near Josephs Coat Basin. The group was from Cleveland, Ohio, and consisted of two older adult men and six teenagers. I asked the leader of the group how they had heard about this place. "We read about it on the web," the leader replied. I naturally assumed that the men were very experienced in exploring Yellowstone's vast wilderness, and asked them about some of the other areas in the park they had visited. "This is our first ever visit to Yellowstone," came the unbelievable reply! "You mean you have never hiked into Shoshone Lake or Heart Lake Geyser Basin?" I asked, thinking out loud that both of these thermal basins represent must-see areas for any serious Yellowstone backpacker. "No," the leader replied. "Then why in the world are you attempting to hike into *this* place?" I asked. "Because only 500 people have ever been there, and we want to make it 508!" the man replied. Obviously, this man had also come across the infamous website!

Our own party of six took a snack break as we watched the group disappear into the dense forest. Soon we were ready to venture out as well, but first we had to ford Broad Creek. During our snack break most of our group had proceeded to take off our boots and don sandals for the upcoming ford. For some reason John kept his boots on.

As we walked along the creek looking for a good place to ford, I noted the thermal features on the hill above us, but the terrain along the creek where we were walking was rather grassy and muddy. The area appeared rather innocuous, as there was no evidence of steam or thermal activity along the bank. John was walking in the lead followed by Alison and me. Suddenly I heard a loud "arghh" from ahead. John was on the ground writhing in pain. His right foot had broken through the muddy surface and found extremely hot mud.

Instinctively, John rolled into the creek, placing his leg into the cold water. He then took off his boot and socks to find an ugly-looking burn, about the size of a golf ball, below his calf. The skin was already beginning to peel which indicated at least a second-degree burn. Hank, a certified EMT, stepped in with his first aid kit, and immediately sized up John's injury. "This does not look good," he said. He applied a medicinal ointment to the wound and then wrapped his leg with gauze.

When John tried to put his boot back on he found that the upper part of his boot came into direct contact with the wound. There was no way that he could wear his boots. So he put on some thick wool socks, sturdy sandals, used his axe to cut a stout hiking staff, and pronounced himself fit and ready to hike. Hank was not amused. "John, you really need to get out of here and have that seen by a doctor." John would not hear of it. "I'm finishing this trip," he insisted. And he did.

In retrospect, Hank was right. Although John did amazingly well in his sandals with his hiking staff, his doctor would later tell him that the wound should have been professionally cleaned and treated sooner than it was. It took almost a full year for the golf-ball sized burn to completely heal.

John's accident was bad enough, but I could not help but think about what would have happened if either Alison or I had broken through into the scalding mud while wearing sandals. If this had occurred, we would have most likely been looking at a crippling injury, since the foot—with thin skin over bones—is one of the worst areas to recover from a burn. Fortunately, John's high top leather boots had protected his foot.

About an hour after our ford of Broad Creek, we encountered the party of eight from Cleveland struggling to find their way back to Josephs Coat Basin. They had become disoriented in the dense forest. We showed them the small drainage that we had followed to this point, and told them that it should lead them back to the basin. We also gave them a full account of John's accident, and warned them to proceed with extra caution through the area.

When we reached the spot where Broad and Shallow Creeks unite, we found a horrendous 800-foot steep descent into the tri-canyon where the basin is located. The trip down would have been extremely treacherous, if not impossible, had John not brought along plenty of climbing rope. The canyon walls here consist of the typical loose, crumbly volcanic rock found throughout the Yellowstone plateau.

After our trip each member of our group agreed that the hike was the toughest we had ever taken in Yellowstone, and that we would not go back.

The "risk-reward ratio" was certainly not favorable. One might as well attempt to backpack through the Grand Canyon of the Yellowstone!

I was sorry that the area had been publicized on the Internet, because I knew that more groups such as the one from Cleveland that we had encountered, would most likely try to find this place. I shuddered to think how difficult it would be for a NPS Search and Rescue team to respond to an emergency in this area.

The Internet publicity was bad enough, but I was absolutely shocked when a friend told me that *Backpacker* magazine had published a feature article on how to reach the basin! At first I thought my friend was kidding. After all, I had enjoyed reading *Backpacker* over the years, and had even written several feature articles for them covering such topics as ski-touring in Yellowstone, how to hike and camp in grizzly country, and an "Elders of the Tribe" piece on Bob Marshall. Over the years *Backpacker* had been a reliable source of information for backpackers. Surely, a reputable magazine such as this would not encourage anyone to visit a place this dangerous and fragile!

But when friend Kathy Russell, who works with the Yellowstone Association, brought me a copy of the April 2004 issue, I could not believe my eyes. There it was in full color: "Secret Hikes in Yellowstone National Park," and it included a story on Yellowstone's "Fairyland Basin." Even though Rick Hutchinson was apparently the first person to document this basin, calling it the Totem Forest, subsequent visitors to the area had used the more romantic term "Fairyland".

Publicizing a dangerous and fragile place in a magazine is bad enough, but the article actually provided detailed information on how to get there! It is one thing to provide instructions on how to use a map, compass and GPS. However, it is altogether a different matter to persuade someone to travel *off trail* to dangerous locations that contain extremely fragile resources.

The article was certainly accurate in its descriptions of areas along the way, such as a canyon filled with "steaming fumaroles" and "sizzling hot springs." The problem is, there are no maintained trails that lead through this extremely dangerous region. Given the fact that over twenty people have died in Yellowstone due to thermal injuries, I found it unfathomable that a magazine would entice readers to go there.

As far as I am concerned the Totem Forest is overrated. Yellowstone has over 1000 miles of trails that traverse its vast and diverse backcountry. There are beautiful thermal basins, which can be visited with a reasonable degree of safety. The Totem Forest is not one of them. During the summer of 2002 a substantial fire, called the Broad Fire, completely burned the forests all around the Totem Forest basin. Perhaps this was nature's way to convince us to stay away from this dangerous and difficult to reach place!

Part V

To Leave Them Unimpaired

The Work of a Yellowstone Ranger

To most Yellowstone visitors, a ranger is a ranger. Anyone wearing the green and gray uniform with a flat hat meets the criteria of "ranger." Many folks use the term "forest rangers," but that identifies a ranger with the U.S. Forest Service. The term "park ranger" properly identifies a ranger with the National Park Service. However, most visitors probably don't realize that rangers work in different divisions. There are basically three kinds of seasonal rangers in Yellowstone: those that are commissioned law enforcement officers whose duties consist primarily of enforcing park regulations; interpretive rangers who give walks, evening programs, rove and staff the visitor centers; and those who work in resource management.

The distinction between rangers in law enforcement and interpretation is not as subtle as it used to be. The heavy belt with gun and other defensive gear should make the distinction easy to recognize. Also, the law enforcement badges are now larger. Although some duties overlap, there is a dramatic difference in primary responsibilities. When I began my career in 1974 as a seasonal park ranger in Yellowstone, the duties overlapped more than they do today.

Seasonal ranger Ted Weight provided my first law enforcement orientation at NPS training. Ted issued us "ticket books" in the event we came into contact with visitors who violated park regulations. Even though we called them "tickets," I believe the documents were actually "field interrogations," which basically consisted of written warnings.

Only a few years later following a serious incident at Yosemite National Park, the National Park Service wisely decided that all law enforcement rangers should be commissioned and have the same basic training as police officers and state troopers. After that, interpretive rangers ceased issuing "FI cards," and instead promptly called a law enforcement ranger when a violation of park regulations was reported or observed.

I have met many outstanding law enforcement rangers over the years, but I always considered Ted Weight to be at the very top of the list. Ted was a big, strapping fellow who taught school during the winter and coached sports as well. Given his size, strength and demeanor, Ted could be as tough as nails if necessary during a difficult law enforcement situation. He was very proficient in backcountry and horsemanship skills as well.

One day during the summer I worked at Mammoth, I was down at the corral saddling up a horse to take out on the trail for a couple of hours. This particular horse had a mind of his own and would not take the bit into his mouth no matter what I tried. Ted happened to be at the corral at the time and walked over to me. "Butch, is this horse giving you problems?" he asked. "Well, I just can't seem to get him to take this bit," I replied. Ted took the bit from me, but I really didn't think he would have any luck either with this stubborn horse.

Was I ever wrong! With one hand he twisted one ear of the horse and yelled into the other one, "Open your mouth you son of a bitch!" That horse opened his mouth so wide you could have stuck a boot down his throat!

Despite the toughness that Ted could display, I found him to be as genuinely a nice a guy as you could ever find. There was nothing he wouldn't do to assist you or make your job easier. He seemed to take extra pride in helping those of us on the staff who were relatively new. Over the years I have observed a few law enforcement rangers, not many, who seemed to think they had to portray the "tough guy" image around the clock, and consequently were, at times, not very helpful to or cooperative with interpretive rangers. Ted Weight proved to me from the very start that it was possible to be one hell of a tough law enforcement ranger when the duty required it, but also be a prince of a nice guy and a wonderful team player.

Law Enforcement rangers may deal with unpleasant incidents dealing with violations of park regulations, but they also make many visitor contacts that require the interpretive skills of providing information on the park's resources. By the same token, interpretive rangers might find themselves to be the first on the scene regarding a medical situation, an accident or a resource-related issue. Therefore, it is vitally important that the different divisions of rangers work together as a team in serving the visiting public and protecting the park's resources.

I was fortunate to spend my first season with the NPS stationed at Norris Geyser Basin. My duties primarily consisted of roving the basin and giving walks and an informal campfire talk at the Norris Campground. However, I was transferred to Mammoth Hot Springs for my second season and there I had a ton of responsibilities. My interpretive duties included giving living history programs on the role of the early mountain man in the Yellowstone country, as well as the role of the U.S. Army at the old Fort Yellowstone. I also developed an evening slide program for Mammoth Campground, and an informal campfire talk at Indian Creek Campground. Giving several guided walks at the Mammoth Hot Springs Upper and Lower Terraces, roving, and staffing the visitor center rounded out the rest of my job duties.

Despite the geometric increase in job responsibilities from Norris to Mammoth, things were going fairly well. Then I committed a royal goof that caused my ranger confidence level to take a big dip. My good friend, Al Duff, had driven down from Great Falls with his friend, Larry, for a long weekend trip, and they stopped by the visitor center to ask me for advice for a three-day backcountry outing. I immediately thought of a wonderful loop trip that Rod Busby and I had taken the previous summer from Hellroaring Creek, up and over the Buffalo Plateau, and out at Slough Creek Campground.

When I suggested this trip to Al he eagerly agreed. I issued the two of them a backcountry permit and wished them a good trip. I would later regret issuing that permit.

A couple of days later during the evening Ranger Don Frazier appeared at my front door. "Did you issue a backcountry permit to two people for a trip on the Buffalo Plateau?" he asked. "Yes," I replied. "They are a couple of friends of mine." Don frowned. "Well, yesterday a park helicopter pilot thought he saw two hikers frantically waving for help. It appeared that one had almost drowned attempting to ford a swollen stream. We think they are now stranded across Slough Creek at the campground, and we are going in with a rescue team in the morning."

I was practically in a state of shock when Don left. I realized that Rod and I had taken this marvelous backpacking trip during the month of August when the streams were relatively low. It was now late June, and I had not even thought about the difficulty that Al and his friend might have attempting to ford the Buffalo Fork, and especially Slough Creek at the campground.

That night I could barely sleep. "What in the world did Don mean when he said that one had almost drowned up on the Buffalo Fork?" I wondered. The next morning I got up at first light and frantically drove to Slough Creek Campground. I didn't know what to expect.

When I arrived, I immediately saw Al and Larry on the other side of Slough Creek, which was running too high to risk fording. However, they appeared to be just fine. When they saw me, they both grinned and waved. "Are you both okay?" I shouted across the fast-moving stream. "Yeah, we're fine," Al yelled back. Then Al tossed his car keys across the stream to me.

"Open my trunk. I have a two-man raft in it and we'll just paddle across the stream," Al yelled. I found a sturdy raft with pump and suddenly felt a tremendous sense of relief come over me. The stream was swollen here but there were no rapids, so paddling across was going to be an easy task. All I had to do was pump up the raft, paddle over, and one by one, get everyone across. We would then get in the car, and let the ranger station back at Mammoth know that a rescue was not necessary. These guys were just fine.

As I was pumping up the raft, I yelled over to Al, "What kind of trouble did you have up on the Buffalo Plateau? I heard you guys tried to signal to a helicopter that you were in trouble." Al looked at me with a puzzled expression. "I don't know what you are talking about," he said. "We didn't have any trouble up there. We saw a helicopter and waved to it but we had no serious problems." "I heard that one of you almost drowned," I said. "Oh no," Al replied. "When we came to the Buffalo Fork we found a nice big log that we walked across. Of course, Larry slipped off the log and fell in over his head, but he promptly recovered and made it across just fine." "Well, that's probably what the helicopter pilot saw," I thought.

When I finished pumping up the raft I dragged it over to the bank and prepared to paddle across. Suddenly, all hell broke loose. A convoy of four green NPS vehicles sped on to the scene. A ranger jumped out of his truck and yelled, "Search and rescue. Clear the area!"

I looked over at Al and his face just sank with the look of total embarrassment. Another ranger, Dunbar Susong, came over and asked me if the search and rescue team could borrow the raft. "Sure," I weakly replied. All I could do now was limp over out of the way and watch the rescue effort unfold.

I soon saw the name badge on the ranger leading the operation. It read "Ted Scott." I knew he was the head ranger at Mammoth. I had traded several letters with Ranger Scott prior to my taking the eighteen-day ski trip a couple of years earlier. Ted Scott had quite a reputation. I knew that he was an expert in backcountry skills, and that he took long backcountry ski patrols during the winter.

Rangers Scott and Susong were now in full rescue mode. It was obvious that they were experts at this. They had probably completed many a training course in this type of rescue not to mention the hours of actual experience. Susong promptly took out a fishing rod. "What the hell is he going to do with a fishing rod?" I thought. An answer was quickly forthcoming. He cast a plug over to Al. Then Dunbar tied the fishing line to a small cord and finally to a climbing rope.

He eventually rigged a rather sophisticated rope pulley system for using the raft to transport the two stranded hikers across Slough Creek. I had planned to simply paddle over, but these guys were pros. They weren't even going to risk the paddle without a safety rope.

After Al and Larry had been transported across the stream, Ranger Ted Scott barked at the top of his lungs, "What idiot sent you on this trip at this time of year?" My heart sank. Al looked at me with a hurt expression on his face. "Sir," I weakly managed, "These are my friends. I issued the permit. I wasn't aware that Slough Creek was unfordable at this time."

Ranger Scott was probably about fifty years old at the time. I was in my twenties. He glared at me about the way a U.S. Marine Drill Instructor greets his new green recruits. Ranger Scott got right in my face, just like a DI. "These are your *friends*?" he screamed. "I would sure as hell hate to see what you do to your enemies!"

Having spent four years in the U.S. Air Force, I had been yelled at by tough men in authority before, so it wasn't Ted Scott that bothered me. What really troubled me was that he was absolutely right. I had screwed up royally. Al managed a weak "thank you" to the rescue team as they climbed into their vehicles and drove off.

"Butch," Al managed, "I'm so sorry." "That's okay," I said. "It was my fault. I should have never suggested this trip. I didn't even think about this ford being a problem. I just wish I had come thirty minutes earlier, and we would have taken care of the situation ourselves."

After wishing Al and Larry a safe drive back up to Great Falls, I began the twenty-five mile drive back to my quarters at Mammoth. It was a long twenty-five miles. I was overcome with doubt over whether I had what it took to be an effective ranger. It was bad enough to have put Al and Larry though this, but the entire spectacle was featured in front of some of Yellowstone's toughest and most experienced rangers.

When I finally dragged in to my quarters, I told Margaret the whole sordid affair. I shared with her my doubts on whether I had what it took to be a Yellowstone ranger. Margaret has always been my builder-upper, and I have been hers. "How were you supposed to know the stream was out of its banks if you have not been over there?" she asked. On that she had a point. In fact, incidents like this helped lead to the excellent system in place today for accurate and current information on trail conditions.

Today, backcountry situation reports are transmitted to all park ranger stations and visitor centers. This allows park employees to be on the same page regarding providing information to visitors on stream fords, snow conditions, mosquitoes, bear observations, fire conditions, and overall trail conditions. Fortunately, the park didn't give up on me after this incident, for the following summer, I was assigned to the backcountry office at the Old Faithful Visitor Center, and was also entrusted with leading twenty-mile overnight interpretive backpacking trips.

The most common law enforcement issue that interpretive rangers encounter in the Old Faithful area involves the park regulation requiring visitors to stay on the trails and boardwalks in the thermal basins. It is unlawful to step off of boardwalks, and there are two reasons for this. First, is the safety angle, since scalding water may be just under thin-crusted mineral deposits; second, the mineral deposits are very fragile and could not withstand significant foot traffic.

The vast majority of visitors comply with these important regulations, but a small percentage of three million visitors represents a substantial amount of potential vandalism. For example, once while I was on roving duty in the Upper Geyser Basin, I happened to walk up behind a young lady just as she was heaving a large log into the beautiful Solitary Geyser. I immediately radioed for a law enforcement ranger. After I escorted the lady back to the Old Faithful Visitor Center, ranger Joe Beuter promptly met us and issued a bond to the lady with a hefty fine of several hundred dollars.

Volunteers spend hundreds of hours each summer cleaning out objects that visitors toss into hot springs and geysers. Unfortunately, many of the objects sink so deep into the thermal features that they cannot be retrieved.

The area around the cone of Old Faithful Geyser is considered to be sacred ground for a good reason. Old Faithful is the most famous geyser in the world and is practically the icon for our national park system. Therefore, the law enforcement and interpretive staff tend to be very protective of the geyser by making certain that immediate action is taken if someone leaves the boardwalk. Such violators are referred to as "cone walkers."

When a cone walker is spotted, we immediately notify law enforcement and head out to entice the violator to return to the boardwalk. In most cases, the violator will receive a ticket and a fine. The most unusual cone walking incident that I ever experienced occurred just a few years ago during the busiest part of the summer, which typically runs from about early-July to mid-August. Old Faithful was nearing eruption, so there were about two thousand folks out on the benches waiting. There was also a line of visitors at the window and desk in the Old Faithful Visitor Center.

Suddenly a visitor ran up to the window and shouted, "Ranger, there are people all over Old Faithful about to be scalded—you better get them out of there!" I managed to look past the people at my window, and to my horror, saw not one or two visitors, but about *twenty* people standing practically on top of Old Faithful. Not only was the geyser in danger, but so were these people.

I immediately called law enforcement for assistance, and then Sam Holbrook and I began an all-out sprint to the geyser. At the same time, Jim Evanoff, an NPS maintenance supervisor, was sprinting toward the geyser from the Old Faithful Lodge. The distance that we had to sprint was about 100 yards. Normally, I am in pretty good shape for hiking and biking around the geyser basin, but my body simply was not acclimated to a 100-yard dash at an elevation of 7400 feet. As the three of us, all in uniform, ran out to the geyser, the crowd of over two thousand visitors back on the benches erupted in a loud cheer. They were ecstatic that justice was about to prevail. I felt as though I was running for a touchdown, and the crowd was cheering me on.

Sam, Jim, and I arrived at the group at the same time, but we all had a big problem. All three of us were so winded that we were just gasping for air and could not talk. Normally when you apprehend someone off of the boardwalk, you ask the person to immediately return to the boardwalk. Once back on safe ground, you go into a detailed explanation regarding their violation and why we have such important park regulations. Sam was the first to find enough wind to say anything, but it was short and to the point: "You're all under arrest!"

Of course, they really weren't, but Sam got their attention and they followed us back to the boardwalk, where a law enforcement ranger took over for us. It turned out that one person on the backside of Old Faithful left the boardwalk, and about twenty others inexplicably followed him out to the geyser.

The serious problem with visitors getting off of the boardwalks in Yellowstone's geyser basins is definitely not helped by the irresponsible television ads that depict such behavior. For example, an ad for Metamucil Laxative depicted a park ranger dumping the substance right into the vent of Old Faithful, to insure the geyser's "regularity." Avis ran an ad inexplicably showing a man tossing a rock into a geyser (the viewer is left to assume that it is Old Faithful Geyser in Yellowstone).

One day while I was on duty at the Old Faithful Visitor Center, a visitor came up to the desk and commented, "I didn't know you could hit a golf ball into Old Faithful." "You can't," I answered. "Well, someone is out there with a pitching wedge, and he says that he is going to hit his golf ball in during the next eruption," the man added.

I knew better to assume that this visitor was kidding, so I hustled out through the crowd awaiting Old Faithful's eruption. Once I got out on the boardwalk, I found a man decked out just like pro golfer Payne Stewart used to dress prior to his untimely death. The man had on golf shoes, knickers and a golf cap. A professional photographer was all setup to capture the event on film. It turned out that a golf magazine was going to put this photo on the cover for its lead story, "Golf Courses of the West."

I asked the man if he had received permission from our Public Affairs Office to film this ad on site. "No," the man replied, and then Old Faithful began its eruption. I stepped directly in front of the man so that he could not swing his golf club, and also to prevent the desired photograph from being taken. "Get out of my way," he said, as he tried to get off his shot. I just tilted my ranger flat hat down a bit, got in his face, and said, "Sir, you cannot take this photo until you get authorization from Public Affairs."

At this point the man gave up and followed me into the Visitor Center. I explained to him why such a photograph on the cover of a major magazine might cause problems, since almost all of Yellowstone's nearly three million visitors stop by to see Old Faithful erupt. Nevertheless, he still wanted to request permission from Public Affairs to film this ad, and it certainly came as no surprise to me when the request was denied.

To illustrate how rangers from interpretation and law enforcement work together, a few summers ago I was driving down to the Lower Geyser Basin where I was scheduled to rove for the afternoon. As I passed Whiskey Flats Picnic Area, I observed a young lady and little girl walking along the side of the road. I thought that perhaps their car had broken down or maybe a tour bus had driven off without them.

When I pulled over to inquire, I noticed that the lady was holding a handkerchief to her bleeding mouth. She told me that her husband had slugged her in the face and then had driven off, abandoning both her and her daughter on the side of the road. I asked the lady to take a seat at a picnic table while I called Old Faithful Law Enforcement to apprise them of the situation. Rangers Lane Baker and Patty Murphree answered and told me they were on their way.

At this point the lady shrieked, as she saw her husband drive by and then turn around. I got back on the radio. I told Lane that the husband was returning. "What is your ETA?" I asked. "Less than five minutes—insure your safety!" came the reply. Even without law enforcement training, I knew that domestic disputes could be very dangerous. Katy Duffy, West District Interpretive Ranger and my supervisor, also understood the potential danger. Katy was on her way to Madison when she heard the radio traffic and pulled into the picnic area to assist.

Just as the husband pulled into the picnic area, Lane and Patty arrived in their patrol car with the siren blaring. They immediately took control of the situation by giving first aid to the woman, and also making certain that the man did not further harm his wife. Lane, a career law enforcement ranger, and Patty, a seasonal who teaches during the rest of the year, exuded tremendous professionalism and competence as they took control of this potentially dangerous situation.

On another occasion, I was roving the Upper Geyser Basin one day when a young man ran up to me. "My Mom has fallen off of the boardwalk and can't move!" he exclaimed. I called for help on my radio as I followed the boy to the site where his Mom was down. My worst fear was that she had fallen into a hot spring. Thankfully, that was not the case.

When we arrived, we noticed that the lady had simply backed off of the boardwalk while looking through her camera's viewfinder in the midst of taking a photo. In the process, she had badly twisted her knee and landed right in some soft mud. I was so grateful that she had not landed on any hot ground. Our first task was lifting the woman off of the ground and placing her back on the boardwalk. But there was a slight problem—she weighed around 300 pounds!

By now my colleague and friend, John Rhoades, also a seasonal interpretive ranger, had arrived on the scene along with a seasonal LE ranger. The three of us managed to lift the lady up on the boardwalk, but she could not stand up due to her knee injury. The LE ranger took me aside. "We had better call for some more help and a wheel chair due to her size," he said.

When another ranger arrived, the four of us managed to lift the woman into the wheel chair, but we still had a problem. She could not bend her injured leg, and the wheel chair footrest would not extend out to provide support. For half a mile I had to walk, bending over, carrying this woman's leg. My back was killing me, so John took over the rest of the way. The lady received prompt medical care and was then transported to the hospital. I guess I injured my back in the carryout, because it took about six months of physical therapy to cure my backache.

The next summer, Lane Baker told me that the lady had sued the National Park Service. I guess she had claimed that the boardwalks were somehow hazardous (see the chapter, "For Your Protection Yellowstone National Park Has Been Closed").

In recent years it has become a rather popular practice for radio talk show hosts to ridicule the incompetence and wastefulness of the federal government. However, one federal agency that has remained popular with the public is the National Park Service. Perhaps the rangers have something to do with that impression. I have always been impressed by the quality of the interpretive rangers that I work with, and just consider the qualifications required to be a seasonal law enforcement ranger today.

The qualifications for this position include: a law enforcement commission, certification in emergency medical service, horsemanship, backcountry search and rescue, knowledge of the park's resources, firefighting, and overall people skills. In return for these impressive qualifications, a seasonal ranger is paid about twelve bucks an hour and receives no benefits regarding retirement or health insurance.

In my biased opinion, the National Park Service seasonal ranger is passionate about the mission and deeply committed to carrying it out. No doubt about it, the NPS park ranger represents one of the best deals going in federal government as far as the U.S. taxpayer is concerned.

Sunset on Shoshone Lake

Tale of the Osprey

The mission of the National Park Service, as stated in the Organic Act, includes the purpose statement, "..to conserve the scenery and the natural and historic objects and the wildlife therein, and to provide for the enjoyment of the same in such manner and by such means as will leave them unimpaired for the enjoyment of future generations." The parks have suffered over the apparent conflict between "conserve versus enjoyment" ever since.

A good example is the manner in which the rivers and lakes of Yellowstone are managed today. There is something extraordinary about paddling a canoe along the calm waters of a backcountry lake. A canoe is so functional. The bow and the stern are streamlined, so with just a little effort and a stroke of the paddle, the vessel glides quietly and efficiently across the water. Paddling opportunities in Yellowstone are basically limited to Yellowstone Lake, Lewis Lake, Shoshone Lake, and the three-mile Lewis River Channel that connects Lewis and Shoshone Lakes.

I occasionally encounter visitors who are upset that Yellowstone does not allow more access to wilderness waters, such as the Madison and Firehole Rivers, the Yellowstone River through Hayden Valley, and the Lamar River through Lamar Valley, just to mention a few. As a canoeing enthusiast myself, many years ago I tended to sympathize with these visitors' complaints. One summer early in my career I was working at the Albright Visitor Center in Mammoth. Two young men approached me at the desk and told me that they wanted to paddle all the way down the Southeast Arm of Yellowstone Lake, and then paddle their canoes as far up the Upper Yellowstone River as they could go. I explained to them that while canoeing along the shores of Yellowstone Lake was legal, the Yellowstone River was closed to boats. "Even hand-propelled canoes?" they asked. "Yes," I replied. Then they asked me the tough question, "Why?" At this time I really did not know so I told the visitors that I would call the Chief Ranger's office to find out.

An assistant working in the Chief Ranger's office explained that it was because of two primary reasons: 1) It would disturb wildlife, and 2) Such use would place additional demands on ranger manpower, which was already spread too thin. When I shared this answer with the visitors, they were not happy and stormed out of the office. Frankly, I was not too happy with the answer either, because I thought about the many wonderful float trips I had taken down the Snake River through the Tetons, which did not seem to harm the wildlife. Well, looking back, this is one time when my thinking was seriously flawed and the park's policy was right on the money.

Thank goodness the National Park Service in Yellowstone never let that particular horse "out of the barn" so to speak. Just look at the Snake River today. A couple of years ago on a beautiful August day, I took my rubber raft down for a float from Dead Man's Bar to Moose, a distance of about ten miles. Perhaps I should have launched at dawn to insure a quality experience, but that is not always feasible. First, I had a 100-mile drive to the park, then I had to go by Colter Bay Visitor Center and purchase a boat permit, and finally I had to arrange for my shuttle.

When I got ready to put in, there was a log jam of commercial outfitters all waiting to launch their big rafts full of paying customers. So I politely positioned myself in line until it was my turn to launch. Rangers in the Tetons make a special attempt to promote proper river etiquette to all who float the Snake. They emphasize in their pamphlets on river use to keep a proper distance between vessels upstream and downstream, and to keep noise levels on the river low.

I tried to wait for the commercial raft to get downstream, at least a hundred yards, but the river guide behind me yelled, "Get going or get out of the way!" I moved out of the way and waited another thirty minutes or so for this group of commercial rafts to put in, and then tried to launch again. The same exact thing happened again—another outfitter drove up and yelled at me to put in or get out of the way. This time the river guide was rather curt. He had a Georgia Bulldog cap on his head and seemed to take offense that my truck had a Tennessee plate on the rear with an Auburn University plate on the front (Auburn and Tennessee are two big rivals of Georgia). He also ridiculed my small but sturdy rubber raft. "You float this river in that thing?" he asked.

I moved out of the way to let them on the river, and as he was putting in I asked the guide a question, "Say, you ever floated this river by yourself with no one around?" He just grunted and hurriedly took off. I decided if I was ever going to get on the Snake on that day, I might as well stop trying to allow distance between the rafts ahead of me. So, like a bunch of bumper cars at the carnival, I just eased in. This particular raft concession seemed more interested in having a raucous good time on the river, than trying to quietly interpret the natural surroundings to the visitors. The rafts in front of and behind me were very noisy. Clearly, I had not come down to float the Snake for *this* experience!

The first chance I got, I maneuvered over into one of the many side-channels that form a braid on the Snake River, in order to find some peace and quiet, and hopefully to view some wildlife. The side-channels were even more crowded than the main river channel! Outfitters, fly-fishing from Dory boats, occupied every single one I turned into!

When I got home that day, I immediately sat down and wrote a letter to the Superintendent of Grand Teton National Park, describing how the quality of floating the Snake River had greatly diminished over the years from the first time I ever floated it in 1968. I'm not sure how a park determines a carrying capacity for such activities as floating a river, but as far as my own experience on this day was concerned, it had clearly been exceeded. I also wrote the commercial outfitter a letter describing my experience. While I did receive nice letters from both the park and the outfitter, nothing has been done, that I am aware of, to improve the situation on the Snake.

So, if years ago Yellowstone had opened its waterways for floating, there is no question in my mind that we would see the same crowded setting along the rivers. Instead of being able to view the wonderful natural scenes of wildlife in Hayden Valley, Lamar Valley, Elk Park and the Madison Canyon, we would be watching lines of rafts and dealing with the constant traffic of outfitter shuttle buses going back and forth. The animals would most likely be back in the woods out of view.

Yellowstone has come a long way with its policy on boat use, but in the opinion of many, still has a ways to go. Prior to 1959, powerboats were allowed on the Lewis River Channel, Shoshone Lake, and the three arms of Yellowstone Lake. Superintendent Lemuel "Lon" Garrison had a tough issue to resolve—one that is inherent in managing national parks: preservation versus use of the resource.

Yellowstone Lake, a spectacular high altitude lake that Ferdinand Hayden in 1871 had described as "...a vast sheet of quiet water, of a most delicate ultramarine hue, one of the most beautiful scenes I have ever beheld...Such a vision is worth a lifetime, and only one of such marvelous beauty will ever greet human eyes" was by the late 1950s dotted with speeding powerboats. Concerns had been documented regarding the impact speeding boats were having on waterfowl at the tips of the arms of Yellowstone Lake, not to mention the intrusive impact the boats were having on the wilderness setting in these areas.

Superintendent Garrison began floating proposals to restrict the use of powerboats in these pristine park waters. The powerboat lobby promptly spoke loudly, and contacted their friends in Congress, especially Senator McGee from Wyoming. Although this took place over forty years ago, the same battles still occur today regarding restricting jet skis, jet boats, and of course, snowmobiles within national park areas.

Several years before his death, Lon Garrison spoke to our staff of interpretive rangers during training at Mammoth. He gave one of the most moving and inspirational speeches I have ever heard. He described how politicians threatened to end his career if he tried to restrict the use of powerboats in Yellowstone. However, Mr. Garrison was determined to do what was right for the park and its future. The proposal under consideration would ban motors on Shoshone Lake, the Lewis River Channel, and the three arms of Yellowstone Lake. The pressure being applied on Garrison against implementing this restriction was enormous. Boating associations and certain chambers of commerce were applying heat. Finally, Superintendent Garrison decided he needed to be by himself to make the final decision.

He decided to examine the resource closely by taking a horseback ride through some of Yellowstone's most primitive backcountry. Garrison rode his trusty steed that he called "Stormy" along the east shore of Yellowstone Lake, staying overnight in patrol cabins along the way. Eventually he arrived at Thorofare Ranger Station, located over thirty miles by trail from the nearest road. From here he traveled up Lynx Creek to Fox Creek cabin, and then across the Two Ocean Plateau to Trail Creek cabin on the Southeast Arm. It was here that Mr. Garrison said he noticed an osprey perched on a branch overhead. The osprey launched from the tree, soared overhead, and began emitting a mournful *kyee, kyee, kyee, kyee!* Mr. Garrison immediately thought of the abundance and variety of birds and waterfowl that depend on this magnificent lake—eagles, osprey, pelicans, herons and many species of ducks.

The Superintendent mounted his horse and rode several more miles. The osprey accompanied him along the way, swooping in so close that he thought the majestic bird was going to either tear into his head or light on his shoulder. This continued over and over until Garrison realized that this osprey was escorting him through its territory. He decided to name it "Omar," and Garrison began a conversation with both Stormy and Omar. Garrison had management problems on his mind and he decided to discuss them on this day with Stormy and Omar.

Garrison looked out across the wild, spacious scenery that enveloped him. Though pleasing to the eye he knew that all was not well here. Motorboats were having a terrible impact on birds. The loud roar of motors would frighten adult birds, causing them to abandon nests, leaving fledglings exposed. The wake caused by speeding powerboats was overwashing low-lying nests with eggs.

That night Garrison looked across the splendid waters of Yellowstone Lake and thought about the osprey. He began to search his soul regarding what the future of Yellowstone Lake should hold. The next day Garrison continued his ride along the east shore of the Southeast Arm. Twice more he stopped to relax along the lake's shore. Both times his newfound friend, Omar the osprey, had followed him, soared overhead and repeatedly sounded its piercing call.

By now Garrison was deep in thought. He had become genuinely moved over the flight of this osprey. Was this osprey trying to speak to him? Garrison thought deeply about the many impacts speeding powerboats had along the shores of this lake—the nesting osprey and eagles, the rookeries of herons, the nesting waterfowl. He knew the number of boats here, already alarming, would only continue to increase. If the osprey was trying to speak to Garrison, he knew in his heart that the right decision to make was to restrict powerboats, no matter how unpopular the decision might be, no matter what the impact might be on his NPS career. It was time to head back out of the wilderness. As far as Superintendent Garrison was concerned, the decision had been made.

I never forgot that speech and have thought about it many times. In fact, once while paddling the Little Tennessee River in 1979, just before the Tennessee Valley Authority destroyed it with the closing of the Tellico Dam, I had a similar experience. TVA had already stripped the shoreline of the big trees, but the remaining vegetation was bustling with birds. A flock of cardinals followed our canoe down the river. It was almost as if they were trying to speak to us to stop this gorgeous place from being flooded.

The tremendous courage that Lon Garrison exercised in restricting powerboats in Yellowstone is the type of leadership we need in our national parks. Unfortunately, politicians often interfere with professional land managers by manipulating budgets to alter the outcome. Such was the case even with Garrison's bold proposal. The political pressure became so intense against the ban that according to *National Parks Magazine*, President John F. Kennedy took the decision out of Secretary of Interior Stewart Udall's hands, and a watered down version of Garrison's proposal was implemented.

Rather than completely banning powerboats from the South and Southeast Arms, they were barred only from the tips of the arms, and their speed was limited to five miles per hour. This is the policy that remains in effect today. Taking powerboats out of Shoshone Lake and the Lewis River Channel was thankfully upheld. This was critical. After all, Shoshone Lake, which measures seven miles from the west to east shore, is the largest wilderness lake in the contiguous forty-eight states!

Over the years the NPS did what they could to strengthen the restriction on Yellowstone Lake. Launching sites and campsites were limited. However, today many conservationists feel that the time has come for Lon Garrison's original proposal to be revisited. Of Yellowstone Lake's 134 square miles of surface area, only nineteen square miles are set aside for hand-propelled craft; of the 110 miles of shoreline, only thirteen miles are protected from powerboats.

The two problems that I have observed with the current situation are excessive speed in the five mph zones, and the noise intrusion in the non-motorized zones. Some powerboats do not observe the regulation. And it is very difficult to enforce.

On several occasions I have been canoeing deep in the backcountry of these superb arms and have had to endure a streaking powerboat piercing the solitude of the wilderness. Once I had my radio with me and called in a violation to Lake Patrol. Unfortunately, there was only one ranger on patrol in the arms at the time, and his transmission back to me was, "What do you want me to do, chase him down in my canoe?"

A few years ago a new draft backcountry management plan for Yellowstone National Park again called for completely banning motorboats from all the arms of Yellowstone Lake. For reasons unknown it has yet to be implemented. Perhaps one day another courageous leader like Lon Garrison will encounter an osprey while on patrol on Yellowstone Lake, and take the necessary actions to strengthen the integrity of the wilderness in the arms of Yellowstone Lake.

Bighorn Sheep

Evidence of Earlier Visitors

Yellowstone's human history is as fascinating as its natural history. Native Americans have visited Yellowstone for centuries and European Americans began exploring the area as early as John Colter's journey in 1807. Although most historians credit Colter with being the first non-Indian to explore the region, I wouldn't be surprised if one day a researcher finds evidence of some trapper having visited even earlier.

Finding evidence of earlier visitors when in the backcountry provides an unexpected thrill. A few years ago I was teaching a one-day map and compass course for the Yellowstone Institute, and was out in the field with fifteen students near the Firehole River. We were running a compass course toward the river that took us along the edge of an old lodgepole forest. One of the students noticed a small depression in the soil. Upon closer examination, we found that it was filled with obsidian chips.

Given the remote location away from any trail, we had to assume that this was a site that Indians had used to shape the glass-like obsidian into tools such as arrowheads and spear tips. Our group stopped for a snack, and we could easily envision the native American Indians sitting there with us working away, only at an earlier date by perhaps some 150 years. I have not returned to this site and hope the chippings remain untouched for another 150 years.

Several years ago Ranger Harlan Kredit called me to express excitement about a teepee ring he had discovered the previous day, not far from a trail near Fishing Bridge. He gave me precise directions to its location, and the next time I was in the area I managed to find it. What I found was a perfect circle of rocks measuring about twenty feet in diameter. The rocks were placed very close to each other, and over the years the forest duff had partially covered them. There were some trees that measured about six inches in diameter growing in the middle of the ring.

The circle of rocks just did not appear to have been used for a teepee to me. Why would anyone use so many rocks and place them so close together? A few days later I called Harlan to discuss the ring of rocks, and he agreed that it was probably not used for teepees. So just who put this ring of rocks here and for what purpose? Some think it was a type of ceremonial ring, but no one knows for certain.

Perhaps the most fascinating relics to come across in the backcountry are old cabins. Park Historian Lee Whittlesey told me about a couple that I marked on my map with the intention of visiting. Both of the cabin remains were in extremely remote locations. One was located nearly ten miles from the nearest road in the far reaches of Hayden Valley, and the other was over ten miles away on the Mirror Plateau. John and Deb Dirksen, Clyde Austin and Dave Wood accompanied me into the upper reaches of Hayden Valley in search of the old cabin.

We found it not too far from a thermal basin and the old cabin actually exceeded my expectations. Although the roof had fallen in the log walls were still in good shape. There was a stone fireplace in the cabin. On the high Yellowstone plateau, winters are long, and the air is dry. Therefore, wood tends to decompose very slowly, taking over 100 years to return to the soil. It was obvious that this cabin was very old. So the palpable questions are, just who built this cabin and what was it used for? Was it an Army scout's patrol cabin? Could this have been a poacher's cabin? No one knows.

Even more fascinating were the old cabin remains near Wrong Creek on the Mirror Plateau. These cabin remains are located deep in Yellowstone's wilderness, well away from the nearest trail. An extended backpack trip is required to visit this site given its remote location. John and Deb Dirksen, Hank Barnett, Alan Martin, and my daughter Alison, accompanied me on this trip. If it had not been for Alison, we probably would not have found it. She somehow managed to spot the old cabin, which sits back in the woods well away from the creek.

This cabin appeared to be quite old and had fallen in. The old door was still fastened by leather hinges. When Lee first came across this cabin, he found an old shovel with the name "X. Biedler" carved on the handle. Mr. Biedler was actually a vigilante in Virginia City, Montana during the 1860s. So what in the world was he doing with a cabin in such a remote area? Keep in mind that Yellowstone was not even "officially" discovered until the Washburn, Langford, and Doane expedition of 1870.

That expedition, and those that ensued, primarily traveled along the area's major rivers and valleys. Wrong Creek is far removed from any of the historical routes. It is located in perhaps the wildest, most remote location a fellow could possibly select in the 1860s. To me, this is one of Yellowstone's great mysteries to discuss around the campfire.

Once while canoeing along the southern tip of the Southeast Arm of Yellowstone Lake, Jim Lenertz and I came upon a logjam near the mouth of Beaverdam Creek. One of the logs contained the large, and obviously very old, carvings of two sets of initials, "PB" and "BT" and a date of "1893." I took a photo of the inscription and sent it to our Park Historian. He felt that it was probably carved by some Army scouts, and did not consider it to be significant. I was in hopes that he would want to retrieve this section of the log for possible display at a later date.

The next time I canoed through this area, I inspected the logjam and noticed that several of the logs had washed away with the spring floods, including the one with the inscription. It is probably now sitting on the bottom of the lake. I am certain that the present Park Historian, Lee

Whittlesey, would have taken action to retrieve this interesting piece of evidence of past human visitation.

Of course, some of the intriguing evidence of past human visitation found in the backcountry is not really all that old. During the late 1980s the U.S. Geological Survey (USGS) began a project to replace the park's fifteen-minute topographical maps, dating back to the 1950s, with new 7 ½ minute maps. Aerial photographs are used to help construct the new maps. One day Park Geologist Rick Hutchinson came over to my quarters in the proud possession of several of the photos that would be used to make the maps.

He showed me one particular photo taken near Douglas Knob in the southwest corner of the park, and pointed out a tiny dot about one mile to the west of the Knob. "Do you know what this is?" he asked. I had no idea. Rick said that it was a U.S. Air Force B-47 that had crashed in 1963. Three crewmembers perished in the crash, but the copilot was able to eject. He was found the next day after spending a harrowing cold night in the snow.

I found Rick's photo fascinating because former Yellowstone Ranger Bob Maury had once told me the details of that crash. It had occurred during early May, when there was a significant accumulation of snow on the ground. Bob was one of the rangers who skied in following the crash and had shared with me what he found. He said that the plane crash site was very different from that of most crash sites in that the plane had gone into a spin, and had "pancaked" straight down into a dense spruce-fir forest.

There had been several feet of snow on the ground that served to cushion the crash, and thus preserve the plane. Bob told me that when he skied to the plane he tied ribbons to the trees so he could find it when he returned in the summer. The plane was located about a mile from the Bechler River trail, and when Bob hiked into the site the following summer, he could not find the ribbons. He eventually located the plane, but the ribbons seemed to have mysteriously disappeared. Finally, Bob solved the "mystery." The ribbons were there all right, several feet above him in the tops of the trees! Bob had forgotten just how deep the snow had been when he had tied the ribbons on the trees while on skis.

Bob told me this story in the late 1960s, so I had always had an interest in visiting the plane one day but had no realistic hope of being able to find it. Rick's photograph changed that. I now had a pinpoint location with reference points nearby. Tom Caples, who worked for NPS maintenance, and I plotted a compass course to find the plane, and headed out with high hopes. Since it was twelve miles along the Bechler Trail from Lone Star Geyser and then another mile off-trail, we planned a three-day, two night trip.

Using Rick's copy of the photo we found a point where the Littles Fork made a sharp bend in the meadow just west of Douglas Knob. From here we plotted a compass course that we would follow for 1.1 miles, which would take us directly to the plane.

Once we left the trail and crossed the meadow, we entered the dense spruce-fir forest that we had anticipated. We knew that if we were off by twenty or thirty yards we would miss it. Typically you travel about one mile per hour when following a compass course off-trail in a forest, so we figured that we should be at the plane in a little over one hour.

Tom and I spread out so that we would increase our chances of seeing the plane in the dense woods. After an hour Tom was the first to spot it. We were amazed at the setting. It seemed as if someone had placed the plane directly on the forest floor amidst the tall, dense stand of spruce and fir trees. There was absolutely no evidence of any trees being damaged or sheared off when the plane crashed, providing further evidence that the aircraft did indeed spin down and pancake into the forest.

The plane was intact and had not disintegrated. Even the tires were still inflated. The fuselage had been compressed by the impact, but the rest of the plane was in surprisingly good shape. We climbed up on top of the plane and walked from the nose to the tail and from wingtip to wingtip.

Tom is quite a photographer and was very frustrated by the thick forest preventing him from getting a decent photo. He astonished me by climbing completely to the top of a tall spruce tree to obtain a bird's eye view and photo of the plane.

This B-47 had crashed over twenty years prior to our visiting it, and to us it was part of Yellowstone's unique human history. Therefore, it came as quite a surprise to learn that the Park Historian considered the plane to be unnatural "litter," and wanted it removed. After all, the plane was twelve miles from the nearest road, one mile from the nearest trail, and perhaps most importantly, the plane could not be seen until you were practically right on top of it.

Furthermore, the plane was not visible from the air, so you did not have the problem of other pilots mistakenly reporting it as a possible downed plane. The fact that the high altitude aerial photo by the USGS had picked up the tiny dot through the dense forest was nothing short of remarkable.

I don't recall ever meeting a visitor or another NPS employee who considered the plane to be an unnatural intrusion in the park's backcountry. However, there are always differing opinions on such things. For example, I find Mount Rushmore to be inspirational. I am thrilled when I come across petroglyphs—ancient drawings on canyon walls—in such places as Canyonlands National Park. However, my old friend and former Park Geologist, Rick Hutchinson, had strong feelings about such carvings and drawings in wild areas. Rick would point out to me that such carvings and drawings amounted to nothing more than vandalism. Rick was first and foremost a geologist, and he did not think that humans could improve upon the natural setting, whether it was long ago or recent.

The Register Cliffs along the Oregon Trail near Guernsey, Wyoming contain some beautifully scripted, carved signatures in the limestone cliffs. Unfortunately, there are also plenty of "Bob Loves Suzie"--type inscriptions carved on the cliffs as well. To me, the signatures made by travelers on the Oregon Trail are historical, while Bob and Suzie simply defaced a unique treasure. Again, Rick considered *both* to be equal examples of defacing a natural feature.

I thought the B-47 was an exceptional piece of Yellowstone's human history that should have remained. However, some park officials considered it an unnatural intrusion on the resource. In September of 1993, thirty years after being hidden in the remote Yellowstone wilderness, the plane was indeed removed during a training exercise by a National Guard unit. The plane was sliced up into small pieces, and flown out by helicopter. What had been a fascinating piece of Yellowstone's history was conceivably recycled into thousands of beverage containers. Was it removal of history or litter?

The Wyoming Ghetto

There is an old saying among National Park Service rangers that most of the pay and benefits are provided in the form of "sunsets." Few rangers join the service because of the promise of financial and material rewards. For example, the quality of housing varies considerably from park to park, especially for seasonal employees. However, over the years Yellowstone has been somewhat infamous for its rather poor seasonal housing. Many employees are housed in trailers that are several decades old. The smaller, older trailers are commonly referred to as "dog trailers." Fortunately, most of these have been phased out of the park over the past several years.

My first season with the Park Service, in 1974, was spent at Norris Geyser Basin. Margaret and I and our nine month old daughter, Caroline, were assigned to a one-bedroom "apartment" that was basically part of the old Norris Museum built in 1929. A wood stove provided the heat and the floors were cold linoleum—not too conducive for a baby to crawl around on! Plus, the old building seemed to house quite a few mice. Since the quarters were adjacent to the museum, it was not unusual to have folks knock on our front door late at night asking if we knew when Steamboat Geyser was going to erupt. On several occasions, I had to explain this to inquisitive, late night visitors. As far as they knew, our little apartment was simply an extension of the visitor center, and I was on duty twenty-four hours a day. Steamboat was dormant throughout our season at Norris.

One geyser that was *not* dormant during our summer at Norris was Harding Geyser, which is located only a few yards away from the building. On several evenings we would awaken in the middle of the night to the strange sounds of gurgling, splashing, and roaring water, as Harding Geyser would erupt. Even though our quarters at Norris were woefully inadequate for a family of three, we did enjoy the unique isolation of living in the heart of Norris Geyser Basin. The building is situated on a bench separating the Porcelain Basin to the north from the Back Basin to the south.

I will never forget waking up in the middle of the night to complete silence except for the plops, gurgles, and hisses of the surrounding thermal features, and the yips and howls of the coyotes out in the basin. Or gazing out at the brightness of Porcelain Basin on the night of a full moon. Or the constant "rotten eggs" smell of sulphur (particularly more noticeable during the evening). Later in the summer an old, but much roomier, trailer in the government housing area nearby became available, and we moved out of our little rustic apartment.

In subsequent seasons spent at Mammoth, and mostly Old Faithful, we were assigned to a type of government quarters called a "transit-home." The transit home is basically a square metal building—kind of like a heavy-duty trailer without wheels. The rooms are quite small, but the place is rather functional, *if*, and that's a big if, they are properly maintained. The transit homes at Old Faithful contain inventory labels stating that they were in use by the Bureau of Reclamation in 1947, so they are rather ancient metal cabins.

The transit homes are located across the highway from the geyser basin and are thankfully out of sight from the thousands of visitors who enter the Upper Geyser Basin each day during the summer. Most of the housing units are situated in close proximity, thus the popular term that most employees use to describe the Old Faithful housing area: "the Wyoming Ghetto."

One spring my family and I returned to our transit home at Old Faithful to find quite a few problems. The roof had developed a leak, which of course had gone undetected, and the floors were covered in water. The linoleum had buckled up and there was an unpleasant stench about the place. The stove and refrigerators were not working properly, and about this time I received a notice that my rent was going up. Printed at the bottom of the notice in small print was a statement saying it was possible to appeal this rent increase. I figured if I ever had justification for appealing an increase in rent this was it. I submitted an appeal to the Chief of Housing in Yellowstone pointing out all of the maladies our old transit home suffered.

My appeal was denied, though we did get our stove and refrigerator repaired. The park was under such budget constraints, that improving the seasonal employee housing was at the bottom of the priority list. Apparently, however, my appeal listing all the problems with our transit home was forwarded to the Superintendent's Office.

Toward the end of the summer I received word from my supervisor, Tom Farrell, that I was to be available at my quarters for an inspection by U.S. Senator Craig Thomas of Wyoming, and his wife. Also in the party were the park's Chief of Maintenance, Tim Hudson, and Yellowstone Superintendent, Michael Finley. Senator Thomas was on a fact-finding mission to see for himself if the park was as short of funds as Superintendent Finley had been claiming to Congress for the past several years. I suppose my plain little transit home had been selected to display to Senator Thomas just how deplorable the housing was in Yellowstone.

The inspection was scheduled for 2:00 p.m. on Friday, prior to my two-day weekend. At 4:00 p.m. I was off and had planned a lengthy backpacking trip through the Bechler Canyon with my eight-year-old daughter, Alison, and our good friends John and Deb Dirksen. Margaret was off attending an art workshop. By 4:00 p.m. the guests had not arrived so I called Tom to inquire what was up. We were anxious to head down to Bechler in order to make our first campsite before dark. Tom said that the party had been delayed at Grant and had changed plans. He said that I was officially now on my lieu days, and to go ahead and take off. I told Alison that I needed to take a quick bath first—after all, I had been roving in the geyser basin all afternoon on this rather warm day.

I had barely eased into the bathtub before I heard Alison knocking on the bathroom door: "Dad, they're here!" "Oh Alison, don't play any tricks on me," I said. "I'm not, *they are here!*" she shouted. All I had to put on were my green Park Service backcountry shorts—which looked like lizard brief swim shorts. I pulled them on and walked out the bathroom door dripping wet. There in the living room stood Senator Thomas and his wife, Superintendent Finley, and Chief of Maintenance Tim Hudson. Finley glared at me as if to say, "What the hell are you doing standing here in front of us in your swimming trunks?"

Tim began pointing out all the problems inherent with maintaining such an old facility as this. Senator Thomas and his wife asked several interesting questions about what it was like to live in such quarters, and I did my best to answer them. His wife picked up on my southern accent, and she asked where I was from. I told her that I was a teacher and lived near the Great Smoky Mountains in East Tennessee. Superintendent Finley had been silent to this point but now he looked over to me and asked, "Why do you choose to work in Yellowstone rather than the Great Smokies?" Obviously, hopping out of a bathtub in my lizard green shorts had not impressed the Superintendent! I got the impression that he would have arranged my transfer in an instant. In any event, I think the tour of the housing area helped Senator Thomas better appreciate Yellowstone's budget situation.

One summer I arrived at Old Faithful ahead of Margaret, who planned to join me in a couple of weeks. Alison was attending school at Montana State University at the time, and met me at the metal cabin. As soon as we opened the door we knew we had problems. The stench almost knocked us off our feet.

"Dad, you better take care of this odor or Mom will get back on the plane and go home," Alison opined. I promptly called over John and Carl from maintenance, but, at first, they could find nothing out of the ordinary. Then they noticed that the smell seemed to be emanating from the wall. Some "exploratory surgery" was required and they hit the jackpot, at least if you are an archaeologist. For in the walls they found piles and piles of bones. As it turned out, it was not some ancient civilization, but rather an old nest of a pine marten.

Pine martens feed primarily on squirrels, and apparently many a squirrel corpse had been lodged in this wall over the years, especially during the winter. After removing all of the mess, Carl poured Clorox and Pine-sol into the wall and set up a fan to pull out the horrendous odors. Two weeks later the smell was noticeably less, but nevertheless still present.

When Margaret arrived she took a sniff and said, "I smell gas." "But honey," I assured her, "our cabin is all electric. We don't have any gas." As the summer progressed and the weather became warmer, the smell became bad again. I called Carl and John back over while Margaret was at work.

This time they found a family of dead mice rolled up in a nest in the floor under the bathtub.

I have always felt that just because someone chooses to work for the National Park Service, they should not be relegated to third-class living conditions regarding the housing provided. Some of the buildings used for seasonal housing in Yellowstone over the years would probably have been condemned in most U.S. cities. However, in all fairness, the NPS Division of Maintenance does a good job in attempting to "patch up" and maintain the marginal housing facilities. It certainly is not their fault. Rather, it is simply a fact that with the huge backlog of needed maintenance in our national parks—visitor centers, restrooms, picnic facilities, campgrounds, trails, roads, bridges, etc.—housing for seasonal employees does not rate as the highest priority.

During the mid to late 1990s our nation's economy boomed and federal deficits turned into huge surpluses. I was so hopeful that we would finally see the National Park Service receive the appropriations it needed to begin making a meaningful dent in the huge backlog of maintenance projects, including upgrading seasonal housing. Most polls that I read showed that the American public wanted to see Congress use a portion of the great surplus to adequately fund the National Park Service.

Unfortunately, Congress failed to take advantage of this window of opportunity. Rather, huge tax cuts were enacted, the stock market tanked, the economy dipped, terrorists attacked our nation, and the huge federal deficits returned. Translated, that means rangers will probably continue to be paid in "sunsets" for the foreseeable future!

Humor in Uniform

Art Linkletter glorified the funny things that kids say and do. I'm surprised that no one has ever written a book titled, "Park Visitors Say the Darndest Things." At Old Faithful we keep logbooks on hand in which we record unusual natural resource happenings, but we also have a book in which we note humorous events involving employees and visitors. We are always careful to include incidents that are in good taste.

After all, you have to empathize with park visitors. I still remember my first visit to Yellowstone and the many strange thoughts and questions that I had, like "Ranger, do you know why there are short fences that aren't connected along some of the highways in Wyoming? Seems like those fences would not contain livestock." Margaret and I actually did ask this question. We were told that these "fences" were actually snow railings designed to prevent snow from drifting across the highway (we never saw such a fence back in Alabama).

So when visitors occasionally display their genuine ignorance about the park, I am always careful not to laugh or display any disrespect in answering their questions. We do get many unusual questions when on duty at the visitor center, like "Can you tell me where I came from to get here?" The following stories provide an idea of some of the humor that is frequently just part of the job in Yellowstone.

During the summer of 2004 a bison had died near the Nez Perce Creek crossing on the Old Faithful-Madison road. Hundreds of bison frequent this area early in the summer, and apparently this young animal had died from an injury sustained from another member of the herd. Several cars had stopped and about twenty visitors had gathered nearby with scopes and binoculars in the hope of seeing a wolf or grizzly bear coming in to feed on the carcass. Suddenly, a visitor in a truck pulled up, stuck his head out the window, and pronounced to the gathering, "Folks, just a little further up the road there are some *live* buffalo you'll be able to look at!"

During June there are dozens of young buffalo calves romping and playing in the herds around the Madison Valley and Fountain Flats. The calves are a reddish-brown color. More than once I have been asked, "How do you train all of those little red dogs to follow the buffalo around?"

One of the funniest stories that I ever heard involved the venerable old seasonal ranger, Tim Bywater. During the difficult period in the late 1960s and early 1970s, bear jams were common along park roads as a result of begging bears conditioned to human foods. Park officials were attempting to remove these roadside beggars by relocating them into remote areas of the park. Most of the efforts to transplant problem bears were not successful, but officials tried anyway.

One day Tim was working a bad bear jam on the east side of the park. Park rangers had decided to immobilize the bear with a drug dart, and relocate it. Tim was trying to keep visitors away from the operation as a ranger shot a dart into the bear, but the drug did not take effect. Apparently more of the drug was needed so another dart was shot into the bear. Still the bear showed no signs of the drug, and lumbered over to the highway where a family of four in a sedan had just pulled up. Of course, they had not seen the darts shot into the bear. "Folks, move away from this bear," Tim shouted.

Before Tim could move closer to this car to talk to the family, the Dad committed the unpardonable sin: he threw out an Oreo cookie. The old bear walked over, picked up the cookie, and ate it. Just at that moment the immobilization drug took effect. The bear keeled over like it was as dead as a doornail. "Dad," the little boy in the back seat shrieked, "you killed that bear! You poisoned it!"

"Sir, you have got to move on," Tim instructed as he approached the car. The little boy was just sobbing. In an attempt to sooth the little boy's feelings the Dad said, "Here son, shut up and eat an Oreo cookie." Tim said that the little boy's face lit up in horror as he screamed, "I'm not eating any of those cookies!" The car drove off before Tim had a chance to explain what had happened. Somewhere, there is still a family that firmly believes they murdered a Yellowstone bear with an Oreo cookie!

Some of the funniest incidents involve not only visitors but also employees. In the late 1970s we had a delightful young lady on our interpretive staff at Old Faithful by the name of Julie Dreher. Julie just bubbled over with enthusiasm and humor, and kept the staff in stitches much of the time. She was also an outstanding interpretive ranger. One day Julie was leading a walk through the Upper Geyser Basin, and had stopped at Grand Geyser to point out its unique characteristics as it approached an eruption.

What Julie did not know was that actor, Robert Redford, had signed up to go on her hike. Several of us in the visitor center were aware that Redford was visiting the area, but you never knew where he would show up, since he was using another name when he signed up for our walks. Julie probably had about forty visitors on her walk, when suddenly, she made eye contact with Redford. She abruptly tripped over her words and stared at Redford as if to say, "Are you who I think you are?" Redford returned a friendly grin as if to reply, "Yes, it's me." Julie became seriously tongue-tied again, but somehow regained her composure and completed the hike. For the next week or so, Julie made such entries in the logbook as, "The second day after Robert Redford went on my hike; the third day after Robert Redford went on my hike; the fourth day…"

During my first summer at Norris in 1974, the park-wide radio system was much different than it is today. There were only a few channels, so it was possible to listen in and pretty much know what was happening throughout most of the park. Today, there are many more channels to handle the traffic, so you typically hear only local radio traffic.

Looking west from Norris Geyser Basin, you can't help but be impressed with the Gallatin Range. The dominant peak is Mount Holmes, upon which sits one of three fire lookout towers staffed in the park during the summer months, the others being on Mount Washburn and Mount Sheridan. I always found it interesting to listen to the lookout transmit his grocery order in to the fire cache about every two weeks. The supplies were then transported in by helicopter, since Mount Holmes is a remote lookout. The roundtrip hike to the summit measures about twenty-two miles, as the trail climbs over 3000 feet to an elevation of 10,336 feet. One day, though, the lookout's grocery order was very different.

The lookout had just placed his order to 700-Fox (the fire cache). About fifteen minutes later, 700-Fox called the lookout to clarify part of the order. When the lookout answered, he had some serious problems. "Uh, it looks like I'm going to need you up here right away," he said. "Well, we weren't planning on bringing up your supplies until tomorrow," came the reply from the fire cache. "Can you please come right now?" asked the lookout.

At this point the Fire Cache knew something was wrong, but they were having a hard time getting a full picture from the lookout. Finally though, the lookout had to describe his embarrassing plight. He had been out in the pit toilet using the bathroom, when a sudden strong wind had come up, blowing the small structure over. Try as he might, the lookout could not get out of the facility. Apparently there were no injuries, other than to the lookout's pride.

I knew that this accident could have happened to anyone. Those of us on the staff at Norris gazed up at the summit of Mount Holmes, as we listened to the incessant radio traffic between 700 Fox and the lookout. It was hard not to chuckle over this amusing incident. Lookouts are trained to always be available to answer radio traffic, and this was one event where it was a good thing the lookout had his portable radio with him!

Restoring the Missing Link

People often ask me why in the world I would work in one park for over thirty summers. "With all the spectacular national parks in America, why spend all of your time working in only one?" they ask. That's a good question, but I have a pat answer—or perhaps three answers: I am enamored with Yellowstone's wildness, diversity and wildlife. Actually, I have worked two seasons in Great Smoky Mountains, and one in Glacier, and enjoyed them both. But as far as I am concerned, the Greater Yellowstone Ecosystem stands alone, given the unique combination of these three attributes.

Take the wildlife. As we enter the 21st century, Yellowstone's abundance and variety of wildlife are pretty close to what they were when Lewis and Clark headed west in 1804. When I embark on a wilderness trip in Yellowstone, I realize that I will be sharing the trails with lions, grizzlies and wolves. I have been fortunate to see all three of these predators in the Yellowstone backcountry, but the gray wolf is a relative newcomer. When I saw my first wolf in Yellowstone during the winter of 1973, I did not really appreciate the significance of that sighting. That wolf was obviously a loner passing through the area, because subsequent research made it clear that there were no viable wolf packs in the park at that time.

Once I began my career as a seasonal interpretive ranger in Yellowstone in 1974, I quickly learned of the tremendous void that had been created by the removal of the wolf from the park. I found it fascinating that park rangers actually helped to exterminate wolves in the 1920s. The last known wolf in Yellowstone was killed in 1926. With each passing decade more and more visitors wanted to see this regal predator restored to the Yellowstone ecosystem. We came to call the wolf the "missing link." The gray wolf was the only animal known to be native to Yellowstone, that humans had removed. For all the right reasons, it deserved to be restored.

Throughout the decades of the 1970s and 1980s, I heard all of the sound reasons why the wolf needed to be brought back into the Yellowstone ecosystem. But, as is often the case, "bio/ecopolitics" prevailed. By the time the decade of the 1990s rolled around, the topic of wolf reintroduction was a hot one, but I had become a serious skeptic. I just did not think the political landscape would allow sound science to prevail. On trips into the backcountry, I would often fantasize about hearing wolf howls reverberate across the mountain valleys.

Eventually, my skepticism was proven to be unfounded. In 1995, fourteen wolves from Canada were reintroduced to Yellowstone; the following year, seventeen more were released. The question was now,

223

would the wolves stay in the ecosystem and successfully form packs and reproduce, or would they run for the border? As it turned out, the restoration program was fabulously successful, and was completed ahead of schedule and under budget. I wonder how many other federal government programs can make a similar claim?

In order to help visitors better understand and appreciate the reintroduction program, the Park Service hired wolf expert Rick McIntyre to work in Lamar Valley as an interpretive ranger. Rick had extensive experience with wolves in Alaska, and was extremely committed to the reintroduction program underway in Yellowstone. During most seasons Rick would actually raise the necessary funds for his own salary by giving interpretive programs throughout the country on the Yellowstone wolf restoration program.

I recall the first time I had the privilege of seeing his evening slide program on the wolf at the Madison Campground Amphitheater. He literally brought tears to my eyes as he explained how our nation had plainly declared war on the wolf, and killed it to extinction throughout the West.

He has also written a wonderful book, *A Society of Wolves*, that provides a moving account of the wolf's plight in North America. I got to know Rick pretty well during our training sessions, and was always amazed at how proficient he was at spotting wolves in Lamar Valley. Biologists had predicted that visitors would rarely see the wolves once they were released. Rick was supposed to hopefully occasionally spot one every now and then, and also lead interpretive hikes in Lamar Valley. However, as so often happens in the natural world, the experts were proven to be wrong. Wolf sightings were becoming very common from along the road, crowds were beginning to gather, and Rick's hikes were proving to be very popular—often filling up days ahead of time.

In the summer of 1997, given the problem with the crowds of wolf observers in Lamar Valley and the limited pullouts along the road, park officials apparently changed gears and decided to transfer Rick to Old Faithful. Rick had become the park's wolf "guru" and "Pied Piper." He did indeed attract significant crowds when he was in uniform roving at different spots in Lamar Valley. Perhaps the thinking was that at Old Faithful he could give his wolf talks without causing any problems with traffic congestion. I guess you could say Rick had become a victim of his own success!

It was the summer he was stationed at Old Faithful that I really got to know Rick well, and came to fully appreciate his expertise, knowledge, passion, and commitment to the successful restoration of the wolf in Yellowstone. Even though he was stationed over two hours from most of the wolf activity in Lamar Valley, this did not stop him from spending every possible off-duty hour observing wolves there. Rick kept a detailed journal on his wolf observations that no doubt will be quite valuable to biologists and researchers years from now.

Each time I would see Rick after his days off, he would give me a thorough account of his wolf sightings. His excitement and enthusiasm were amazing. Rick kept egging me on to join him on one of his trips. I knew that on his days off he headed out to his observation post on the Blacktail Plateau before dawn. So in order to join him, I would have to leave Old Faithful at about 3:30 a.m. for the long drive up. I guess I was not sufficiently motivated for a few weeks, but then one day Rick convinced me.

He told me that during the last week he had successfully observed new pups from the Leopold pack. "Rick," I said, "You have talked me into it. Just tell me when and where to meet you." Rick took out his map and pointed out the pullout where he parked his small compact truck. "Meet me here at 5:30 a.m." Rick instructed. "From this spot we will hike about a mile up to the top of a knob, which affords a great view of the Blacktail Deer Plateau."

When the appointed day arrived, I managed to pull myself out of bed at 3:30 a.m., and was on my way, though a bit bleary-eyed. After two hours of driving in the dark, I finally arrived at the pullout along the road where Rick had told me to meet him. There was no moon out and it was still pitch dark, but I did see his truck already there. "Butch, is that you?" he asked. "Yes, I actually made it," I managed to murmur through my grogginess. "Good, let's get up the hill before it gets light," he said. It was late in the summer and on this morning the temperature was below freezing. We started hiking up a ravine in the dark without the benefit of a trail. "Rick, don't we need a light?" I asked. "Nah, I know the way up," he casually answered.

About five minutes into the climb we suddenly encountered an explosion of noise from directly in front of us, as some large animal or group of large animals, had clearly been surprised, probably awakened by our intrusion. "Good God almighty Rick, what is it?" I blurted out. Rick calmly stood still then said, "Must've jumped a big bull elk. Good thing. Last week I jumped a grizzly up here." "Well, gee Rick," I whined, "thanks a lot for letting me know about this now!" I was clearly shaken. I'm not in the habit of walking around in grizzly country in the pitch dark. My body was still trembling as I continued to follow him up the hill. Finally we arrived at a really neat outcropping of rock that provided a wonderful view of the surrounding countryside, but especially to the south of the Blacktail Deer Plateau.

Researchers had constructed a small lookout post to store materials, and duck in out of the weather, if conditions really got bad. Rick handed me a high-powered telescope, as the early pink rays of light began to bathe the plateau. I started to look through the scope and immediately felt as though I was looking for a needle in a haystack. "We'll never find these wolves," I began to think. However, after about two minutes, I heard Rick exclaim "Got'em!" Rick was ecstatic as he helped me line up my scope to also find the wolves. It took me a while, but I finally found them and brought them into focus. I had seen Rick quickly spot wolves out in Lamar Valley before, and was amazed at his wildlife viewing skills.

Once I had my scope on the wolves, I took a seat on a log. Soon, a couple of small pups walked into view and began to play with the adult wolves. The pups and adults were playing with each other just like a family of German shepherds. In fact, I will never forget what went through my mind. It was still a bitter cold morning, and I was groggy from lack of sleep. I was also hungry, having had no breakfast or coffee. I had been scared out of my wits by the big bull elk that pulled the great imitation of a charging grizzly in the pitch-black ravine. Now I was looking at some puppies through a telescope. The thought going through my mind was, "I can't believe I got up in the middle of the night, drove two hours and hiked up a frigid, pitch-black ravine to look at some German shepherd puppies."

Just as this thought had gone through my head, Rick leaned over to me and whispered, "Butch, do you realize that you are looking at the first wolves born into the wild in Yellowstone in over sixty years?" His question hit me just like a punch in the stomach. A tremendous sense of guilt swept over me, and then tears welled up in my eyes as I realized the significance of what I was looking at. This was indeed a moment to be treasured. Suddenly, my concern over my lack of creature comforts disappeared.

Rick had adjusted my attitude, and I was now into my surroundings. I felt a true sense of wildness, as I stood on this remote outcropping of rock with a man I deeply respected, who had spent so much of his life and energy studying, researching, and promoting the role of wolves in the wild. We observed the wolves for over an hour, and Rick recorded their every move and activity in his journal. As I looked out over this spectacular view of the valleys and mountains around us, I just felt wonderful! I knew that this great big wilderness that I loved so much had just gotten even wilder.

In subsequent summers, thousands of visitors have enjoyed the thrill of observing wolves in a wild, natural, ecosystem. Researchers have also gained a wealth of knowledge on wolf behavior by tracking and studying their actions and movements. I have had the privilege several times of receiving in-depth reports from biologists during our seasonal interpretive training each summer. One impression that they have made on me is the fact that even though the wolf is very high on the food chain, it is tough being a wolf in Yellowstone.

A good example of this is a marvelous observation biologists shared with our interpretive staff at training. They were watching a pack of wolves surround a lone bull bison in Pelican Valley during the winter. The wolves seemed to have a great game plan to take down the old buffalo. The bison would move from wind-blown knoll to wind-blown knoll, and in the process would travel through belly-deep snow between the knolls.

The wolves waited for the bison to reach the deepest snow, then several pounced on his back and latched on with their vise-like jaws. The bison hardly seemed to even notice, given the full thickness of its winter coat. The bison just continued to slog through the deep snow up to the next knoll with three or four wolves hanging on. When the bison reached the top of the wind-blown knoll, he simply began to shake his massive body, similar to the way a dog would shake off when getting out of water. Suddenly, the wolves were flying in all directions, some being kicked, and others getting gored. What had looked like an easy meal for this wolf pack turned out to be anything but! Although I didn't see this encounter for myself, just hearing the details of it and knowing that Yellowstone once again has a viable population of wolves produced feelings of pure joy.

The restoration of the wolf in Yellowstone will undoubtedly go down as one of the greatest wildlife protection projects in the history of U.S wildlife management. A major wrong has been righted. The missing link has been restored, and as a result the Greater Yellowstone Ecosystem is a wilder and healthier place.

Backcountry Campsite in Thorofare

Camping in the New Millennium

During August of 2003 Margaret and I decided to take a camping trip to one of our favorite areas, the southwest corner of Yellowstone, known as Bechler region. We had taken many long hikes and backpacking trips into this region, but on this weekend, we were simply going to find a relaxing campsite at the Falls River campground in the Targhee National Forest, then take some short hikes to enjoy the lush scenery along the Bechler and Falls Rivers. The campground is remote and quite primitive, just the kind we like.

Getting to the campground requires driving down a narrow, winding road, which leads to several campsites along the Falls River. However, when we reached the campsites, we simply could not believe our eyes. There, deep in the woods at the end of the road, were some of the largest, most extravagant trailer homes we had ever seen. I guess some people call them camping trailers, but to me these were not camping units. These were mobile homes.

For the life of me, I could not imagine how anyone could maneuver these trailer homes down this snaking road. At first, I thought that perhaps some folks had decided to spend most of the summer living here, but upon further scrutiny, it was obvious that these "campers" were here, like us, just for the weekend.

Our rig was pretty simple by comparison. For most of our camping life, the Bach family always camped in a tent. Then a few years ago, Margaret and I graduated to a small camper that slides into the bed of our pickup truck. It's still similar to a tent though, because the little camper pops up about three feet. The canvas sides have windows that zip open, allowing us to adjust the flow of fresh air in our sleeping area. We absolutely love it and would never imagine wanting or needing anything bigger or fancier.

After spending several hours hiking along the trails of the area, Margaret and I returned to our campsite to cook dinner. The trailer homes around us had brought all the adult toys as well. There were satellite dishes so the television would not have to be sacrificed out in the woods; generators were running for who knows what, and the campground was full of motorbikes and ATVs.

The next morning was quite cool, so I stepped outside to build a fire in the fire pit to warm us up. The folks in the trailer next to us simply turned on the furnace. Somehow, having to listen to the roar of a furnace, and being surrounded by fifty-foot trailers detracts from the camping experience. This all deeply saddened me. These families were denying themselves the true joys of camping out in the woods. I don't know what you should call it when you lug a fifty-foot trailer home into the woods. Maybe "trailering" or "motor homing" or I guess "Rving," but it sure isn't camping!

During the summer of 2002, Margaret and I were camping for the night at what used to be one of our very favorite places, Lonesome Hurst campground on Hebgen Lake, a few miles to the west of the town of West Yellowstone. We were attracted to this location because of the beautiful bay adjacent to the campground that supported an array of wildlife, including moose, sandhill crane, ducks, geese, osprey, eagles, and a variety of shore birds. We also frequently observed owls in this vicinity.

I was sitting out by the campfire, and there was a small hill that separated our campsite from the one next to us, which was actually right on the water. I overheard a conversation that was intriguing. "Men," a voice began, "tomorrow we are going to see what you are made of. Your scout leaders have trained you to properly handle your watercraft, and in the morning we are going to put those skills to work!" I turned to Margaret and told her that I really admired men who took the time to become scout leaders, and teach boys how to paddle a canoe along with the skills of camping. I was looking forward to looking these scouts over in the morning, and watching them paddle their canoes. The bay here was perfect for canoeing, since it was sheltered from the wind, and it supported an abundance and variety of wildlife.

The next morning as we were preparing our breakfast, I heard the scout leaders barking orders again, "Okay men," one shouted out, "let's find out if you have learned the skills you have been taught." I told Margaret I wanted to walk over and take a look at these admirable scout leaders, and the fine young boys as they prepared to launch their canoes. However, just as I stood to walk up the hill, an ungodly noise shattered the peaceful silence of our morning. I ran up the hill to see what terrible event had occurred, and there to my shock, were about twenty boy scouts revving up a big fleet of jet skis! The noise and air pollution were dreadful! I could not believe it. Boy scouts? On jet skis? In this beautiful natural setting?

This particular section of Hebgen Lake, which for years had been so beautiful, and peaceful to visit, soon became a Mecca for jet skis. I complained to the campground host, and he enthusiastically agreed with me, saying I should take my complaint to the Forest Service. This I did, but I was told they had no jurisdiction out on the lake's waters. So I complained to the Montana Department of Fish, Wildlife and Parks. I told them that visitors for years had come to this beautiful bay on Hebgen Lake to enjoy the sights and sounds of nature, not to hear the roar of machines and smell their fumes.

This is precisely what folks try to leave behind in the cities when they come out here to camp! I suggested that a simple "no wake" rule in this bay would solve the problem. After all, for years anglers had launched their boats here and headed out on the lake. But these jet skis were a different breed. They launched, but they didn't leave. They stayed right off shore and played, running around in circles and jumping the waves. The air and noise pollution were incessant, and it dislocated the bay's wildlife.

Later that same summer Margaret and I were camped at our favorite site overlooking the bay. The next morning we noticed a grandfather and his grandson fishing from a small boat about 100 yards offshore. Suddenly, two jet skis roared by and decided to run circles around the little boat. The ensuing waves created unstable water conditions for the man and the youngster attempting to fish. I looked through my sixteen-power binoculars and noticed the elderly man motion to his grandson to just ignore the jet skis. The mischievous side of me wanted to pick up a rock and throw it at the young men on the jet skis harassing the old man and boy, but I resisted the temptation. I believe this was the last time Margaret and I camped at Lonesome Hurst campground. As far as I know, the Montana Department of Fish, Wildlife and Parks has not taken any action to reduce the use of jet skis in this area of Hebgen Lake.

Given the revolution in "camping" vehicles, the Park Service should attempt to keep some campgrounds rather primitive for the tents and small trucks and popups. Yellowstone has done a good job with this. Fishing Bridge is the RV campground complete with hookups. Given the prime grizzly habitat in the area, tents and other soft-sided camping units are not allowed. The park's larger campgrounds—Grant, Madison and Canyon Village—take reservations and are better suited for large RVs. Other campgrounds, like Pebble Creek, Slough Creek, Norris, Indian Creek, Tower Falls, Mammoth, and Lewis Lake, are smaller, do not take reservations and are better suited for small camping units.

Several of Yellowstone's campgrounds—Lewis Lake, Grant, Bridge Bay and Fishing Bridge—are situated near the shores of the park's two major lakes: Lewis Lake and Yellowstone Lake. Thankfully, the National Park Service in Yellowstone had the wisdom and foresight years ago to prohibit jet skis on park waters.

For Your Protection Yellowstone Has Been Closed

Yellowstone National Park is a natural, wild ecosystem. It is not Disney World. Potential dangers include grizzly bears, scalding water, rugged mountains, deep canyons, swift rivers and ice-cold lakes. However, it is difficult to make a strong case that Yellowstone is really a dangerous place to visit, since only a few people out of three million visitors annually suffer serious and/or fatal injuries. I have always maintained that you are safer in the backcountry than anywhere else. From a statistical point of view this is true. Most serious injuries and deaths in the park involve automobile accidents.

However, there are no guarantees in the backcountry. Accidents do happen. I have had a few close calls myself. So what should you do if a loved one tragically dies in the park as a result of a bear mauling, thermal burn, bison goring, climbing accident, or a boating accident on a stream or lake? Unfortunately, some turn to, *or respond to*, an attorney.

Anytime an individual dies from an accident in Yellowstone, it is truly a tragedy. One day at Old Faithful we received the report that an elderly gentleman had fallen into the Yellowstone River while fishing and was presumed drowned. The man's son was out touring the park and did not know of his Dad's terrible accident. An "important message" bulletin was posted at all park visitor centers in an attempt to locate the son as soon as possible. I was on the desk when the young man approached and inquired as to why his name was posted on the important message board outside. I followed protocol and put him in contact with the communications center in Mammoth, so they could relay the message. I will never forget the young man's reaction upon learning the awful news about his father.

However, one person's calamity should not be allowed to lead to a disaster of a different nature that could negatively impact the visiting public. For example, during the summer of 2000, a dreadful accident occurred near the vicinity of the Lower Geyser Basin. It involved some concession employees who fell into a hot spring that measured 178 degrees F.

The young employees had hiked about a mile into the backcountry to go swimming in a river that runs right through a thermal basin. From all indications the accident was the result of a combination of bad judgment and bad luck. The bad judgment involved the young people waiting until after dark to hike out of the area. There was no moon and they reportedly had no flashlight, so they were unable to see where they were stepping.

The bad luck occurred when they apparently mistook the sound of a hot spring runoff channel with that of the river and tried to jump over it. The three landed directly in the hot spring. One young lady died and two young men were badly burned but survived.

There was an outpouring of sympathy for these young people and their families following the accident. Then, amidst all of the hopes and prayers for the two surviving young men came the disturbing news that one of them had filed a lawsuit against the National Park Service. His suit claimed that the accident was the result of negligence by the Park Service. Specifically, the suit stated that the entire area should have been closed at night, and there should have been barriers placed around the hot spring.

When I read the specifics of the lawsuit, I felt a sense of remorse that so much time, money and energy would be invested in something that clearly is not in the public's best interest. I wished that same time, money and energy could have been invested in an effort to raise funds to assist this young man and his family pay what must be sizeable medical expenses.

The region where these young people were traveling is a backcountry area with no officially designated trails. There are an estimated 10,000 hot springs in Yellowstone National Park. Should the National Park Service build a fence around each and every spring? Wouldn't this destroy the very natural beauty that visitors come to Yellowstone to see? There are also many thermal features scattered around the park's backcountry. In fact, two noteworthy geyser basins, Shoshone and Heart Lake, are both deep in the backcountry. Should the NPS build fences around the hundreds of beautiful thermal features found in these two backcountry thermal basins?

What about the backcountry camping that occurs in the park? Many of the designated campsites are near such thermal basins, including Shoshone and Heart Lake. Should the NPS ban backcountry camping at these pristine, wild places? All employees who work in Yellowstone attend orientation sessions given by park rangers. The potential dangers that are present are strongly emphasized in these sessions.

Some people might say that such lawsuits are simply the American way. Everyone knows how the game is played. You file a lawsuit for millions of dollars of damages, but you really have no intention of ever going to trial. All you want to do is settle for a few hundred thousand out of court. Trouble is, this is not the way such lawsuits are handled by the Park Service, and for good reason. If the NPS settled with plaintiffs in such suits, just imagine the precedent it would set. The restrictions that would follow could be severe.

For example, over the years I have had a couple of unpleasant accidents while floating the Snake River through the Tetons. Both occurred while I was attempting to navigate narrow channels and I ran into a cottonwood tree that had been felled by beavers, thus blocking the channel. I once asked a Grand Teton river patrol ranger why he did not bring in a saw and remove these hazardous trees. His response was interesting. "We can't do that," he said. "Our goal is to keep the river in a natural situation. The first time we start cutting trees we will have set a precedent for removing river obstacles. Then, when accidents occur we will be sued for negligence."

Therefore, the NPS does its best to post warnings of these hazards at the launch sites along the Snake River, but they do not attempt to "groom" the river. After all, it is a wild river, not a golf course. Why should they attempt to "manicure" the banks of this wild river? The Snake River is not some type of theme park raft ride. It is a river that flows through wild, untamed country!

In my opinion, the NPS in Yellowstone does everything humanly possible to warn visitors and employees of potential hazards while striving to protect and preserve the natural scenery. Information containing warnings on possible dangers in the park is given out at entrance gates, and at backcountry offices when obtaining a backcountry permit, and is also posted at trailheads. In addition, all concession employees are required to attend orientation sessions that cover prospective dangers in the park.

The accident involving the three young people occurred in a backcountry area that is not accessible by trail. Unless the NPS erected signs every ten yards along the road system, certainly not a practical suggestion, it is hard to imagine what else could be done within reason.

In 1972 a young man from Alabama was tragically killed in the Old Faithful area by a grizzly bear. He unfortunately broke just about every safety rule in the book regarding hiking and camping in bear country. First, he and his friend hitched a ride into the park, so they did not formally receive the NPS publications, which point out the potential dangers in the park along with park regulations. However, according to later court testimony, the person who had given the young men a ride had warned them about bears, and had told them to go to a ranger station.

Second, the young men camped illegally in the woods near Grand Geyser. There were no legal campsites anywhere near this spot. Third, they left food out in their camp when they left to visit facilities in the Old Faithful area. When the men returned later that evening, they found a grizzly rummaging through their illegal camp. The grizzly attacked and killed one of the young men. The other man ran through the geyser basin in the darkness to get help. It is a miracle that he did not fall into a hot spring or a geyser in the process.

Despite the fact that this young man violated so many park regulations, which have been established for the safety and protection of park visitors (and also the protection of native wildlife), the deceased man's family sued the National Park Service. Unbelievably, a judge ruled in favor of the deceased man's family. Perhaps this judge thought that Yellowstone should keep its animals safely behind fences, like at a zoo. Or perhaps the judge felt sorry for this family, since the young man was probably being counted on to help with the family business endeavors.

After all, the federal government has access to plenty of money. Why not use some of it to aid this family regarding this tragic incident? In any case, it was a decision that would have set a terrible precedent for our country's national parks and the public that visits them. For this reason the NPS appealed the judgment and fortunately prevailed. The judge's ruling was overturned.

Following this I was shocked to observe a U.S. Senator from Alabama present a bill before Congress requesting a sizeable settlement for this family. The Senator claimed that it was only fair that the federal government pay a settlement to this family from Alabama, since the young man had been killed by a "federal grizzly bear." At the time I was attending graduate school at Auburn University in my home state of Alabama. I decided to write my Senator a letter to express my frustration regarding his actions.

I asked him this question: "If I ever fall off of a "federal" mountain, drown in a "federal" river or lake, am gored to death by a "federal" buffalo or fall into a "federal" hot spring, will you also come before the U.S. Congress and ask that tax dollars be awarded to my family?" The Senator responded that he was doing the correct thing and was only attempting to help one of his constituents from Alabama. As far as I know, the Senator was not successful in convincing his colleagues to pass the bill.

The point is the American public is headed down a slippery slope with litigation against the government when injuries and deaths occur in our national parks, which were established for the very reason to preserve and protect a small semblance of our country's natural heritage. You never know what a judge or a jury will do. We have all read the headlines from court rulings that seem to defy common sense.

Regarding the lawsuit filed over the thermal burn in 2000, fortunately, a judge eventually ruled that this suit had no merit. But all it would take is for one or more of these types of ludicrous lawsuits to be ruled in favor of the plaintiff to lead to unprecedented restrictions by the Park Service. Obviously, the safest and easiest restriction would involve federal officials simply posting signs that read: "For Your Protection This Area Has Been Closed to the Public."

You Can Never Go Home—the Value of Public Lands

I first came to Yellowstone as a college student in 1968. I have fond memories of that summer as a twenty-two year-old, exuberant kid discovering the wilderness and hiking into such glorious places as Grebe Lake, Dunanda Falls and Osprey Falls. Today, I can go back to those places and enjoy the same, natural setting as I did over three decades ago.

I wish I could say the same for my boyhood memories back in central Alabama. The beautiful ravine where I spent many summer days perched in a tree house listening to songbirds is now paved over. The wonderful city parks of my youth in Montgomery were sold off and developed to avoid being integrated. The adventure of finding arrowheads along the wild tributaries of Jordan Lake and Martin Lake is no longer possible. The shores are now lined with summer cabins.

My grandparents lived on the outskirts of town adjacent to several hundred acres of pristine, hardwood forest, replete with meadows and a number of ponds. The area was literally teeming with life—hawks, songbirds, turtles and frogs—a naturalist's paradise. It was in these woods that my love of the natural world was born and then blossomed.

My Mom told me that the land had been willed to a nursing home with the stipulation that it could never be developed. However, when I was in college taking courses such as Resource Economics and Regional Planning, that emphasized the need to use some foresight in setting aside natural areas close to cities to provide quality living, I was dismayed to learn from my Mom that somehow the land was scheduled to be sold to the highest bidder.

The next week I called officials in Montgomery to urge them to utilize federal matching grants to set some of this wonderful land aside. Even if only a quarter of the land had been preserved, it would have been a superb investment for the citizens of Montgomery. However, apathy prevailed and today this land that was such a natural treasure in my youth is wall-to-wall commercial and real estate development. Not a single acre was set aside for recreation.

Therefore, my cherished boyhood memories of growing up in Alabama are now just that—only memories. It is impossible for me to share with my children and grandchildren those special places. They are gone.

The development and subsequent loss of natural areas is an insidious process. A piece of land here and there and before you know it, the cumulative effect is devastating. Thank goodness for public lands, whether they be city, state or national lands, so that we can maintain a semblance of our natural world. When I discovered Yellowstone, a fragment of our once wild country that was still intact, undeveloped and actually protected, it is no wonder that I fell in love with it.

Aldo Leopold once made a profound statement: "Wilderness can shrink but it cannot grow." You would think that with our growing population and shrinking wild areas, setting aside and preserving additional public lands would be a popular thing to do, especially in the West, where we still have an opportunity to avoid making the same horrendous mistakes we made in the East and South. But if anything, Westerners appear even less concerned, at least based on the politicians they elect and send to Washington to represent them.

Many of the politicians from the three states that make up Yellowstone— Montana, Wyoming and Idaho--almost seem to be anti-Yellowstone and anti-wilderness. It wasn't always like this. In fact, when I was stationed at Malmstrom Air Force Base during the early 1970s in Great Falls, Montana, I was in awe of Montana's two U.S. Senators, Mike Mansfield and Lee Metcalf. These two gentlemen were true statesmen. They represented the people of Montana with great dignity, and they deeply loved the natural outdoor legacy that all Montanans should be thankful for. Today, there is even a wilderness area in Montana adjacent to Yellowstone named for Lee Metcalf.

We Americans, with our economic system, have a tough time using foresight. What would America be like in the 21st century if some of our forefathers had not had enough foresight to protect some of our nation's natural heritage? What will life be like in America in the 22nd century if we do not use more foresight in preserving and protecting what few wild areas we have remaining?

Way back in *1910*, when most of the West was still undeveloped, Theodore Roosevelt, a *Republican*, stated, "I recognize the rights and duty of this generation to develop and use the natural resources of our land; *but I do not recognize the right to waste them or to rob, by wasteful use, the generations that come after us.*" Obviously, Teddy Roosevelt was a visionary. Today's Republicans would do well to study this great conservationist and examine their party's roots.

Public lands are a wonderful way to protect our natural environment for present and future generations. Clearly, management of public lands is critical. Certainly that includes protecting the integrity of the Greater Yellowstone Ecosystem. The national forests that surround Yellowstone National Park provide critical wildlife habitat and an important buffer zone for the park. These lands provide the threads of a greater fabric that we refer to as the Greater Yellowstone Ecosystem. Without them the integrity of Yellowstone National Park would be greatly diminished.

I recall one summer, when I was working in Great Smoky Mountains National Park, I hiked the Cove Mountain trail which skirts the north boundary of the park. I was appalled at the summer home development right up to the boundary line. The same exact thing happened along the Little Pigeon River, which flows out from Greenbriar in the Great Smokies. Fortunately, Yellowstone has a much better buffer zone—if we can make the correct decisions to manage these lands in the best interests of preserving the ecosystem. Sometimes difficult choices must be made.

For example, during the 1990s, a gold mine was proposed very close to the boundary of Yellowstone in the northeast corner of the park. The mine would have destroyed critical grizzly habit in beautiful, sub alpine meadows. While I have nothing against gold mining, you cannot have both a wild, intact ecosystem and gold mines on the border of Yellowstone National Park. Fortunately, the Clinton administration decided in favor of preserving the integrity of the Greater Yellowstone Ecosystem, and bought out the gold mine.

In recent years there have been concerns that Yellowstone's grizzly population is an "island" population, since there are no corridors to other grizzly populations elsewhere. Bear inbreeding can eventually weaken the genetic strength of the Yellowstone grizzly. In Glacier National Park there exists a wildlife corridor where grizzlies from the Canadian Rockies can intermingle and breed with the grizzlies in northern Montana. No such corridor exists for the Yellowstone grizzlies.

Therefore, the U.S. Fish and Wildlife Service was prepared to reintroduce grizzlies into large wilderness areas in Idaho, thus establishing an important corridor for providing genetic diversity with the Yellowstone grizzlies. This plan had been approved by federal and state land agencies, and was set to go forward, but the Bush administration cancelled it due to opposition by Idaho's governor.

Politics always has and always will have a lot to do with maintaining the health and integrity of the Greater Yellowstone Ecosystem. Those who love Yellowstone need to stay involved. The public lands in and around Yellowstone National Park that make up the Greater Yellowstone Ecosystem belong to *all* Americans, not just to some special interests in Idaho, Montana and Wyoming. After all, most politicians in these three surrounding states were opposed to the reintroduction of the wolf to Yellowstone. But since most Americans in all fifty states wanted the wolf restored to its rightful place, our federal government, under the Clinton administration, got the job done.

Public lands are a wonderful gift to our children and grandchildren. The communities around our country that are consistently awarded with high quality of life ratings typically feature such public land amenities as parks, greenways and rails to trails systems. Given the amount of public land in and around Yellowstone, it is no wonder that the ecosystem is facing pressures from more people moving in. People vote with their feet and they love public lands. If only politicians at all levels of government fully understood and appreciated their importance.

Ecopolitics

Having taught college economics for thirty years, I am convinced that Capitalism is the best type of economic system in the world for providing the best standard of living for society as a whole. That being said, there are three necessary ingredients for our free market system to truly excel. First, you must have competition in the market place. Second, you must have necessary regulation (the trick here is how much constitutes too little or too much). And third, you must have foresight.

Foresight, or specifically, the lack of it, seems to be the biggest problem we have with the U.S. free market system. Our free enterprise system does a great job providing us with theme parks and golf courses, but it does not effectively provide us with large, natural wilderness areas such as a Yellowstone, Yosemite or Great Smoky Mountains National Park. This is the role of government, and it requires a great deal of foresight.

The public has certainly demonstrated that they love their national parks. Since our federal government is budgeted by 435 members of the U.S. House of Representative and 100 U.S. Senators with leadership from the President of the United States, this foresight has to come from politicians, and this is where we run into problems with our national parks.

Just about every person I have ever met who works for the National Park Service joined the agency because they have a deep appreciation of our national parks, and desire to protect and preserve them as well as help the visiting public to enjoy and appreciate their parks. It is therefore too bad that we cannot allow the park superintendents, these professional men and women with great expertise and training in managing our public lands, to actually run the parks.

Politicians typically do not have the educational background or work experience to qualify them to run a national park, but that doesn't stop them from trying. In Yellowstone, politicians accuse park management of allowing too many animals, such as elk, to populate the park, but when park management succeeds in reintroducing the wolf, which may dent the elk population, the officials catch hell for that. Yellowstone park managers often find themselves in a "damned if you do, damned if you don't" situation.

Frankly, I never dreamed that politicians would ever allow the National Park Service to reintroduce the wolf. Despite overwhelming scientific evidence that the ecosystem needed the wolf, and that public opinion favored it, it took many years for this momentous event to finally occur. Politicians in the states around the park put up one obstacle after another, but finally the public's will prevailed.

In another example, the fires of 1988 really brought out the worst from some politicians. Forest scientists had documented that forest fires had burned on the Yellowstone Plateau as long as there had been trees there, and it was simply nature's way of recycling nutrients and keeping the forest diverse and healthy. However, after the fires of '88, politicians claimed that the park's forests had been destroyed, the soil sterilized, and that the park would never recover. Of course, they were wrong, but politicians are seldom held accountable for their public statements when it turns out they were 100% wrong. Following the big fires of '88, politicians intervened in the park's fire policy, and for a period of time required that all natural fires be extinguished, even if trained fire experts were certain that the fire would burn itself out.

This resulted in the waste of hundreds of thousands of tax dollars. A lightning-caused fire (which had a zero chance of spreading) would pop up on top of a mountain, but the park was ordered to fly in crews of smoke jumpers—at considerable expense to taxpayers, to put it out. Fortunately, the park was eventually allowed to resume a more flexible and scientific policy in managing forest fires.

During the past several summers the Rocky Mountain West has suffered from severe drought, which obviously results in more forest fires. On one hot August day, with the sound of helicopters racing overhead to transport courageous firefighters to the scene of several fires burning, I opened up a copy of *The Wall Street Journal* to read a column about the fires in and around Yellowstone. The writer said they were burning because of President Bill Clinton. I could not help but laugh out loud. What did Bill Clinton have to do with this severe drought?

The column made the common claim that many politicians make, that if the forests were just "thinned" out in the West, we wouldn't have these fires. Sometimes the constituents of such politicians visit Yellowstone and ask why we aren't thinning the forests. "Why do you just allow all of those trees to go to waste?" they ask. I recall that one summer our interpretive ranger training included a session in the "Art of Verbal Self-Defense." I find myself using the tips learned from that workshop to answer such questions: "How would you suggest that we go about cutting the trees?" I ask in return. "Well, just go out there and cut them down!" "Okay, I understand," I add, "but how would you get out there to cut the trees down?"

At this point the conversation usually progresses into a discussion of what would really have to occur to "thin" the forest. Roads would have to be built all over the park's backcountry to harvest the trees. Visitors usually readily admit that they really don't want to see road scars all over the countryside in a national park.

We often run into the same problem with protection of thermal features. Several times each summer I am asked the question, "Why are you people allowing all of this energy to just go to waste?" Of course, they are referring to the hot water coming out of the ground in the hot springs and geysers in the thermal basins. I have a pat answer to that question: "It is not going to waste. It fires the imaginations of three million people a year!" I then point out that you just can't have it both ways. If you start to drill for energy in a thermal basin, you will bleed off heat, water, and pressure and destroy the geysers. The energy that would flow from such drilling would be rather insignificant anyway.

The fact that drilling for energy in thermal basins can destroy geysers has been well documented in several places in the world, most notably Iceland. There, geothermal drilling destroyed geysers up to fifteen miles away. Yellowstone's most famous geyser basin, the Upper Geyser Basin, is located only *thirteen* miles from the west boundary. While there are protections against unregulated geothermal drilling on U.S. Forest Service lands adjacent to the park, there is no such protection at all for private lands along the park boundary. After a scare with proposed drilling near LaDuke Hot Spring (on the northern park boundary), where scientists had concerns over the impact it might have on the beautiful terraces at Mammoth Hot Springs, the National Park Service expressed concern over being able to preserve the rare thermal features in the park.

Consequently, politicians from Montana and Wyoming proposed a bill in Congress, The Old Faithful Protection Act, that if passed would ensure the protection of the world's most famous geysers in the Upper Geyser Basin. The bill was really quite simple. A private landowner who owned property within fifteen miles of the boundary could drill for *cold* water for irrigation for crops or water for cattle, but they would be prohibited from deep drilling for geothermal energy.

While the Montana and Wyoming congressional delegations supported the Old Faithful Protection Act, politicians from Idaho, most notably Senator Larry Craig, opposed it. Typically, it is very difficult for this type of legislation to pass in Congress, unless it enjoys the support of the local members of Congress who represent the affected area.

So as a result of Idaho's opposition, the Old Faithful Protection Act failed to pass. The reasons given for their opposition centered on the great institution of Capitalism, private property—the idea that the federal government has no business telling a private landowner what he or she could or could not do with their land. Now, the institution of private property is a wonderful part of our economic system, and probably best serves society over ninety per cent of the time. But here is where the problem of not exercising foresight comes into play.

Suppose that some landowner decides to drill a geothermal well near the west boundary. What if that produces the same result that has occurred in other regions such as Iceland? Suppose Old Faithful (the world's most famous geyser), Castle, Grand (the world's largest active geyser), Beehive and Riverside Geysers were all destroyed as a direct result. Millions of present and future generations of Americans would be robbed of their natural heritage. Can you imagine trying to explain to your children and grandchildren how our nation was unable to protect something as rare, unique and beloved as the geysers of Yellowstone?

I once wrote a letter as a private citizen to Senator Craig, asking him if he had ever read the studies and reports that the National Park Service has produced which substantiated the need for The Old Faithful Protection Act, and why he would not support it. Senator Craig wrote back to basically say that he simply did not believe that this legislation was necessary. Well, needless to say, I sincerely hope that Senator Craig is correct. But my concern is, if there is only a one per cent chance that drilling might occur, and another one per cent chance it could hurt the geysers, why take this chance to begin with?

When the National Park Service attempted to design a winter use plan that would reduce the terrible noise and air pollution being caused by snowmobiles, politicians again intervened to prevent the park from carrying out this plan. Most of the concern this time centered not on what was best for the protection and preservation of the park's resources, but what was best for business interests located in adjacent communities. This was interesting because when Yellowstone National Park was established in 1872, there was no such thing as a West Yellowstone, Gardiner or Cooke City, Montana; or a Cody, or Jackson, Wyoming, for that matter.

The towns adjacent to the park really popped up to provide services for visitors to the park. Nowhere does it say in the legislation that created Yellowstone National Park that the park should be managed so as to maximize the wealth of nearby communities. So does it really make sense for business interests in these towns to indirectly dictate policy (through politicians) on how the park should be managed for present and future generations?

The park's winter use plan is still being worked out as of this writing, and it is sincerely hoped that new technology will play a big role in eliminating the unacceptable air and noise pollution currently in the park. My friend Tom Gerrity of Great Falls, Montana once told me a story of how some of his friends from Boston flew in a few years ago, and rode into Old Faithful on a snow coach to visit the basin, hoping to experience its uniqueness during the winter. He said that the air and noise pollution from snow machines was so bad that his friends vowed to never return. "The place sounded like a chain saw convention," he told me.

Personally, I feel the same way. When I visit Yellowstone during the winter, I usually ski in somewhere along the Northwest corner or I drive down to Mammoth and go out to Lamar Valley. I really would love to go see Old Faithful during the winter. As soon as I know that the experience will not include excessive air and noise pollution, I will go.

Perhaps the ultimate example of how politicians just don't always know what is best for a national park was demonstrated in Grand Teton National Park. Members of the Wyoming congressional delegation managed to draft a bill that would have *abolished* the park. The bill then actually *passed*

Congress. Fortunately for all Americans, President Franklin Delano Roosevelt vetoed the bill. But what if President Roosevelt had not vetoed this bill? We would have been denied the preservation of one of our nation's crown jewels.

Park managers attempt to utilize the best science available to protect and preserve resources, which often centers on wildlife. Their efforts to protect the grizzly bear, mountain lion, wolf and other species are sometimes met with fierce opposition from politicians who may try to manipulate park policy by starving the park's budget. Of course, it is always healthy to have a good open dialogue when major policies are being formulated. This is healthy and will only improve the eventual decisions made. Public opinion is obviously very important, as is the use of solid science when formulating park policy. However, political intervention often gets in the way of a healthy decision making process. In the long run, there is little doubt that "ecopolitics" usually hurts, rather than helps, regarding the protection and preservation of our precious park resources.

My friend and former interpretive ranger colleague, Mike Yochim, has recently completed a doctoral dissertation at the University of Wisconsin titled, "Compromising Yellowstone: The Interest Group—National Park Service Relationship in Modern Policy-Making." Mike's research reveals that over the years, much of the park's policy has been heavily influenced by those who view Yellowstone as an economic engine rather than a natural preserve. That influence continues today.

Ideally, you hope that the millions of visitors from all fifty states in the union who visit Yellowstone communicate to their own representatives, senators, and the President, that they want their park to be preserved for their children and grandchildren. If this were to happen, politicians might be more likely to work most of the time to support park managers in their efforts to protect and preserve the Greater Yellowstone Ecosystem.

Bison Walking the Road Along the Madison River

Triumphs and Challenges

Yellowstone's future is fraught with many potential pitfalls that could seriously harm the health and integrity of this magnificent ecosystem in coming decades. It is rather easy to become pessimistic about the park's future; however, Yellowstone has many supporters who work extremely hard to protect it. Not all of the news is bad; let's look at the good news before concluding with what needs to be done to protect the park in coming decades.

When visitors find out how long I have been working in Yellowstone National Park they usually ask me, "I'll bet you've seen a lot of changes over the years haven't you?" The insinuation is that the park was probably a superior place to visit in the "good old days." Actually, I think the park is in better condition today and offers a much higher quality visit than it did thirty years ago. When I worked as a Sanitation Supervisor for the old Yellowstone Park Company at Canyon Village in 1968, a myriad of serious problems existed.

Looking back, it is hard to believe some of the things that occurred in the park. For example, I was basically in charge of dishes, pots, and garbage at the Canyon Village restaurants. Each evening the wait and bus staff would bring us an inordinate amount of leftover food scraps from the dining room, coffee shop and cafeteria, filling up about eight large garbage cans. Around midnight it was my job to roll the garbage cans outside on the garbage dock for the NPS maintenance workers to pick up early the next morning.

It was not unusual to find one or two grizzly bears waiting on the dock for my arrival. The bears would hide behind the dozen or so empty cans out on the dock, and once I started rolling out the full cans, they would stand up on their hind legs waiting for me to leave. This was so common that I would nonchalantly go about my work not thinking twice about sharing that dock with one of the most powerful predators in North America. For some reason these bears would not come out and eat while anyone was standing around on the dock, so at least they had a semblance of wildness in them.

The NPS garbage crews that arrived the next morning would find that half of the garbage had been eaten, which was fine with them. That was just less garbage they had to haul out to the Hayden Valley dump. Yes, there were open garbage dumps in the middle of gorgeous Hayden Valley. I knew better than to hike out to that place to watch the grizzlies, but I did get a good idea of what went on out there from Scott Bryan.

Before becoming an interpretive ranger at Norris in 1974, Scott had worked as a laborer for the NPS, hauling garbage to the Hayden Valley dumps. Scott related to me how the bears would beg almost like little pups,

245

putting their paws up on the truck. He also said that they would get into vicious fights with each other over a select morsel of food (I used to be amazed at the number of untouched Kansas City strip steaks that came back to the dishwashers—sometimes the kitchen staff would eat them, thus depriving the bears of a meal the next day).

Scott said he would also cringe when he witnessed bears wolfing down plastic wrap, aluminum foil, seasoned paper and other such gastro-pleasing victuals. In other words, the entire scene was pretty miserable to watch considering you were in the middle of one of the most pristine ecosystems in North America.

There was a similar dump at Rabbit Creek, where all of the Old Faithful garbage was dumped. Now if you really wanted to see garbage grizzlies, the place to go was the West Yellowstone "Drive-In Bear Show," the nickname the park's concession employees used for the outdoor landfill along the park's boundary just north of the town of West Yellowstone. Here people would line up their cars, just like at a drive-in movie theater, and wait for the grizzlies to come out to feed on the garbage.

Margaret and I attended the "show" once, and it was quite a sight. Just after sunset a few bears began to emerge from the surrounding dense forest, but once it was dark the action began in earnest. People turned on their headlights and enjoyed the entertainment. Occasionally, bears would get into a fight, just as Scott had mentioned to me, but as long as you stayed in your vehicle, I suppose you were relatively safe. However, I recall on the night we were there, an individual with more guts than brains got out of his car, walked right up to a feeding grizzly, and took a photo with a brilliant flash from his camera. The grizzly reared up and I thought we were about to witness a tragic incident right before our very eyes, but the old bear settled back into digging through the garbage again.

Driving around the park in the late 1960s could be a nightmare. Begging black bears, conditioned to human feeding, would line up along the roads, thus grid-locking the traffic flow. The Canyon to Tower road was especially bad. If you were trying to reach a destination within a reasonable time you were often out of luck.

Today, there is some type of animal "theme park" in Idaho not too far from Yellowstone that runs ads on the radio all summer about how you can still enjoy the "good old days" in Yellowstone, when the bears would come right up to your car. If some people think watching a bunch of garbage bears conditioned to humans is entertaining, I guess that's a personal preference, but thank goodness this no longer occurs within the boundaries of Yellowstone National Park.

Looking back at how conditioned Yellowstone's bears were to human foods and how prevalent they were along the park's roads and campgrounds, it is somewhat of a miracle that more people were not killed or seriously injured. Harlan Kredit once told me a story about a camper at Fishing Bridge campground, who was sleeping out in the open in a sleeping bag with no tent. During the night he awoke to find a grizzly stepping right over him. The dazed camper sat up to watch the grizzly mosey right past several other folks who were also sleeping under the stars.

Of course, the National Park Service changed its bear management policies dramatically, beginning around 1970. Today, all the garbage is removed from the ecosystem. Feeding of bears along the roads, in the campgrounds, or anywhere else in the park is strictly prohibited. If you are fortunate enough to see a bear in Yellowstone today, you will be looking at a superb animal feeding naturally in a wild ecosystem, rather than a roadside bum begging for a handout.

If you get caught in an animal jam today, chances are bison, not bears, will cause it. The bison population in the late 1960s numbered around 500; today, the bison number more than 4000. In May of 2004, Margaret and I were driving from West Yellowstone to Old Faithful after dark, and we encountered a herd of hundreds of bison walking right down the middle of the road.

On this evening the herd was moving up the canyon south of Madison, and there was really nowhere for them to move off the road. Ours was the only vehicle on the road at this late hour. As we watched the animals lumber along ahead of us, we figured they were moving at a pace of around two miles per hour. With about three miles to go through this section of road before the terrain leveled out, we realized we were doomed to over an hour wait here. I decided to ease my vehicle through the herd, and felt like I had gone back in time 150 years. There were bison as far as we could see on all sides of us. Today's visitors to the Madison Valley of Yellowstone during May and early June see a sight that likewise takes them back to a time reminiscent of the original, natural West.

There were few, if any, mountain lions within Yellowstone in 1968. Today, the population has recovered somewhat and there is a decent population of fifteen to twenty lions concentrated in the north portion of the park. Of course, there were no viable populations of wolves in the park then either. Perhaps an occasional lone wolf drifted through, but the park was missing a key component of its wildlife—the "missing link." That missing link is restored today to the delight of thousands of visitors each year.

The NPS greatly improved the visitor experience within geyser basins, such as at Old Faithful by re-routing roads. This helped reduce vandalism and impact as well. Several campgrounds were removed to further reduce crowding and impact.

A natural burn policy was adopted in 1972 to allow some lightning-caused fires away from developed areas to burn, thus allowing some recycling of nutrients and insuring forest diversity. From the time that Yellowstone was established in 1872, up through 1987, a rather insignificant amount of acreage burned in the park. At such a high elevation heavy snows and wet summers were the norm. However, this cycle changed dramatically in 1988. A summer of drought combined with the huge buildup of fuel helped produce the biggest burn Yellowstone had experienced in perhaps 200 years. Most scientists agree that the benefit to the ecosystem and its wildlife was substantial. However, from the human perspective, fire is often considered an evil act of nature, even in a wild ecosystem like Yellowstone. It didn't help that the media confused the public into thinking that the NPS was content to let the fires burn without fighting them. A study by Conrad Smith at the Ohio State University concluded that the media's reporting of the fires of 1988 was often very inaccurate. In fact, the park's natural burn policy only applied for remote areas when fire conditions were not extreme.

The effort to extinguish the fires in Yellowstone actually became one of the largest ever in the nation, as over 25,000 fire fighters came to the park to fight the fires, and over $125 million were spent in the attempt to control them. In the end, it was nature's September snows that doused the fires.

Today, most of the burned forest has experienced a tremendous rebirth, and the increased abundance and variety of plants benefits wildlife. However, some visitors still express outrage at the evidence of the great fires of 1988. There still exists the perception that humans have total control over natural events such as forest fires.

During the summer of 2003, a gentleman approached the desk at the Old Faithful Visitor Center where I was working, and demanded to know who the superintendent of the park was in 1988. "Bob Barbee," I answered. "Well, I assume he was fired?" he asked. "No," I replied. "In fact, he received a promotion and became a regional manager in Alaska." The visitor expressed outrage. At this point I asked him where he was from. "Florida," he answered. "Well, let me ask you something," I said. "Remember Hurricane Andrew?" "Yes," the visitor replied. "Did you fire the governor of Florida when Andrew blew through your state?" I asked. The gentlemen chuckled and seemed to pick up on where I was headed with the conversation. Before we were finished the visitor shook my hand and seemed to possess a much better understanding and appreciation of the natural force that fire plays in a wild ecosystem.

So overall, I would have to say that Yellowstone is a much healthier place than it was thirty years ago. There have been many triumphs. But there remain many challenges as we move into the new millennium. One concern I have regarding the management of Yellowstone, or any national park for that matter, is whether or not we document a reliable baseline for assessing how the resource changes over time.

For example, the Bechler region of the park's backcountry is one area where I have unfortunately observed an insidious deterioration of the resource. When Rod Busby and I first backpacked twelve miles into Union Falls in July of 1969, I felt as though we had discovered Shangri-La. We did not see another soul during our two-day trip. We did not even see any human tracks along the way. In fact, we felt as though we were hiking down a moose trail. The trail was full of their sign, plus we came across several during the trip. The trail was in great shape—the soil very firm.

On my last visit there, in August, 2001, we encountered one horse party after another. Heavy use by outfitters and other horse parties had ground the soil into ankle-deep muck in several sections. A horse is basically a 1500-pound cookie cutter, and when enough of them use the same trail, the results are obvious.

Some other areas in Bechler's backcountry that contain thermal activity appear to have suffered from overuse. I recall hiking through this country with Rod during 1972, and we met Paul Miller, a backcountry ranger who patrolled this region throughout the summer. Paul wanted us to see some of the unique thermal features nearby and led us to them. At the time there was not even a trail present.

Fortunately, I took several photographs of the thermal features there. In recent years this same area has suffered from overuse. Vegetation along streams was worn away. As a result spring floods loosened rocks no longer held down by the vegetation, and washed them directly into thermal pools. Before his untimely death in 1997, former Park Geologist Rick Hutchinson had expressed great concern over the deterioration of this area.

A few years ago I learned that West District Ranger Bob Siebert was attempting to alleviate resource damage caused by overuse in the Bechler region of the park's backcountry. Bob was proposing limiting or restricting use and restoring vegetation in some trampled areas. I called Bob and asked him if he would be interested in seeing my photographs of this area taken in 1972, when the streams, thermal features and vegetation were in pristine condition. Bob was excited to obtain the photos, because it would provide him with some baseline data going back thirty years.

To most people hiking through this area today, the setting is idyllic and little concern is expressed about resource damage. But when you compare the photo taken in 1972 to the conditions found more recently, the deterioration becomes obvious. Typically, a district ranger will transfer into Yellowstone from another national park, stay several years, and then move on to still another park assignment. Bob had come to Yellowstone from Glacier. Fortunately, Bob and his staff have implemented restrictions and vegetative restoration that have improved the condition of the resource. However, the condition of some of the trails from overuse by horses remains a serious problem.

The biggest challenges facing Yellowstone in the future have more to do with what happens outside, not inside, the park's boundaries. When Yellowstone was established as the world's first national park in 1872, Congress basically drew a big square on a map that included major geologic wonders such as the thermal basins, Yellowstone Lake, and the Grand Canyon of the Yellowstone River. However, critical wildlife habitat and corridors were not included, and thus protected. The park is merely an island within an island.

The smaller island, the park, appears to be in good shape. But its lifeblood is drawn from the bigger island, known as the Greater Yellowstone

Ecosystem. This big ecosystem includes Yellowstone and Grand Teton National Parks, parts of six different national forests, two national wildlife refuges and state and private lands. Cooperation and coordination among the many federal and state agencies that manage this land are critical.

Threats include real estate development, logging, mining, gas and oil development, political interference with the management of public lands within and surrounding the park, and, of course, the problem of how to manage growing visitor use. Most people have heard the analogy of how popping a few rivets on a big 747 jet would be insignificant at first, but at some point the missing rivets would begin to weaken and endanger the aircraft. The Greater Yellowstone Ecosystem works the same way.

There is no question that the health and well-being of Yellowstone National Park depends on the health and well-being of the Greater Yellowstone Ecosystem A great indicator is the grizzly. This majestic animal requires a large and wild space in order to live, reproduce and perpetuate this key species. If we can provide enough protection to the ecosystem to perpetuate a healthy grizzly population, then the park should fare well. But that is a very big if. The key is to become involved, stay involved, and fight to protect and preserve this magnificent place for our children and grandchildren.

Many visitors ask what they can do to help protect and preserve Yellowstone. Usually when visitors return to their busy lives back in their home states, typically far away from the park, little thought is given to the continuous array of issues facing Yellowstone.

One way to keep up with current issues is to frequently visit Yellowstone's official NPS website at www.nps.gov/yell/. Another way to stay on top of these issues and understand how to take action to protect the Yellowstone Ecosystem, is to join one or more of the conservation organizations listed in the appendix.

Epilogue

Since 1968 Margaret and I have had a unique perspective on observing changes in the West. We have often driven back and forth from the South to the Yellowstone country. St. Louis may have been considered the Gateway to the West to the explorers of the wilderness West, but Margaret and I used to consider Kansas City to be the gateway to the West of our time. The congestion and development rapidly declined, as we would drive into Nebraska and Wyoming.

After spending most of the year in the congested South, it was always a joy to return to the wide open spaces of the West, and to pass through remote little communities such as Muddy Gap, Wyoming, Two Dot, Montana and Arthur, Nebraska. Once, while engaged in the frantic rush hour traffic on the freeways surrounding Atlanta, Margaret pulled out a pen and paper, and scribbled this poem that she titled, *Somewhere Between Two Dot and Muddy Gap:*

> Rubber on asphalt
> Riding, roaring, racing
> Rumbling, weaving on
> Four lanes of armored ammunition
> Coming collision close
> Just give me a weathered
> Pot-holed two laner
> Between Two Dot and Muddy Gap
> Where I can breathe easy
> With the wide open land
> And be free to think
> Unhurried, gentler thoughts
> Somewhere between
> Two Dot and Muddy Gap

Over the years, we have observed the insidious encroachment of congestion and development even into Nebraska and Wyoming. No longer do we consider Kansas City to be the "gateway to wide open spaces." On numerous occasions, I have flown roundtrip from the South to the Yellowstone country, flying in and out of such cities as Knoxville, Atlanta and Memphis in the South, and Salt Lake City, Bozeman and Jackson, in the West. I am always appalled at the incredible lack of open space that I see below around the southern cities, especially Atlanta. When flying over Wyoming and Montana, I find myself looking at a landscape that still has hope. In fact, in my mind's eye, I often think back to the time of Lewis and Clark and imagine what the entire West was like then.

From the air, the subtle but steady encroachment of development in and around the Greater Yellowstone Ecosystem is readily apparent. Today, there are so few wild and unspoiled places left on the map. I have a very difficult time attempting to follow the logic of those who want to reduce what few precious little wild spaces we have left.

Over 140 years ago Henry David Thoreau's simple eight word quote, "In wildness is the preservation of the world," recognized that the human spirit needs wild country as nourishment for the soul. The Yellowstone country provides such sustenance.

The Greater Yellowstone Ecosystem is one of those wild places that we still have a chance to preserve and protect for our children and grandchildren. May its wild spirit live on in perpetuity.

Orville E. Bach, Jr.
Old Faithful, Yellowstone National Park
June, 2005

Appendix

The following organizations work to protect, preserve, and/or support Yellowstone National Park and the Greater Yellowstone Ecosystem:

The National Parks Conservation Association
www.npca.org

The Greater Yellowstone Coalition
www.greateryellowstone.org

The Sierra Club
www.sierra.org

The Wilderness Society
www.wilderness.org

The National Audubon Society
www.audubon.org

The Nature Conservancy
www.nature.org

The National Wildlife Federation
www.nwf.org

The Natural Resources Defense Council
www.nrdc.org

The Yellowstone Association
www.yellowstoneassociation.org

The Yellowstone Park Foundation
www.ypf.org

The Geyser Observation and Study Association (GOSA)
www.geyserstudy.org